PRAISE FOR *LEARNING AND THE METAVERSE*

"This groundbreaking book on the metaverse is a must-read for anyone interested in the future of learning. With expert insights and compelling research, the author illuminates the immense potential of immersive technologies. It is an essential resource for educators and learners seeking to navigate the exciting realm of the metaverse and unlock new frontiers in education."
Sheila Jagannathan, Global Head, Open Learning, World Bank

"Excitement about the metaverse died down towards the start of 2023, its oxygen stolen by the arrival of generative pre-trained transformers (GPTs) – astonishingly capable AI models. But the metaverse will be back: the tech giants (especially Apple and Meta) are still spending vast sums on its development. It is best understood as the internet in 3D, the application of extended reality, including virtual reality (VR), augmented reality (AR) and mixed reality (MR). These technologies are going to be enormously influential in every aspect of life, and perhaps, most of all in education. There is no better guide to this exciting new world than Donald Clark, who has been at the cutting edge of education technology for over 35 years. Not only does he talk and write with deep expertise, but also engagingly and entertainingly. What fun!"
Calum Chace, author, *Surviving AI*, and global keynote speaker

"Donald Clark gives a great overview of learning and the metaverse, easing us in with an exploration of the term before deeply immersing the reader into a myriad of benefits. Part three is particularly insightful, as he shows his specialism in learning technologies. I left with a much better understanding of the topic and recommend the second half to experienced professionals in L&D."
Tom Ffiske, Editor, *Immersive Wire*

T0309292

BY THE SAME AUTHOR

- *Artificial Intelligence for Learning*
- *Learning Experience Design*
- *Learning Technology*

The above titles are available from all good bookshops.

For further information on these and other Kogan Page titles, or to order online, visit the Kogan Page website at: www.koganpage.com.

Learning and the Metaverse

What this technology means for L&D

Donald Clark

KoganPage

Publisher's note
Every possible effort has been made to ensure that the information contained in this book is accurate at the time of going to press, and the publishers and authors cannot accept responsibility for any errors or omissions, however caused. No responsibility for loss or damage occasioned to any person acting, or refraining from action, as a result of the material in this publication can be accepted by the editor, the publisher or the author.

First published in Great Britain and the United States in 2023 by Kogan Page Limited

2nd Floor, 45 Gee Street
London
EC1V 3RS
United Kingdom

8 W 38th Street, Suite 902
New York, NY 10018
USA

4737/23 Ansari Road
Daryaganj
New Delhi 110002
India

www.koganpage.com

Kogan Page books are printed on paper from sustainable forests.

ISBNs

Hardback   978 1 3986 1212 9
Paperback   978 1 3986 1210 5
Ebook   978 1 3986 1211 2

British Library Cataloguing-in-Publication Data

A CIP record for this book is available from the British Library.

Library of Congress Cataloging-in-Publication Data

9781398612105

Typeset by Integra Software Services, Pondicherry
Print production managed by Jellyfish
Printed and bound by CPI Group (UK) Ltd, Croydon CR0 4YY

CONTENTS

LIST OF FIGURES AND TABLES

PREFACE

Learning is about expanding the mind and we have for millennia used stories, writing, printing, movies, broadcast media, internet and now computer games and VR to enter virtual worlds. This progression has headed steadily from 2D to 3D, towards convergence in the metaverse.

As I explored in my last book *Learning Technologies* (2023), all of these media are intrinsically learning technologies, and mixed reality and the metaverse will be no different, in that they will be used for learning. We already have evidence of how this will happen from VR and other sources, including current work in existing metaverse-like environments. This is the first book that uses evidence from the history of our need for other worlds, along with learning theory and learning practice, to tackle 'learning in 3D and the metaverse' head on.

When I first made computerized 3D graphic worlds in the 1980s, we had to render them in expensive studios using very expensive computers that would render them overnight. We built an entire French town, then used it for learners to navigate and buy things in that town to learn the language. We then bought very expensive Silicon Graphics computers so we could do the rendering ourselves. Over the years this task became easier and cheaper, fuelled by the rise of the computer games industry and CGI in movies, so modern packages can produce high-fidelity 3D environments in seconds. At that time we, Epic Group plc, were in both the learning and games industries, the latter the real genesis of virtual worlds, as 2D platform games gave way to 3D worlds in which you as a player were totally immersed. Our two sons had every console – Nintendos, Playstations, XBoxes – and spent more and more time in such worlds. It was clear, even then, and even clearer now, that technology would make 3D immersion the norm.

Jaron Lanier started the first VR company in 1985 and I saw him speak in the early 90s in the US where he had a vision beyond technology. He also gave some warnings. We can use this technology, he claimed, to achieve great things, beyond our imaginations, but we can also use it for more command and control. We shall indeed explore how the degree of decentralization of governance, economics and institutional control can have radically different structures in virtual worlds. I had designed learning experiences in 3D worlds using laserdiscs; these included that French town for language learning, 3D mazes and other environments, but it was Lanier who put me on to VR. Then, in 2005, I became a Board Director at Caspian Learning, which developed an authoring tool for learning in 3D worlds. We did some wonderful work in training, including certified training for gas engineers in the USA, in full 3D environments. It was a true simulation used for both learning and assessment. For example, if you left a window open that could blow away dangerous gases, you failed when you performed the gas test; also care home training to teach care workers to support residents with dementia; then construction work, such as placing ladders at the right angle. All were perfect for this new form of 3D training. This work was way ahead of its time.

I had, like most, several forays into Second Life on a 2D screen. This did not excite me much, although deliberately choosing a female avatar was a revelation in terms of sexual harassment. I wrote and gave talks about these experiences at the time, puzzled at the many academic projects where the goal was to build lecture theatres online. Nevertheless, it was a fascinating experiment and lots of good literature on virtual worlds emerged from that period.

VR had been a professional interest when I was given a DK1 development kit in 2013 by Chris Brannigan of Caspian. With the second DK2 kit I began to experiment with all sorts of applications, from having my head chopped off in the French Revolution, seeing myself back from inside the basket, to doing a space walk in and around the International Space Station using the experience to teach Newton's three laws. At conferences, I would ask large audiences why astronauts floated around inside the Space Station. 'Zero gravity!' they would shout. Most, even academic audiences, got the answer wrong. The astronauts are actually falling to earth at the same speed as the Space Station. Teaching physics is hard; experiencing physics in VR is a fantastic learning experience.

Then out of the blue, Facebook bought Oculus for $2.3 billion in 2014. Technologies have their moments. Early versions are often too primitive to be used as consumer devices. This was true of the early computers, the internet and mobile phones. It took massive leaps of imagination, investments and risks to get where we are today with ubiquitous computers and smartphones. Buying Oculus seemed odd at the time but there are a number of headsets available and all of the major tech companies are moving towards 3D in some form. As soon as AR and VR become the Christmas devices of choice, the shift to 3D will happen.

My eyes were also opened to the power of simulations in the military, and I gave talks at military conferences across Europe and in Florida, where I extolled the power of simulations and online learning. In Florida, I stood in immersive domes, shot rocket-propelled grenades and generally immersed myself in leading-edge simulation technology. It was clear that VR would play a role in reducing the cost of training in this world, along with multi-user environments, and, of course, it has.

Having owned the very first Oculus development kits and seen great projects designed at Caspian Learning, I began to write about this new medium as a channel for learning. It is a medium, not a gadget. I continued to write a great deal on VR and the metaverse, gave keynotes and made podcasts on the subject (one within VR!) and demonstrated it to hundreds of people individually, both here and abroad.

I had taken it into a care home in Edinburgh where the elderly residents had wondrous experiences, taking them back to their younger selves. But it was in Africa that I had the most fun. I will never forget the schoolchildren in Kampala, Uganda, in 2014, who brought forward their friend in a wheelchair. He tentatively put on the headset, did a bungee jump, went on a rollercoaster and did things he had never done in real life. His friends knew exactly what this meant for him and were jumping with joy at his enthusiasm. That memory still moves me. We also had the initially stern Minister of Education shriek with excitement inside the headset, while his aides giggled.

In most cases, those who try VR come away astonished, even amazed, full of ideas and applications. In 2015, I was in Ethiopia demonstrating its capabilities in the African Union Congress Building, where I took part in a huge debate arguing that Africa needed more vocational learning, not more universities, and that technology such as VR and virtual worlds had a role to play in meeting that need. We won that debate.

Witnessing real learning applications in healthcare at Penn State University, in the oil industry at Immerse Learning, in the airline industry at IATA, in robotic education at E-com and in many other training contexts at Make Real, I am more convinced than ever we are moving towards something quite different and bigger than we may ever have imagined. I was also involved in a metaverse project with Metanode allowing me to take a deep dive into the role of AI in immersive environments.

John Helmer and I did a podcast from within AltspaceVR, exploring VR and the metaverse from within a proto-metaverse, covering its origins, early pioneers, such as Lanier, and researchers such as Makransky, along with more philosophical perspectives from Plato, Descartes, Chalmers, Baudrillard and Nozick. This book is the culmination of that long journey both in my own mind and around the world.

For a detailed account of using AR and VR, my book *Learning Experience Design* goes into detail on the learning theory and possible types of experiences, along with a detailed set of Dos and Don'ts on design. This matters, as many of the early vanity projects lacked rigour, design or clear learning goals. It is important that we understand how 'learning' works in these environments.

My book *AI for Learning* proved prescient, as it now sweeps through the world of learning and work, possibly the most significant technology since the invention of the internet. It will also shape mixed reality and the metaverse. 3D worlds, objects and avatars will be created and influenced by AI. Generative AI allows far more pedagogically sophisticated exchanges, what I call pedAIgogy, to occur in immersive worlds. It gives 3D experience a massive boost in terms of creation and sophistication.

We can see, across time, that technology continues to scale, add value and change the learning landscape. AI coupled with a shift from 2D to 3D will have a cumulative effect that allows virtual worlds to flourish. The two will develop in tandem to create new unimagined worlds that expand our culture and, importantly, rebalance learning towards learning by doing as well as enable new types of learning.

ABOUT THIS BOOK

This book is for learning professionals, anyone involved or interested in how mixed reality and the metaverse will affect the learning landscape, from learning designers through to those who like to take a strategic view of learning. It is also a book for those who may be au fait with mixed reality and the metaverse but do not know much about how learning is likely to be implemented in that environment. Those involved in any way in learning technology should be especially interested as it is likely to be part of their world, if it is not already. And for anyone just curious about mixed reality and the metaverse and learning, this book is also for you.

Part One opens with the case that learning may well be one of the killer applications in mixed reality and the metaverse. My argument is that there is a steady pendulum swing from 2D to 3D in learning, as the technology makes it practically possible. We are 3D people who live and work in a 3D world, yet most learning is in 2D, from text or 2D screens. We have a relentless and deep need to create second worlds, as heavens and hells, in both sacred and secular realms. The philosophical and psychological need for other 3D worlds is examined as it is full of ideas and debates relevant to the imagined metaverse.

We focus on how we got here, as this is a key argument for why the metaverse will happen. As explained in my last book, *Learning Technologies*, there is a tendency to deal with an individual technology as a thing-in-itself. As we found, technology in general, learning technologies in particular, evolve and are often combinatorial, bringing other technologies into being. They also envelop past media or content types, so the text, sound and video found in books, radio, TV and cinema, can all now be found delivered in abundance on the internet.

There is a tendency to forget, demote or dismiss past technologies as not being technologies at all. In learning technologies we rarely see writing, printing, pens, paper or books as learning technologies, but they are. To this end, I have gone to some length to lay out the 'origin stories' of the metaverse, to explain how we got here and why it is one of the inevitable next steps in the evolution of technology. It has deep origins going back to when we first told stories, created the magnificent cave paintings, and then an architectural heritage around creating huge spaces both sacred and secular.

We look at monumental metaverses in the 3D architecture we have created as a species. In parallel, we have a rich philosophical, literary and cinematic history, not only expressing but exploring and reflecting on the relevance and moral impact of alternative worlds. Then media metaverses, the 3D worlds created in novels, movies and TV. The digital revolution also provided a different technological background with the great unification that was the internet. Virtual worlds and games metaverses are explained in detail. All the while, virtual reality began to be explored, virtual worlds, also social media, inhabited by billions. Virtual computer games, inhabited by hundreds of millions, and specialist virtual worlds that give us a glimpse of what is possible, especially in learning, have exploded in reach and popularity. They give us real insights into how the metaverse is likely to evolve.

Part Two shows the coalescence of all of this around a single idea – the metaverse. Who knows how exactly it will shape out but there are likely scenarios, so we explore the shape of the metaverse, outlining its direction of travel, likely governance, standards around interoperability, as well as the major players and likely outcomes, as well as the technology.

Part Three is wholly about learning. There is a good case to be made for change in learning, especially on making it more relevant and more vocational. I present that case through some major intellectuals in the field, such as Goodhat, Caplan, Sandel and Schank. Can the metaverse offer something quite new and bold in learning? Perhaps we need an alternative world to deliver an alternative set of services, and effect real change in a sector that remains quite stagnant and resistant to change.

Having made the case, we take our cue from self-determination theory (SDT) as applied in general psychology and the relevant 3D world of games to unpack what are the likely features of the metaverse that will enable learning.

We look at learner autonomy, especially learner presence, identity and action, but also context and transfer. It is important to bring what we know in the science of learning to bear on the problem. In particular, we focus on recent research in VR and learning that illuminates how learning can be best delivered in the metaverse.

We then look at competence and what sort of learning can free us from the tyranny of time, place, text and passivity. What do we know from VR about how to design learning in mixed reality and immersive worlds? We draw from researchers in the field to identify recommended directions of travel. There are, of course, thousands of examples of VR, some in recent virtual worlds, so we explore what we can learn from them. These include the Metaversities and other formal and informal learning projects that have appeared over many years. This evidence is real and points towards what has worked and has not worked.

The *social* dimensions in learning will also be important in what are already social spaces. Evidence from the success of virtual worlds and games suggests this will be a key driver of use in the metaverse, especially in learning.

Pulling all of this together will be data-driven solutions, especially in learning, so we explore the role of techniques such as eye-tracking, haptics and other data-rich sources and activities in learning.

Part Four is a take on the future. Of course, mixed reality and the metaverse is not without its problems; even at this definition stage it has attracted the predictable wrath that attracts all future and imagined technology. Whenever I mention the 'metaverse' I get the same reaction I've had all my adult life to new technology; personal computers in the 80s, internet in late 90s, then smartphones, social media and computer games... the same attitudes that appeared when Elvis appeared in the year of my birth – 1956! Usually, like grief, technology faces the typical five stages of denial, anger, bargaining, depression, acceptance.

With the metaverse, most are in denial, some angry. Satya Nadella, CEO of Microsoft, one of the main players, states the metaverse is 'already here', as the investment is already colossal, the hardware advancing and hundreds of millions are already in virtual worlds. In *Fortnite*, Roblox, *Minecraft*, VRChat and the 3D games industry, 3D worlds are booming. It is not enough to just throw out the phrase 'Second Life', as most of the hundreds of millions of users in these new environments were born after Second Life was launched... and most of the critics before.

Problems do exist at all sorts of levels: first, on governance and standards around interoperability; second, on what seem like unattainable technical demands; third, on user acceptance; fourth, on learning. We tackle these head on. The aim is to be neither techno-utopian nor techno-dystopian, but honest in the appraisal.

Not content with looking at the distant metaverse, we speculate whether this could take us into the far future, in general and in learning. We consider the role other great innovations will play in the creation and operation of the metaverse. This includes the other great technology of the age – artificial intelligence. It is clear that these two technologies are converging to build the metaverse, its inhabitants and their behaviour. Advances in generative AI suggest that the move from 2D to 3D will be easier than we imagined.

Finally, we indulge in some speculation on metafutures, visions of the metaverse around concepts like the super or hive mind. All books are products of the imagination; this is no exception and so we take imagination to the limit.

Scepticism and negativity often accompany new, bold visions. It is premature to write off something before knowing what it is or the evidence that it may have benefits. This is especially true of the metaverse. The word 'metaverse' has become a 'trigger' word with accompanying verbal eye-rolls or predictable references to Second Life, as if that was the end of the matter. We need to be wary and critical of technology but being critical doesn't mean closing our eyes and ears or saying this or that failed in the past, concluding all is bound to fail in the future. It is not what we are familiar with that should form the basis of our judgements on the metaverse but where it has come from, where it has got to so far and where it is going. Dismissing computer games on the basis of *Pong* would have been ridiculous. Dismissing smartphones on the basis of the early brick-sized devices would have been ridiculous. Dismissing the internet on the basis of its simple initial messaging would have been bizarre. We must think about mixed reality and a metaverse beyond our imaginations. The metaverse is coming. Resistance is futile!

ACKNOWLEDGEMENTS

Spending long periods in the metaverse of your own thoughts when writing a book can make you antisocial. Apologies to my wife Gil, family and dog for these spells of introspection.

LIST OF ABBREVIATIONS

AAR	after-action review
AR	augmented reality
API	application programming interface
AWS	Amazon Web services
BIM	building information modelling
DAO	decentralized autonomous organisation
DEI	diversity, equity and inclusion
CGI	computer-generated imagery
IEEE	Institute of Electrical and Electronics Engineers
FNCS	*Fortnite* Champion Series
GAN	generative adversarial network
GPS	global positioning system
GPU	graphics processing unit
HTML	hypertext mark-up language
IP	internet protocol
L&D	learning and development
LMS	learning management system
LRS	learning record store
LXP	learning experience platform
MOOC	massive open online course
MUD	multi-user dungeon
MMORPG	massively multiplayer online role-playing game
NeRF	neural radiance field
NFT	non-fungible token
OER	open educational resource
OS	operating system
SCORM	sharable courseware object reference model
TCP	transmission control protocol
URL	uniform resource locator
USD	Universal Scene Description
VAK	visual-auditory-kinaesthetic

VLE	virtual learning environment
VR	virtual reality
W3C	World Wide Web consortium
xAPI	Experience API
XR	extended reality

PART ONE

Origins of the metaverse?

01

Metaverse

Flatland

Flatland (1884) is a wonderful, satirical Victorian novel, a 2D world inhabited by points, lines and 2D shapes. Equilateral triangles are the middle classes, isosceles triangles soldiers and workmen, squares and pentagons the professional class, hexagons and above the nobility, circles the priestly class. All is well until a Sphere appears from Spaceland, revealing himself by descending through Flatland to show a decreasing circle as he descends.

Change of any sort is frowned upon in Flatland, as threatening and dangerous. Innovation is illegal and suppressed, heretics imprisoned. Flatland is not ready to hear from 3D Spaceland. The residents of Flatland are resistant and skeptical of revelations from this strange other 3D world. We are told at the end of the book that the narrator was mocked as 'the maddest of the mad', accused of heresy as he writes his memoir from prison, where he remains, dejected at his failure to convince Flatland of the reality of other dimensions.

Narrated by 'A. Square', it is a wonderful social satire but can also be read as a critique of those who tend to get trapped in a fixed view of change, sticking rigidly to what they know, always suspicious of the new. It is a tale of the realization of the limits of cognition and the need to be open to innovative, new, even radical ideas.

It can also be seen as relevant to the current debate over the metaverse, where those in the real world seem affronted that another may exist or be created. Not fully understood, even threatening, it confounds those who see it as a potential evil twin of the real world, a dangerous distraction, where all sorts of depravity can take place. What is at work here is often confirmation bias, defending what we are familiar with against what is unfamiliar; also, negativity bias, a basic mistrust of the new.

In Flatland, many years needed to be spent at the 'illustrious University of Wentbridge' to learn the ways of social advancement. All that fail to pass the Final Examination of the University are imprisoned for life or killed. Those from the criminal and vagabond classes are placed in schools to show children how not to behave. Learning in Flatland is about making learners comply with the rules of Flatland.

The wonder of the book is that it can also be read as a critique of learning theory, the idea that teaching and learning is the sole concern of 2D media, such as writing, flat images and speaking (Flatland has audio). Edwin Abbot wrote the book towards the end of his 25-year career as a schoolmaster. He implores us not to be 'confined to limited dimensionality' and not to stay stubbornly secure in the conformity of the present.

Flat learning

Many would affirm, as McLuhan (1962) pointed out, that culture, education and training is somewhat stuck in the flat, linear world of text. Its focus on cognition and knowledge, at the expense of experiences, skills, vocational and contextualized learning, has been the story of learning for a long time. To be fair, schooling is quite recent in our history and we have not had the teaching and learning technology to expand the schoolroom into the real world. This could be possible through the metaverse.

Pedagogy seems to be held captive by voice, supplemented by flat books, textbooks, chalkboards and whiteboards. Even online learning seems stuck in the flat presentation of text, graphics, video and variations of multiple-choice questions. Despite the world being 3D, learning delivery seems stuck in a linear 2D world of print, PowerPoint and presented e-learning. That world is now being changed through generative AI, where text and other media can be generated in seconds. What this new technology does is expose serious flaws in text-dominated learning and simplistic assessment. A new 'pedAIgogy' is emerging, where we learn through dialogue, support and more co-created contexts. This will be expanded on further throughout the book, especially in the final chapter.

Learning in 3D, from experience, is rare, vocational learning seen as secondary and ignored, skills sidelined. Our educational systems, confined to classrooms, lecture halls and training rooms, are unable to cope with the demands of the real world, as they lack context and relevance. The metaverse may be the bridge between these two worlds: the flat institutional 2D world with its flat media and flat tools, and the real 3D world.

2D to 3D

At the dawn of media production, 500,000 years ago, simple marks were made on 3D shells, 50,000 years ago prehistoric sculpture was voluptuously 3D, wallowing in the grace of the human and animal forms, and cave paintings took full advantage of the 3D cave and shapes of the rock contours.

In a sense, the invention of writing heralded a 5,000-year aberration, the 2D representation of ideas in flat symbols, on expensive materials, then amplified by 2D printing. Other 2D media, from painting, which was long non-perspectival, to photography, are also flat and 2D. Screen-based media delivered from cinema screen through to television, computer, tablets and smartphones, are 2D.

Immersion was the method of inducing realism, larger cinema screens, larger TVs, greater fidelity; but this is simply 2D striving to be 3D. Even in gaming, with games that are often completely 3D, 2D screens are still the norm.

We may therefore have swung full circle back to the spirit of earlier 3D representations with mixed reality and the metaverse. We are going back to matching human perception, which is spatial and 3D. Only now can we create 3D media, building on the network, processing and storage technology that supports screen-based 2D media on the internet.

The personal epiphany many have when trying VR for the first time is often an experience that defines their faith that the metaverse will happen. You do not have to be a techno-determinist to see that 3D technologies, as they have unfolded through games, Google Earth and virtual worlds, now point towards digital twinning and eventually mixed reality and the creation of the metaverse. Technologies that scale, combine previous successful technologies and provide compelling experiences, tend to succeed. Think about

FIGURE 1.1 History of learning technology

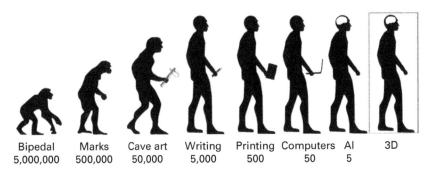

Bipedal	Marks	Cave art	Writing	Printing	Computers	AI	3D
5,000,000	500,000	50,000	5,000	500	50	5	

what compelling experiences you have had in technology, the first time you were inside a 3D computer game, saw Google Earth, played *Pokémon Go*, were first completely immersed in VR, spoke to Alexa, asked ChatGPT a question and got an astonishing reply.

Augmented reality (AR) retains our 3D vision as its backdrop, as it places 3D images into that already perceived 3D world. Layers of reality are then blended together, as we saw with *Pokémon Go*. New AR technologies play to the 3D capabilities of the brain and present data that allows the brain to seamlessly integrate projected images from the smartphone, headsets, glasses or headsets to your retina. All of this is like dreaming with your eyes open.

VR takes this a step further with total 3D immersion, where you really feel as though you are in another place. It gives you full 3D experiences of games, entertainment, locations, imaginary worlds, education, training – in your mind. Access to 3D 'experiences' is what makes VR so compelling. When you first try VR, you get an 'aha' feeling. Wow – I'm in a created world that feels real. That is because all the media you have experienced before has been in 2D. We are so used to being presented with 2D print and screens, that it comes as a real shock to see represented worlds as they really should be – in stereoscopic 3D. The epiphany is that we can now experience experiences as they are meant to be experienced. Like AR, VR and 3D experiences speak to our brains in a way that resonates physically, emotionally and subconsciously. It literally becomes an extension of consciousness.

New media rarely knocks out old media and we have had 50,000 years of evolved 2D media from cave art to screens. But we are at the start of a new era, where media actually deliver what our brains expect – 3D realities, artificial realities, mixed realities, augmented realities, virtual realities. This is as it should be. We are being taken back inside the cave where we can experience 3D images that are exciting, terrifying and new.

The metaverse is a big concept but so was writing, printing, the internet, smartphones, social media and AI. The metaverse is foundational, fundamental and societal and lies at the end of a long trajectory that has seen our species become more virtual and more enthralled by 3D worlds as technology has evolved and matured. The 3D future is here, it is just not evenly developed; still a set of separate rooms that are yet to form a single edifice.

2D to 3D technology

Digital technology is a story of drive, aspiration, imagination, innovation, design and farsightedness. It constantly reinvents and improves itself to

FIGURE 1.2 2D to 3D

move beyond the limits of our bodies and minds. The metaverse does precisely this. It takes us into new territory with a vision of the virtual that really does transcend the limits of the real.

Books such as *The Metaverse* by Matthew Ball (2022) often start with long, convoluted, fixed definitions or end states, whereas actual technical progress is proving to be more of a fluid evolution from 2D towards 3D media. The premise of this book is a measurable, technological shift from 2D to 3D already manifested in hundreds of millions of people working, socializing, entertaining and learning in 3D contexts (Figure 1.2).

It is important to keep this simple, as there is no single, present vision of the future of the metaverse. The future does not exist; the metaverse has still to be created. We should therefore see this as a natural next step in the evolution of technology. The world of media has been flat since the invention of writing, especially in learning, for the last 500 years. This 2D world then underwent a radical technological shift from analogue to digital over the last century with the advent of computers and the internet. It has now been undergoing another shift, already underway since the advent of 3D worlds in games, for around 50 years.

This has not been possible at scale before, as the underlying technology in terms of processing, storage, bandwidth, developed software and capable devices has been beyond the threshold for its delivery. We now see, emerging out of the games world, technology that tackles these issues and delivers proto-metaverses, so some sort of convergence into 3D technology seems certain, if only to make as much content interoperable on as many devices, for as many things in as many contexts as possible.

This is why it is wrong to push fixed definitions of what the metaverse has yet to be. The metaverse must evolve, not be prematurely spirited into existence and foisted upon people. It will take many turns and pivots. There will be failures but also successes, dead-ends but unexpected open roads. This shift from 2D to 3D has only just started and has a long way to go.

3D additive to 2D

The metaverse is more of a paradigm shift towards 3D. Like most technological shifts, especially in digital technology, it is likely to be more of an addition than a replacement of 2D media. Technological revolutions do not always replace one technology wholly with another. They shift the fundamentals but often in a more expansive fashion in terms of deliverable media. The cinema, broadcast radio and television did not entirely replace print; they were largely additive. Similarly with the internet, where text, images and video were made more widely available, rather than any one medium being crushed.

The move to the metaverse may in some cases replace in 3D what was done in 2D, but its real promise is to *add* opportunities, enhance and open up new frontiers for human progress, learning being one of them. Books, podcasts, video and other forms of 2D learning will not disappear but they will be supplemented by new opportunities to learn where 3D is appropriate. The metaverse is an upgrade.

This shift is not at the deep level of AI, which goes hand in glove with 3D development, like genotype and phenotype. AI, as we shall see later, is now integral to the creation, operation and advantages which 3D can offer, but 3D has more to do with what we see, hear and do than the deeper underlying supporting technology. But it is more than just a presentation layer, as 3D changes the very dynamic of autonomy, activity and interaction. This is not merely an interface switch, it is cognitively quite different, more matched to what we actually see, hear and do. It provides agency, presence, context and experiential opportunities, currently limited by 2D media.

Neither is it likely we will all be working, all day, totally immersed and cut off from reality with the current bulky VR headsets. This one metaverse where we all hang out seems, at the moment, unlikely. Glasses and smaller devices will also be commonplace, providing lots of mixed-reality opportunities, most yet to be imagined and realized. Total immersion will be part of the metaverse, it will not be the whole metaverse.

The metaverse should be seen as a more open, mixed-reality future, not as excluding the real world but providing various degrees of the real and virtual with meaningful and fruitful dialectic between them. The metaverse does not pit one reality against the other, it sees lots of different realities as useful, it is not a complete alternative to the real, it can also be an enhancement and option to the real.

Learning in the metaverse

Over time, our species has invented ever richer and more sophisticated virtual worlds from the physical spaces of cave art and buildings, to writing, printing, radio, TV, movies, games, computers and the internet. Every one of these technological shifts changed the world culturally and economically; so it may be with a reimagined internet. In the same way that the internet exploded when opened up to individuals, institutions and businesses, who could all create value, so it will be with the metaverse.

The same is true for technologies that accelerate teaching and learning, as defined in *Learning Technologies* (Clark, 2023). Writing brought about literacy, mathematics and data-led science; printing produced books, textbooks and academic publishing; broadcast media took learning to the masses; computers and the internet brought all of these and more into one global network. So it is likely to be with learning in the metaverse.

The metaverse is not a platform, so will not be built or bought by a single, global tech company, even a handful of these companies. It may even lead the fight against this distorting monopolization of the internet. Neither will the metaverse turn into one great gameverse; this is not feasible, as there is no compelling reason for huge existing games to make that effort. It would provide a metaverse of sorts, but not the sort that would be compelling to people outside that audience. In terms of creating value, learning in the metaverse is a strong candidate, as learning gives the metaverse meaning. It is a universal need that links the virtual back to the real world. As a bridge from cognitive learning experiences, especially experiential learning, it offers real benefits to individuals, institutions and society.

There needs to be a strong bridge to and from the metaverse and the real world. One of those bridges is learning. All new experiences affect the brain in some way and are learning experiences, but some learning experiences are better than others. The focus should be those relatively permanent changes in long-term memory as well as the transfer of that cognitive change back into life and practice, a renewed effort to apply and transfer knowledge and skills to actual tasks. Indeed, the metaverse could help solve age-old problems in learning: ease of access, cost, autonomy, learning by doing, context, social learning, practice and transfer.

This is just one area where value can be realized in the metaverse; it is not the only one, but one that holds huge promise. Just as there is a vast physical network of schools, colleges, universities and training spaces in the real world – any learning space can be created in the virtual world, such as a digital twin or newly imagined places and services. It is also likely that new, fast, innovative players, with a real focus on value in their domains, will create learning in the metaverse.

The metaverse is not really about being in a 3D world, it is about creating meaningful experiences in those mixed-reality and 3D worlds. The point of the metaverse is not to create places where people just hang out; it must create compelling places and activities. You can't have a mall without shopping, a library without books, a school or university without learning. This is why a focus on virtual worlds providing real solutions to real problems must be at the forefront of the metaverse effort. metaverse experiences must offer something more than real world experiences and improve our lives. The point is not to simply mirror or move from the real to the virtual, but for the virtual to transcend the real and provide fulfillment. It must also offer better social and economic opportunities than currently exist in the real world. This is more than just creating the future; it is about creating a better future.

The yearning for virtual worlds has been around since we have had the imagination and language to create such worlds. Our ability to imagine other places was a practical form of cognition, useful for survival in a dangerous world, as both episodic memory and, as a consequence of those imagined memories, forward thinking in terms of planning. These are clearly evolved forms of cognition.

We then created spaces both physical and psychological that originally satisfied basic, practical needs but grew to satisfy many other needs. From Palaeolithic caves to architecture, ideas have been made concrete and the largest buildings for centuries were separated-off places that encouraged us to contemplate the afterlife. Even in theatres and sports arenas, we had an urge to create spaces for spectacles. With writing and print, other worlds could be conjured up through words, from religious texts and philosophy through to novels that create virtual worlds which we willingly enter.

This book produces a world which you enter by reading and printing. With the electronic age, we also created and escaped to virtual worlds through cinema. Broadcast media brought these other worlds into our homes through radio and television. With digital technology, we created other worlds we could enter and participate in with others, such as computer games and social media. We have always endeavoured to build, enter and be part of one metaverse or another. All of this is the result of one simple drive: our curiosity to imagine, contemplate, explore and even strive to live in worlds other than the real. These were also seen as informing our lives in the real world. Our imagined and created proto-metaverses were often a reaction to, or conversation with, our real lives and the real world.

Immersion and learning

Eventually, we created technology to allow us to totally immerse ourselves in newly created worlds through VR and the coming metaverse. Rather than paint, build, write and watch such worlds, we made them and climbed inside them. We could be in these worlds, feel our presence and the presence of others, do things, interact with others. There is therefore an inevitability about this natural move towards a more singular vision of virtual worlds.

In all of these cases, learning lay at the core of the activity. In these proto-metaverses, we learn how to deal with real life or find solace in the belief that there is another, better world waiting for us beyond death. We also literally learnt from writing, printed books, film, television, radio, computers and the internet. We are all virtual learners now, mixed reality and the metaverse merely an extension of the technologies we have invented to be at the disposal of educators, trainers and learners. Immersive learning will therefore be one of the drivers of the metaverse. Value will be created in the metaverse by useful, meaningful experiences, especially *learning* experiences.

VR has already become a common method of training and the metaverse is a natural expansion of this. There is a great deal of academic evidence from VR and other virtual environments to show it works, what types of learning work best in such environments, as well as researched criteria for success. This book draws on evidence to see what we know so far and how likely and in what form learning will take place in the metaverse.

Hundreds of millions of users are in proto-metaverses, such as *Fortnite*, Roblox and *Minecraft* (which has a *Minecraft Education* product). Others in VRChat and many other spaces share in open VR environments, where there is some fascinating teaching and learning. We have a substantial body of good research, both on what works and, just as importantly, what does not work. This is very useful for the education and training world, as these media are relatively new. It is clearly applicable to many tasks that involve learning by doing, as well as social learning, even soft skills.

So, solid research already exists on how we can use this immersive technology in learning. We know way more than many think about what can be taught and how it should be taught in virtual environments, through existing 3D worlds and researched trials, so we can come to some conclusions from the research about what features of the technology matter, such as presence, agency, competences, social, context and transfer. These also bring problems, such as distraction, novelty and cognitive overload. What clearly works is often deliberate learning design, rather than just immersion, but other more informal forms of learning will also emerge.

The internet was born from blue-sky research in public institutions and eventually opened up to business. The genesis of the metaverse is the opposite, being funded by the world's largest organizations: Facebook, Google, Microsoft, Nvidia, Amazon, Apple and Tencent, to name but a few, yet the issues of interoperability and governance have to be developed communally.

Economic forecasts for the metaverse have been consistently in the trillions of dollars. Jensen Huang, CEO of Nvidia, has even claimed that the GDP of the metaverse will be greater, at some point, than the real world. It is clear this will be a huge market. This is also true of those in the learning game.

The learning world has to take the metaverse seriously. Some immersive learning has been around for a long time, more is coming fast and it is now only a matter of how big it will become. Whatever its size, there is a current thirst to know what it is and how it can help in learning, specifically in learning by doing, often neglected in education and training.

The metaverse moves beyond the existing world by providing freedoms. We already inhabit virtual online worlds as they offer freedom from the tyrannies of distance, time and other constraints. We can communicate virtually, face to face, with anyone around the globe any time for free. Yet learning seems to be constantly constrained by old pedagogies, scarcity, institutional inertia and costs.

What is the metaverse?

The metaverse has been an emergent phenomenon. There was no single event, as the idea has been around as long as we could tell stories. The idea exists not because it was mentioned in early sci-fi novels, such as *Snow Crash* in 1992, but because it emerged from a basic need to create other worlds. This drift towards the metaverse is akin to the problem of polytheism and monotheism. As polytheism led inevitably to monotheism, multimedia led inevitably to the internet and will eventually create the metaverse.

There is, of course, a tendency to get carried away by the power of a single word, especially one as grandiose as the 'metaverse'. The metaverse is therefore thought of, and spoken about, as a replacement for the existing internet, more 'verse' (totality) than 'meta' (above). This is possible but unlikely in the short term. The existing internet is a massive global phenomenon with an enormous physical infrastructure of cables and satellites, optimized through data packet transmission, to deliver a massive range of services and media. It is difficult to see how this will be wholly replaced or swapped out by a 3D alternative.

The metaverse is more likely to be more 'meta' than 'verse', in being a system that sits above but is integrated with the existing internet, a place where one goes for mixed reality and a range of more presence-oriented activities. Given the affordances of different media, some of which are 2D – text and graphics, even video – along with activities that do not require the user to be present in any 3D form, it seems unlikely we would need a 3D world to access, let's say screen-read fiction, traditional TV or movies.

Neither will the metaverse overturn the invention of writing, which can be produced quickly and read much faster than audio. The web is still text dominated, with billions posting text on social media, messaging and reading text. Even online social activity is still a largely text-based phenomenon. Text is searchable, can be hyperlinked, is quick to read and has its own characteristics that would be degraded in 3D.

In learning at all levels, text remains a fundamental medium. It gives access to definitions, articles, journals and books and will remain the medium of choice for abstract ideas. In the same way that radio, TV and movies did not supplant text, indeed the internet led to a renaissance of reading and writing text, so the metaverse will not wholly supplant text in learning. Symbols were one of our greatest inventions as a species: the representation of language outside our minds, that could be captured and transmitted using the simplest of tools. But communication is not their only function. They help us remember things by being able to manipulate them in working memory and store large amounts of information in long-term memory. They help us learn more than we could if we were illiterate. Writing remains the Big Bang of learning technologies (Clark, 2023). Only invented in four places from around 5,000 years ago, it led to most of what we know as culture and civilization. Without writing, and its offspring mathematics, which arose at the same time, there would be no computers, no internet and no metaverse.

How would you read this book in the metaverse? Do you really need to be sitting as an avatar in a 3D world? No. Do you need to be in the presence of other 3D avatars? No. The metaverse is likely to stick to what it is good at: mixed reality and 3D experiences. Similarly with TV and movies. If I settle down to watch a movie with someone, it is unlikely we will search out two headsets and sit as avatars to watch it, and I'll pass on the virtual popcorn. The first 3D movie was *The Power of Love*, shown in 1922 in Los

Angeles. A century later, 3D movies have never caught on. Why? Because 2D suffices as a form of 3D illusion for that sort of entertainment. It is therefore highly unlikely that *all* learning will ever be delivered in the 3D metaverse.

Every new technology, especially a learning technology induces an automatic backlash. Our confirmation and negativity biases kick in and we see the new and unfamiliar as destructive, even dangerous. The metaverse is no different. It has the added handicap of being partly the marketing brainchild of the tech companies, one in particular, Facebook. There are, of course, a whole rack of ethical issues around personal safety, data, privacy and so on, yet this is true of all learning technologies. Criticism is always easier than creation, and all technology has its good and bad. In the absence of information, people tend to focus only on the bad. This book, hopefully, is an antidote to that tendency. It is important to calm fears about the metaverse in learning, as many are skeptical. This book takes a detailed but sober look at what is possible, as well as pointing out the inherent dangers.

When will the metaverse arrive?

Wrong question. We shall see that the metaverse has been around for as long as we have had language, and certainly since the advent of cave paintings. It is already here. It will not be as sudden as the arrival in the Yucatan of the asteroid that wiped out the dinosaurs and 80 per cent of all species. Nevertheless, there will be some disruption, as some dinosaurs will go out of business but many new species, like birds, will evolve and take flight as the shift happens.

We have been moving from bricks to bits since the electrical telegraph was invented in 1831, just short of 200 years ago. Over that period, we have seen virtuality appear as cinema, radio, television, personal computers, internet, social media, games, AR and VR. What we saw with the internet was a network that grew exponentially, but technology is always ahead of sociology and we are still in the process of catching up, moving from the real to the virtual.

Some movements take millennia, then rush towards being a mainstream technology. With artificial intelligence, for example, there was no sudden, miraculous appearance but a long 2,500 history of mathematics from the ancient Greeks and Euclid through hundreds of years of probability theorists, statistical theorists, logicians and algorithmic geniuses, like Bayes and Laplace, then a more recent galvanizing force in 1956 with the Dartmouth conference, followed by a series of summers and winters, leading to the remarkable successes of the last few years. Technologies often have much longer gestation periods than people think.

Yet some technologies move at an extraordinary pace. It was only 66 years between the Wright brothers' first flight to putting a man on the moon. But it took 50 years from the first movie to the first movie with spoken words and a century to the first film on VHS videotape and another quarter of a century to get YouTube and streaming.

With the metaverse, some, like Microsoft's CEO, say it is already here, and he is right. Zuckerberg says 5 to 10 years, and he is also right. Epic and Nvidia's CEOs say the coming decades. Others, like Google, remain non-committal. They are all right, to some degree, as there is no year zero, no BC to AD, no before and after, no Big Bang. Things simply start to come together, as technology is combinatorial (Clark, 2023).

The virtuality of computers, internet, VR, AR, gaming and virtual worlds have been heading towards a combinatorial goal. That is evidenced by the fact that we as a species have been spending more and more time in virtual worlds. My parents spent a lot of time at the cinema. My generation spent more time than they would like to admit watching television. The next generation are social media addicts. A gamer generation is now a consumer, adult gaming generation and the coming generation, in their hundreds of millions, have spent huge amounts of time in virtual worlds. We thought the revolution would be televised; it is in process of being virtualized.

There comes a point of no return when enough intent, investment, existing worlds and momentum turn into a critical mass. We have reached that moment, hence this book.

Metaverse in motion

Some metaverse origin stories and visions may be overshaping our perceptions of the metaverse. Virtual reality is amazing but it is not *Snow Crash, Ready Player One* or *The Matrix*. Within our bigger picture of the history of technology, what is clear is that we spent more and more time throughout the 20th century, first in the alternative worlds of the written word, then print, then radio, film and television. Clay Shirky's *Cognitive Surplus* tracks the shift from broadcast to online, claiming that at least when computers and the internet came along we were active not passive participants in these alternative worlds. The first two decades of the 21st century have seen an explosion of this 'experience economy'. The amount of time we spend online has been increasing steadily both at home and work. Covid-19 was a further accelerant and we now live in a blended world of blended work increasingly from home. We also have blended entertainment through social media, YouTube, gaming and streamed TV services, blended finance with online banking, blended health via telephone and Zoom appointments and even blended eating with the massive rise of home delivery of recipes and ingredients or full meals. The future is blended with more and more of our experiences shifting online. Indeed, we now exist in a blizzard of other-world offerings and consume ever increasing amounts of narratives delivered from this virtual world.

The future of the metaverse is partly tied up with the future of work. Companies are setting up experimental places in the metaverse to see what works best. Although it is important to recognize much of this as marketing hype, the early experiments give some idea of how such virtual work may take place. Metaverse offices have been set up for social communication, online meetings, events, product demonstrations, interaction with international clients and innovation hubs. If it follows the past, it seems likely the metaverse will develop and evolve over time with increasing quality, capability, scope and use cases, rather than explode into being. Many can see how meetings may, and I stress 'may', be enhanced in a metaverse, or some specific training. Yet it is not at all clear that all work-places will transfer easily to the metaverse. On the other hand, collaborative projects, prototyping and design using digital twins, already largely digital, are likely to thrive.

The metaverse will be a place where all organizations and brands play. It will become the focus of huge marketing spend because the target audience will be there. The important point to understand is that the metaverse proposition is that almost everything will have a 'digital twin' and so the digital world becomes not just a replica of many aspects of the real world but also a world in itself, with its own structures and economies. Imagine the metaverse as another planet, intimately linked to planet Earth but in many ways wildly different, as there are fewer constraints.

So although the Multiverse is no longer a work of fiction, neither is it real. We are in the low foothills looking at a mountain in the very far distance. Like the early days of personal computers before the internet, a confusing landscape of different devices, standards, tools and crude attempts at networks are scattered around like playthings. Nothing has yet been fully realized. A good description of the state of play is Gibson's 'The future is already here – it's just not evenly distributed', but the metaverse does promise to create an open, social, collaborative world of avatar experiences that open up opportunities for learning.

Manifesting the metaverse

Novels and movies have provided thought experiments for the metaverse, but are there any that envision what *learning* could look like in the metaverse? The modern metaverse is unlikely to turn out to be wholly utopian or dystopian, a heaven or hell. Like most leaps in technology, it will be a blend of both, something in-between. Douglas Adams' always sound advice included, 'Anything that's invented between when you're fifteen and thirty-five is new and exciting and revolutionary and you can probably get a career in it. Anything invented after you're thirty-five is against the natural order of things.' It would be foolish to dismiss any technology on the basis of one early failure, namely Second Life, as early failures were features of almost all online technologies; early browsers, social media sites and smartphones to name but a few.

The starting point is the 'physical' world. You are a physical person in a physical world. Your self is also a mass of 'data' points, physical (biological) and represented (financial records, health records, education records and so on). These dimensions have to be represented or taken with you into the digital world of the metaverse and go with you wherever you go in those digital worlds. There is the question of who 'you' are exactly in the virtual world, as your body shape, appearance, age, accent and other things can be changed. Identity in the virtual world is not a simple transfer and can introduce ambiguities.

Imagine these other worlds, with which you currently interact, probably online, such as work, entertainment, government, health, finance and learning, as each having their own requirements or needs in terms of authentication and data. The internet is a useful precedent, as it became the substrate for a huge range of largely 2D content and services at different 'levels' of scale, complexity, demographic and geographical reach. The metaverse substratum, however that turns out, whether as something new or built upon the existing internet, will enable the shift to 3D, but that shift will be a general 'Meta' move with many layers and species of 'verses'.

In *Metaversed* (Wolfe and Martins, 2023), a range of sectors are examined in relation to the metaverse: Arts and performance; advertising, PR and marketing; retail; gaming; entertainment; production; sports and fitness; automotive; aviation and aerospace; military; healthcare; hospitality and tourism; architecture and real estate; manufacturing; education and training. The authors use these sectors to show what things are likely to happen in the metaverse. We focus on the last of these, learning, as this is likely to be one of its important successes and needs specific and special treatment.

Metaverse and learning

A great starting point for learning in the metaverse is Toni Parisi's seven-point manifesto. He wants to see some unifying, open, democratic principles at the heart of the metaverse. They may seem utopian, but there is a genuine wish that such an open path will be followed. Tempered by realism, the workable technology will need investment and sustainable business models; nevertheless, it is a useful statement of intent (Table 1.1).

Learning has for a long time been fuelled by learning technologies (Clark, 2023) and been moving in the direction of 3D worlds. The process of open distribution, democritization and disintermediation has been largely realized by a hardware-independent internet. As a source of both informal and formal learning, the internet has delivered FirstSearch, one of the most important pedagogical shifts in the history of learning technology, shifting agency to the learner. Wikipedia is the largest, free, open knowledge base, in the most languages, that our species has ever seen. YouTube has seen free video explode as a medium in learning; with other more formal layers of learning services, such as MOOCs, Khan Academy and others. We also see the emergence of AI-driven, smart services, such as Duolingo in language learning, and generative AI services that deliver generated design, content and co-learning.

The metaverse is a natural extension of this shift towards what is open, free and accessible. Information may want to be free, but it is even more important that the human good – education and learning – be free. For this to be realized, autonomy, learning by doing and learning with others have to be part of the mix. Parisi's manifesto gives us guidance about what is possible if we transcend the tendency for learning to be closed, elitist, controlled by commercial interests, needing proprietary hardware and software, fragmented, institutionally bound and costly.

TABLE 1.1 Manifesto

Parisi manifesto	Learning manifesto
There is only one metaverse	There is a new learning world
Metaverse is for everyone	Metaverse learning is for everyone
Nobody controls the metaverse	Nobody controls metaverse learning
Metaverse is open	Metaverse learning is open
Metaverse is hardware-independent	Metaverse learning is hardware-independent
Metaverse is a network	Metaverse learning is networked
Metaverse is the internet	Metaverse is a learning world

The great triumph of the internet was its openness and access. A habitat can grow and evolve if it is built on solid earth and open to the sky. With a sound set of standards and the ability to set up easily, quickly and cheaply, anyone could enter the learning game, from the individual to large organizations; a vision of open education was therefore made possible. This is the current intention with metaverse technology, with discussions around standards being held in an open and collective fashion.

We have seen technology emerge that brings education closer to the disenfranchized. With smaller, faster, cheaper connectivity and devices; along with the delivery of connectivity through global, no-blind-spot technologies, such as Starlink, we will be creating a metaverse delivered from a layer above our planet, opening up learning for anything to be available to anyone, at any time, in any place. At that point, the metaverse will have a solid and successful existence.

Shifts in perspective

2D learning came relatively recently in our evolution, around 5,000 years ago with the invention of writing, manuscripts, books and eventually 2D screens for film, TV and computers. Yet we have two eyes evolved with stereoscopic vision and if we have to learn about the real world, reality is 3D. We also hear, feel and smell in 3D – as we have two ears, two hands and two nostrils. Our immediate transportation into another world is made easy by this evolutionary background. It is not that you suspend disbelief in VR but that belief is suspended automatically, as the mind is fooled into being there, having presence in this new world.

To understand the metaverse, one must understand not only our evolutionary past, which allows consciousness to be swapped out with ease, but also the technologies we have developed to progressively shift perspectives and power into the hands of users and learners. All of these media inventions involve perspectival shifts.

In the physical *theatre*, from the ancient Greeks onwards, the viewing distance is fixed; it is one long, fixed perspective of the stage. Yet the stage was a 3D model of reality with real 3D actors, props and scene changes to indicate changes of place and time. The 'fourth wall', where actors pretend you are not there but we see through the wall to observe and feel the performance, is invisible but solid.

In *cinema*, the close-up, medium, long, pan, cuts and other techniques gave more freedom with multiple perspectives. You the viewer, as the camera, could be anywhere relative to the action, although you have no choice on where you are taken. These are more than mere scene changes; you are taken closer, further away and moved around within a scene. It is still essentially a multiple perspective 'theatre' experience, with a 2D screen replacing the 3D theatre, the great illusion being, of course, that it is shown on a 2D screen but appears to be 3D. This cinema experience has been remarkably immune to change. Improvements to talkies, from black and white to colour, also in sound and vision, have been gradual.

With *broadcast media*, radio and television, we took cinema into the home, especially as affordable screen size grew. This is significant, as this is the user's personal not public space.

Video on demand was the next move, first on videotapes, then DVDs, where content was time-shifted, free from fixed schedules, weekly releases and half or one-hour slots. YouTube and Vimeo were instrumental in shifting us towards the expectation that films and TV could be watched when it suited the viewer. In learning, we saw corporate videos and recorded lectures. Eventually, with larger screens and streaming, viewers had complete control in terms of what they watched and when.

Personal computers arrived with 2D screens, bringing huge amounts of autonomous user freedom, not only to consume but to create new worlds. They had visual metaphors, such as files and windows on 2D screens.

The internet was a combinatorial technology that brought video, radio (podcasts), computer content, interactivity and 3D computer gaming together. Both 2D and 3D media were available but the big difference was scale. One could access almost anything at any time from anywhere. The user therefore had massive and complete control.

Social media brought an added dimension in that groups of people could converse, co-opting images and video into their deeply social activities. This is now massively user-driven as the content is largely user-generated.

Computer games were another advance, with their created worlds, freeing you as the viewer to roam and do things within these worlds. This is a big shift as you are an active agent within these created worlds.

Virtual reality was the next step, as it literally swaps out the real world to present worlds that are virtual but social, with many of the possible dimensions of real life. Multi-user VR took things further, as social experiences with the 3D presence of your own and other avatars. This led to more sophisticated levels of learning, where teams and groups, with teachers or instructors, inside as avatars or outside giving guidance, could teach new skills.

As technologies have evolved, the pendulum has swung from teacher to independent learning (Clark, 2023). The history of consumer technology has also been one of shifting user control. From broadcast media with nothing more than channel switching, to computer control, search and the internet, video on demand and the box set released all at once. You can see where this is leading, as the metaverse puts you in almost complete control. It is not just a replica of the real world but a range of new spaces that allow the user to create new and unimagined worlds. You can see the progression here in terms of the increasing presence and agency of the user as both consumer and creator.

Conclusion

As with all new technologies, the metaverse has tended to be dismissed outright, as an evil idea in the minds of evil corporations, designed to enslave us all, something that will never be accepted by right-thinking people and that will fall like Icarus under the glare of right-minded criticism. The truth, as always, is more prosaic. The metaverse will happen and no one yet knows how it will shape up or what it will be.

Not everything in technology and its uses can be identified in advance. Indeed many hugely popular phenomena were never predicted at all. There is therefore no definitive definition of the metaverse. Our definition is a loose and tentative '*scalable shift from 2D to 3D, an interconnected, interoperable set of mixed-reality and virtual spaces where people can engage, as digital avatars, in fun and useful social endeavours.*'

As our minds evolved a faculty of imagination, millions of years ago, we have been turning away from the limits of the real world. Since storytelling began and we first painted the exquisitely decorated caves of Chauvet and Altamira, it has been our constant endeavour, over thousands of years, to build places, write, make movies, play games and create ever more elaborate and wonderful new worlds.

We have been holding our heads in the clouds for as long as we have told ourselves stories, spending more and more time immersing ourselves in those other worlds. The metaverse is just the latest realization of that human need, the need to escape from the harsh reality of the real. We may catapult ourselves a few miles out into the infinite space of the universe and hit a few barren rocks but our real effort has been in creating our own new worlds in the here and now.

With the metaverse, we have an open book. Far from being defined up front, it is likely to surprise us. There are no rules because it transcends the limitations of the real world, its biology, physics and sociology. Virtual worlds are more limitless than real ones. We see glimpses of it in the various species of existing immersion in books, movies, games and other immersive worlds but it is a yet-to-be-written book open to unimagined opportunities.

Learning may be the killer app for the metaverse. There is congruence between the needs for attention, focus, embodiment, doing, context and transfer, which makes it ideal for immersion. We don't see it yet because we have never had it. It has yet to happen, but it will.

People are not satisfied with being ordinary people in ordinary places; they want to be extraordinary people in extraordinary places. The metaverse will be that extraordinary place. The metaverse, our desire to create other worlds in which we escape from this world, is nothing new, so we will now explore the roots of our desire to create such worlds.

Bibliography

Abbot, E (1884) *Flatland: a Romance of Many Dimensions*, Dover Publications, New York

Adams, D (2005) *The Salmon of Doubt: Hitchhiking the universe one last time*, Ballantine Books, New York

Ball, M (2022) *The metaverse: And how it will revolutionize everything*, Liveright Publishing, New York

Clark, D (2023) *Learning Technology: A complete guide for learning professionals*, Kogan Page, London

Cline, E (2011) *Ready Player One: A novel*, Broadway Books, New York

Gibson, W, The future is already here – it's just not evenly distributed, *The Economist*, 4 December 2003

Kindig, B, The key to unlocking the metaverse is Nvidia's Omniverse, *Forbes*, 2 September 2021, www.forbes.com/sites/bethkindig/2021/09/02/the-key-to-unlocking-the-metaverse-is-nvidias-omniverse/?sh=4ebf7e85e17e (archived at https://perma.cc/8KBZ-96KD)

McLuhan, M (1962) *The Gutenburg Galaxy: The making of typographic man*, Routledge, New York

Parisi, T, The seven rules of the metaverse [blog] *Medium*, 22 October 2021, www.medium.com/meta-verses/the-seven-rules-of-the-metaverse-7d4e06fa864c (archived at https://perma.cc/KW6W-XTW6)

Shirky, C (2010) *Cognitive Surplus: Creativity and generosity in a connected age*, Penguin, London

Stephenson, N (1992) *Snow Crash: A novel*, Bantam Books, New York

Wolfe S G and Martins, L B (2023) *metaversed*, Wiley, New Jersey

02

Philosophy of the metaverse

It may seem odd to bring philosophy into a book on the metaverse, but it is a solid starting point as there have been thousands of years of profound thinking about the real and virtual, how we define reality and our understanding of it, not only philosophical speculation about what is real but also about ethical issues.

Philosophy teaches us to look at issues such as the real and virtual in new ways, to be less certain of our certainties, less attached to binary distinctions and more open to new possibilities and definitions of what is real. Some philosophers are interested in the specific implications of the metaverse and consider questions about the nature of reality and the boundaries between the physical and virtual worlds.

When we really examine being in the world and cognition, things get a lot more complex, and previous, intuitive simplicities turn out to be wrong. Virtual worlds, as products of our imagination, are more common than we think. A philosophical understanding of where this impulse for second worlds comes from is useful.

We need to consider what we see as experiences in relation to consciousness, cognition and our need for generating metaphysical speculation and beliefs in other worlds, most commonly seen as some form of afterlife. metaverses are not unusual in *metaphysics*, as the other world is seen in many philosophical systems as a reality either unavailable to us or the recognition that there is no material reality at all, even that we are in a simulation or multiverse. There has been intense debate around the very nature of the real and whether it differs from the virtual, even the possibility that the virtual is just as real as that which we normally regard as real.

Similarly in *ethics*, moral philosophy and thought experiments force us to face up to what we actually mean by ethics and the moral challenges we face when dealing with new forms of being and technology. There is often a confusion in ethical thinking about technology, as if moral philosophy were about sniffing out the 'bad'. That is lopsided and not ethics at all. Ethics is a complex subject that investigates the very nature of ethical judgement and the nature of rights and wrongs, not just the wrongs. So much so-called ethical investigation around technology is barely disguised confirmation and negativity bias, attempts to simply find fault. Rarely do you see an ethical approach that truly attempts to also see the benefits and common goods that technology brings. They quite often descend to the level of witch-hunts.

One fair ethical lens is to take a utilitarian look at both the benefits and possible harms. If we do this with another technology, say vehicles, we know that well over a million people die every year in vehicle crashes, with many more injured. Yet we see the benefits of personal and public transport as outweighing that harm, so driving has become a normalized technology. Any reasonable look at new technology, learning technology or otherwise, such as the metaverse, can also be subjected to this form of analysis.

There are certainly possible harms, some philosophical, some existential, others around personal safety and privacy. But there are also benefits – social, financial, medical, fun and, the subject of this book, learning. As with most technology, it is a matter of eliminating or minimizing the potential harms and maximizing the benefits and social goods. Some are interested in the social and political implications of the metaverse and consider issues such as the potential for the metaverse to either free us or reinforce existing power dynamics and inequalities.

The metaverse is an intangible second world and these worlds have been part of human culture for as long as we have had language sophisticated enough to tell stories that can describe such worlds. These stories were sacred but became secular with the rise of philosophical speculation and it is in our two and a half millennia of philosophy that we find deep and rich veins of thought on the subject of second worlds. From Plato to the scholastics and on through the hard stop of Descartes to Baudrillard and Chalmers, along with moral reflections by Nietzsche and Nozick, philosophy has debated these topics at the highest of intellectual levels.

Philosophy of the metaverse

In caves from 50,000 years ago, we created enclosed worlds, full of useful instructional images through the inspired, visual spectacle that was cave art. Aspirational, alternative worlds have been similarly imagined in religious thought for millennia, as heavenly realms, free from the pain and suffering of earthly existence and were represented, in print and art, as places of peace, pleasure and harmony. The fascination and pull of the idea of a metaverse is similar to these religious, transcendental ideas – the metaverse as a heaven on earth.

Many different religions and spiritual beliefs have a concept of heaven or a similar afterlife realm. In Christianity, Heaven is often referred to as the Kingdom of God, a place where the souls of the selected faithful go after they die. In Islam, Heaven is Paradise, described as a place of abundant beauty and delight, where the souls of the righteous enjoy eternal bliss. In Judaism, Heaven is known as Olam ha-Ba, a future world in which the dead will be resurrected and live in a state of eternal happiness. In Hinduism, Swarga is one of several potential reincarnated destinations for the soul after death, depending on the individual's karma. In Taoism, Heaven is called T'ien, and is seen as the realm of the celestial deities and the source of all goodness and virtue in the world. The Vikings had Valhalla. There are many other examples of the concept of heaven or similar afterlife realms.

While the concept of heaven may share some similarities with the metaverse, such as the idea of an ideal, virtual realm in which people can interact with each other and with their surroundings, they are not the same thing. Heaven is a spiritual, the metaverse a technological concept. Yet, although the metaverse is concrete and examinable, not heavenly, what matters is the evidence it provides of our drive towards creating such alternative worlds, a drive that is fairly universal across cultures and time. Only 16 per cent of the world's population claim to be secular; most of the other 84 per cent believe in a religion that has a supernatural dimension, the existence of another world as a separate realm, heaven or paradise.

This is no dry, esoteric debate. A consequence of creating worlds such as heavens, and hells, is the common belief, among the billions of humans who believe in the Abrahamic and other religions, that they have a soul (or avatar) that will exist after death and that there are other realms (metaverses), heavens or possibilities of reincarnation, that make our 'souls' persist across time into these metaverses. As a species we seem to have a propensity towards the creation of worlds beyond our own, a propensity towards the creation of desirable, second worlds.

Throughout history, and prehistory, as a species we clearly had a drive towards imagining, worshipping, even devoting and sacrificing our lives for such second-realms. The metaverse may be the latest manifestation of that same drive to escape from the real world. But rather than stories, novels and movies informing us of other worlds and their dangers, some of the greatest minds that ever lived have considered ideas similar to the metaverse.

Metaphysics of the metaverse

The metaphysics of the metaverse are fascinating. This may be the first major medium, alongside artificial intelligence, that invokes serious philosophical discussion. One major book, *Reality+* (2022) by the philosopher David Chalmers, even argues that our new virtual worlds are just as 'real' as what we call the 'real' world. He goes through much of Western and Eastern philosophy to show that virtual worlds have been the subject of intense philosophical debate for over 2500 years, all the way back to Plato.

What is real?

In *The Republic* (375 BCE), Plato famously imagines his allegory in a cave. It gave life to a philosophical problem that has been at the heart of philosophy for over two millennia – what is real and what is appearance? Plato divides reality into the 'visible' and 'invisible' and asks us to see ourselves as being imprisoned in a metaverse of sorts, a cave, where we can only look at the shadows on the far wall of the cave, unaware of the source of light from the entrance. There is also a candle between you and the wall that creates shadows of things for your eyes. The lesson is that we only see appearances, not reality and that is all we ever see. We are trapped in a metaverse.

Plato goes on to argue that there is a way out of this world of appearance, to search through reason for the truth. The pursuit of truth was escaping from the bounds of our perceived world. Here one would find mathematically precise worlds of perfect forms. This is not far from the mathematical Platonism that would emerge with the 'world as simulation' theories of the computer age, two thousand years later.

This search for the truth was something Plato thought dangerous, as returning to the cave after realizing the truth could be hazardous, as evidenced by the death of Socrates. It raises, by analogy, another problem, later raised by Nozick, that when this choice becomes real, and we start to spend considerable amounts of time in other, virtual worlds, are we choosing a good life or not?

This first detailed consideration of our predicament, being trapped in our own metaverse, was to shape philosophy for the next two thousand years.

Religion

Nietzsche saw negation in the Christian need to create a transcendent world, a hatred of the real world, and many would agree that time spent in virtual worlds is a modern escape from the real. But suppose we agree with Nietzsche that 'God is Dead' and nevertheless create a transcendent world that augments and affirms life. Does the created metaverse obviate the need for metaphysics?

Nietzsche – who famously said, in *Beyond Good and Evil* (1886), that 'Christianity is Platonism for the masses' – identified this philosophical disposition, to create worlds, over and above the existing world, as a moral tendency. We imbue the current world, the one we find ourselves in, with moral deficits and create an aspirational world free from suffering and sin. In the Christian religion it is a rather rarified vision of a Heaven where access is for the virtuous only. Plato, with his definition of a divided world of appearances and perfect forms, was co-opted into this vision to give it metaphysical shape through St Augustine.

The metaverse, therefore, has this familiar pull, a heavenly world free from the friction and physical restraints of the real world, a world that Nietzsche saw as beyond good and evil.

The evil demon

As we emerged from the religious scholasticism of the Middle Ages, a new line was drawn over the past with the applied scepticism of the rationalist René Descartes. Like Plato, he constructed another thought experiment, one of philosophical doubt. Descartes introduces the idea of an 'evil demon' in his *Meditations* (1641). In searching for indubitable knowledge, he first puts forward the idea that everything we see may be the result of a dream state, therefore what we experience may not be real at all. Swapping our mind's perception of one metaverse with another in VR would have been a perfectly normal thought experiment for Descartes! He goes one step further in imagining a God that has created this illusion, but his third step is to imagine an 'evil demon' who sets us up to think 'that the sky, the air, the earth, colours, shapes, sounds and all external things are merely the delusions of dreams which he has devised to ensnare my judgement. I shall consider myself as not having hands or eyes, or flesh, or blood or senses, but as falsely believing that I have all these things.' This eventually leads to his famous conclusion that the only thing of which he can be certain is that '*I think therefore I am*', as even an evil demon must have someone to deceive.

This is a thought experiment, and Descartes saw that one defaults back into normality, the common sense belief that the world is real. We also have, in Descartes, the separation of mind and body or mind and the machine. As a dualist, he saw the mind as lying outside of the realm of the world. That world was the mechanical world, the world at that time experiencing a scientific revolution based on the mechanical workings of clocks and astrolabes. Just as the computational model grips us today, the mechanical model gripped Descartes and his contemporaries.

Nevertheless, this idea of reality being illusory, a metaverse of sorts, has stuck around stubbornly in Western philosophy, especially in the long tradition and various forms of idealism. George Berkeley, the 18th century idealist philosopher, held a *Matrix*-like belief that the real world is nothing but our perceptions of it – *esse est percipi*, essence is perception. This perceived world is not unreal; it is reality as there is nothing but perceptions. All of this is, rather conveniently for a bishop, held in the mind of God. This subjective idealism or immaterialism remains an interesting idea in philosophy, often seen in contemporary discussions of reality being a simulation. It may seem esoteric but it is not entirely clear, to this day, that there is a 'material' world.

Coming back to the more rationalist tradition, the Descartes debate has continued into the 20th century with the 'brain in a vat' hypothesis, variously describing the idea that we may be the subject of deliberately induced hallucinations. The idea of a dystopian intelligence goes back, as we have seen, to Descartes and his evil demon, the basic idea behind the film *The Matrix* (1999). Neo thinks he is in 1999, but it is actually 2199. He thinks he has a body but his brain is in a vat and has no body; it is merely fed hallucinations. Call the metaverse a matrix and you get the point. Simulated bodies are avatars and it is a world of hallucination. Twin World hypotheses have also been imagined by Putnam (1975). Putnam's famous refutation of this idea is that it is self-refuting, in that it assumes we have a brain and body in the first place.

This Cartesian argument on reality being an illusion has been revived in the age of artificial intelligence and computers, with the idea that we are in a simulation and that all we experience is within that context. The rise of the idea that cognition is computational has led many to hypothesize about the possibility and probability that we all exist within a computational simulation. This computational hypothesis, that the universe is fundamentally founded on computational principles, has its advocates. Note that this doesn't change anything. The world as we know it remains the same, it just changes the underlying explanation and structure. It is not an outrageous hypothesis, no more outrageous than those who believe in God, who speculate at this same level, and there are plenty of those.

Hans Moravec argues that the key to understanding this is the consistency and realism of mathematics, a realm of mathematical idealism that defines the possibility of us being in a simulation. Nick Bostrum argues that this is possible but that we are unlikely to ever know whether it is true or not and the fact that any evidence may also be simulated leads to an infinite regress of nested simulations, making proof difficult, if not impossible.

Consciousness as metaverse

Is there a parallel between consciousness and the metaverse? Consciousness is the state of being aware of one's thoughts, feelings and surroundings. It is a fundamental aspect of human experience. The term 'metaverse' refers to a collective virtual shared and social space. While consciousness and the metaverse are related, in the sense that both involve mental experiences and the creation of virtual environments, they are not the same thing. Consciousness is a personal and subjective experience, while the metaverse is a collective and constructed space.

Yet consciousness is a construct and to daydream is to find ourselves suddenly lost in the reverie of our own imagination, to enter a personal metaverse. We do this more frequently than we think; while sitting, walking, doing physical tasks, even while speaking to others; our minds drift into our internal metaverse.

Even more extreme is sleep, where we daily enter a dark, virtual metaverse, for around eight hours, punctuated by episodes of surreal imagination. It is wholly disassociated from the actual world. You are inside another world, the world of your unconsciousness with occasional conscious-like wanderings. These products of our imagination can be overwhelming, realistic and vivid. The fact that they can include people we know, or do not know, and interactions with these people, also gives them a social dimension.

Dreams during sleep fit most definitions of the metaverse – totally immersive, risk-free interactions with other people and things in imagined worlds – but the vision of the metaverse is not a vague dream. It needs concrete proposals on a full stack of infrastructure, standards on interoperability, agreement on governance and, above all, value-creating reasons for being there.

We also induce dream-like metaverse experiences. Evidence for drug use goes back millennia, from alcohol to hallucinogens that created alternative realities to normal consciousness. The 'drunken monkey' hypothesis, posited by Robert Didley, claims that we took to alcohol when we started to descend from the trees and search for rotten, over-ripe fruit, a new dietary niche. A single mutation has been identified at around 10 million years ago, ADH4, which allowed us to metabolize alcohol, which would otherwise be poisonous to us and we have, so the story goes, been fond of the stuff ever since. Psilocybin mushrooms have also been part of human culture. Images of mushrooms in rock paintings in the Sahara go back to between 9,000 and 7,000 years and we have definitive evidence of hallucinogenic plant use from the 15th century onwards in Central America. From the simple blunting of consciousness to feelings of reverie to full-on hallucinogenic states, where images and other worlds appear in consciousness, magic mushrooms, LSD and other hallucinogenic drugs remain, for better or worse, part of many modern cultures as recreational drugs and forms of escape. Drugs are induced metaverses.

The extended mind

Andy Clark is a philosopher at the University of Sussex, who, with David Chalmers, an Australian philosopher and cognitive scientist at New York University, proposed the extended mind thesis (EMT) in their paper 'The Extended Mind' (1998). Some, such as Panksepp and Lakoff, see embodied cognition as an extension of the mind within the body, but Clark and Chalmers extend the mind, or cognition, beyond the body.

What is mind? As you read this from a screen, the text is in your mind. The technology seems invisible, part of your consciousness. When we lose our smartphone or laptop, we feel the loss, it is thought, because they have become part of our extended consciousness and mind.

Clark and Chambers see the use of technology, such as pens, diaries, calculators, computers and smartphones as extensions and part of consciousness. We, as humans, have minds that reach out beyond our skulls and bodies into the world; literally extended minds that treat technology, which we can store and retrieve memories to and from, as being part of our minds. It is an active form of externalism where the environment can drive cognitive processes. External objects function as part of the mind. These objects must do what internal processes do – the external objects must function with the same purpose as the internal processes, store and retrieve memories, help minds solve problems and so on.

Imagine a person looking at geometric shapes and holes on a computer screen. One uses their mind to fit shapes to holes. The next uses a 'rotate button' to match the holes. A third has an implant to rotate the shapes. How much 'cognition' is present in all three of these cases? They all think about the same thing and get it done.

Clark and Chalmers see no distinctions and regard the external process as on a par with what one would simply do in one's head. When using this technology, we are using a coupled system that has the same causal effect on behaviour as relying just on memory and thinking. Whether it is in the head or not is immaterial. Language they also see as one major example of an extended technology being 'in the loop' of cognition. There is a reaching out or extension of consciousness into reality or virtual realities that is all too familiar when discussing the metaverse and learning within the metaverse.

Extended mind and learning

While not presented as a learning theory, one can immediately see how the same extended mind idea can be applied to the cognitive process used in learning, and Clark and Chalmers do discuss the extended mind's role in learning. Learning itself involves the extensions we use to learn, the 'physical and computational artifacts' we use in schools and work in a 'densely coupled system'. More than this, they speculate that this coupling with external tools and artifacts may have been involved in the development of cognition.

Clark and Chalmers call this learning technology 'environmental supports' and use the examples of pen and paper to do (or learn) long division. This theory matters in learning, as the tools we use for input, such as pens, pencils, keyboards (physical and touch-screen), audio and video recording devices and even musical instruments can be seen as extensions of the mind. Learning is almost always an active engagement using these mind extensions.

The idea, they think, has some interesting consequences. Take morality – it may be that as data about us is out there and used in interactions with us, the old idea of a moral agent trapped inside our own heads becomes more dilute, as part of who we are is out there. Chalmers has suggested a redefinition of the extended mind in terms of sensori-motor interactions with external tools and technology.

Others still see a clear boundary between mental states, cognition and external entities. There is also the slippery-slope problem of determining where the extended mind stops out from, say, a smartphone to the internet to other devices, satellites and so on. Does the use of a GPS device involve, as a cognitive act, the triangulation of many satellites and data collected from cars tracking traffic jams? That's a stretch.

Clark and Chalmers have had some traction through popular books on learning, such as *The Extended Mind* by Annie Murphy Paul (2021), and the extended mind is discussed in detail in *AI for Learning* by Clark (2020). Margaret Boden, in her magnum opus, *Mind and Machine* (2006), thinks that the topic of cognitive technology will hold our attention for the next 100 years.

Metaverse and hyperreality

From another philosophical school, the postmodern hall of fame, Jean Baudrillard has proved relevant as a philosopher, cultural theorist and prophet of the metaverse.

In *The Matrix*, Neo carries a copy of Baudrillard's 'Simulacra and Simulations' (1981), and what we now call the Multiverse is close to the Baudrillian world of 'hyperreality', although Baudrillard thought the film's directors had got this wrong! Baudrillard, rather than seeing the world in terms of the old binary oppositions of appearance and reality, subject and object, oppressors and oppressed, sees us as increasingly being in this world of simulacra and simulations – ads, TV news and soap operas – and with the metaverse we literally step into these worlds on scale, inhabiting them and creating new economic models and economies within them. He mapped out the way in which this develops. It is not difficult to imagine a tipping point, when we spend more time and attention in the digital world than in the real world. This may be the point at which the metaverse starts to bite. metaverses start first to reflect a reality, they then mask and pervert that reality and increase the absence of that reality, then finally bear no relation to reality, a bit like Disneyland, in which Baudrillard sees the US embalmed and pacified.

When we not only spend more time there but, through VR, AR, glasses and other forms of extended mind technology that replace and mediate the real world, to find our way around, project on to and augment it, then the metaverse can be seen as being dominant. Beyond this, if we are in the metaverse looking out at the real world through AR or mixed reality, as opposed to being on the internet looking in, then the metaverse will have gone one step further.

Baudrillard's point is that we are increasingly masking and perverting reality, so that it becomes increasingly absent. We then see this new reality as being reality itself, which may pull us into different ways of being.

Astonishingly, all of Baudrillard's work was written in the era of broadcast media, before the internet. Now that his simulacra are being realized in technologies such as computer games, social media, virtual reality and the metaverse, he is more relevant than ever.

Baudrillard is also the philosopher of 'consumerism', which he thinks is a refutation of 'communism'. Rejecting the economic explanations of traditional Marxism, the actual world is now a complex nexus of consumerism, communications and commodities. People are no longer economic agents within a process of production, they are agents who consume and occupy digital and hyperreal worlds. The fact that one of the largest, most valuable and globally pervasive companies on the planet has adopted Meta as their brand and the metaverse as their goal, now confirms the view that physical production is no longer the essence of capitalism. Facebook makes its money from advertising. It is a consumer-driven company, harvesting and selling data from social activity, and may well be creating a perfect market which people willingly inhabit as target consumers.

Baudrillard's position on all of this was brave and honest. He saw such worlds as being more than extensions of humanity. They capture our attention and hold us hostage. As the world has become de-anchored as God's creation, we began to build our own worlds. It is not yet clear where all of this is going, or more accurately, taking us. The metaverse may not, if Baudrillard is right, work out as many think it will. He thought it was inevitable that we as a species would drown ourselves in our own simulacra, as their all-consuming nature smothers and consumes us. Baudrillard really (or unreally) is the philosopher of the Multiverse.

What would we choose?

Long before *Snow Crash* and *Ready Player One*, the philosopher Robert Nozick, in *Anarchy, State, and Utopia* (1974) proposed a thought experiment that has, for the last half century, been a catalyst for serious discussion about alternative worlds. Incidentally, the book is also a brilliant demolition of the sort of anarcho-capitalism that often underlies Web 3.0. He came up with the thought experiment as an argument against utilitarianism's position that 'happiness' or 'well being' should be our goal in human activity and morals, and that our yearning for heaven on earth is misplaced.

His famous thought experiment is that an 'Experience Machine' is available and you have a choice; either to stay as you are in everyday reality or enter a simulated, metaverse-like reality where any and all desirable and pleasurable experiences are provided. In his thought experiment, scientists can stimulate an individual's brain with happy experiences indistinguishable from experiences in the 'real' world. If you make this hedonistic choice, of a 'lifetime of bliss', you can't come back, and in a clever twist, your memory of making the choice is erased. Nozick then asked a provocative question: if given a choice, would we choose the metaverse over reality?

He concluded that we wouldn't, arguing that it is better to experience the highs and lows of this world than to experience the artificial, never-ending high of the simulated metaverse. We want, fundamentally, to be a person in the real world, we want to do things not just have the experience of doing them, and that such a machine limits us to what the machine can make, not deeper realities.

Nozick would have seen the metaverse as a move towards inauthenticity and his experiment warns us against the utopianism of imagined, other worlds, heavens on earth. It is so easy to get carried away with this quasi-religious idea that such a world will be better, even in the sense of being more useful. It is certainly questionable, according to Nozick, that it would bring us contentment.

At a more practical level, to spend one's life in the metaverse would be like spending one's life in a submarine. It may seem exciting for a while and you will experience some great things but after a while you will long for real life and the breadth and realism of that experience. There are several lessons to be learnt from Nozick's thought experiment. First, that the choice matters. Will people choose to spend their time other than for specialized experiences, such as games? Second, that the ethical choice between an idealized alternative world and the real world ignores our attachment to the real, even with all of its limitations and faults.

Some, like Frischmann and Selinger (2018), argue that this is not so speculative after all, as we are being lured into digital worlds that trap us, that the Experience Machine is already here and continues to present a slippery slope towards enslavement, through lots of tiny, personal steps into the all-embracing digital. We are, in effect, moving towards a more inauthentic life, where contests, places, objects and activities are created for us.

We have here an interesting philosophical speculation on what the metaverse may hold for us, the choices we may have to make and the possibility of it sucking us in and holding us in an inauthentic world that damages our appreciation of the real world.

Conclusion

We thought the metaverse would be a quirky idea, quickly thrown aside, the product of Zuckerberg's geeky imagination. It turns out to have been the subject of intense philosophical speculation for the last two millennia, the metaverse as metaphysics. Philosophy does indeed give us some general and fundamental ideas on the likely nature and consequences of the metaverse.

Philosophical reflection on the metaverse is worth the effort, as so many have thought about the nature of other worlds in our long philosophical tradition. It also throws light on some of the epistemological and ethical issues we face, when we consider the creation of such worlds. The idea of a metaverse is not new. It has been imagined, and argued over in philosophy, for millennia.

What an actualized metaverse is likely to do is stimulate more philosophical debate around the idea that, in swapping out consciousness or at least spending more time in simulated, virtual forms of consciousness, we may be increasingly revealing the very nature of consciousness. Actually experiencing the Cartesian dream within simulated worlds is likely to spark interest in the bigger philosophical debate about the very nature of what is real, and not real.

We can conclude that three millennia of religious and philosophical beliefs and speculation show that metaphysical beliefs are commonplace. Philosophical reflection has dealt in detail with issues around real and virtual worlds, appearance and reality. Philosophical reflection has also dealt with the ethical issues around virtual worlds.

Everything we think about the real world may need to be rethought, even turned on its head as the metaverse develops and evolves: what it is to be a human, live in the world, or different worlds, how we engage with others and think about ourselves. The metaverse may allow us to transcend the current limitations of what we can do, learn and experience.

Although these thought experiments and visions inform us of what the metaverse could be, they are still largely inadequate. They are signposts to, but not maps of, the metaverse. Without real-world benefits, the metaverse will be merely a virtual dreamworld or playground. To be able to hang out and play is necessary, but it is far from being a sufficient condition for success.

Bibliography

Baudrillard, J (2019) (1981) Simulacra and simulations, in C Greer (ed) *Crime and Media*, Routledge, New York

Baudrillard, J (2018) On consumer society, in J D Faubion (ed) *Rethinking the Subject*, Routledge, New York

Berkeley, G (1982) *A Treatise Concerning the Principles of Human Knowledge*, Hackett Pub. Co., Indianapolis

Boden, M A (2008) *Mind as machine: A history of cognitive science*, Oxford University Press, Oxford

Bostrom, N (2014) *Superintelligence: Paths, dangers, strategies*, Oxford University Press, Oxford

Clark, A (2001) Reasons, robots and the extended mind, *Mind & Language*, 16 (2), 121–145

Clark, A and Chalmers, D (1998) The extended mind, *Analysis*, 58 (1), 7–19

Chalmers, D J (1996) *The Conscious Mind: In search of a fundamental theory*, Oxford Paperbacks, Oxford

Chalmers, D J (2022) *Reality+: Virtual worlds and the problems of philosophy*, Penguin, London

Descartes, R (2008) *Meditations on First Philosophy*, translated by Michael Moriarty, Oxford University Press, Oxford

Dudley, R (2014) *The Drunken Monkey: Why we drink and abuse alcohol*, University of California Press, Berkeley

Frischmann, B and Selinger, E (2018) *Re-engineering Humanity*, Cambridge University Press, Cambridge

Nietzsche, F W (1968) (1886) *Beyond Good and Evil*, Penguin, London

Nozick, R (1974) *Anarchy, State, and Utopia, Volume 5038*, Basic Books, New York

Paul, A M (2021) *The Extended Mind: The power of thinking outside the brain*, Harcourt, New York

Putnam, H (1975) The meaning of 'meaning': Language, mind, and knowledge, *Minnesota studies in the philosophy of science*, 7, 131–193

Sheldrake, M (2021) *Entangled Life: How fungi make our worlds, change our minds & shape our futures*, Random House, London

03

Monumental metaverses

We have created fictional and virtual worlds for as long as we have used language, tell stories and create media and technologies to distribute those experiences. We have in parallel built buildings that reflect these imagined beliefs. A monumental building is the realization of an idea or ideas. Architecture is the manifestation of the virtual, the embodiment of an imagined set of beliefs and purpose. If you want to envision the future, it is wise to look at what has been done in the past, so let us look at the history of our building of monumental metaverses, both sacred and secular.

Monumental metaverses

We have created other separated worlds, physical metaverses, within the real world for 50,000 years. This started with the wondrous caves created as the result of our cognitive revolution, decorated with some of the finest images we have ever seen of the animals we feared and hunted, in places used as a social space when we were still hunters and gatherers. Then, with the Neolithic, came the megalithic builders who astonish us with their dolmens, barrows and stone henges.

Our attachment to religious worlds beyond our own led to some of our finest ecclesiastical architecture; temples, mosques and churches containing huge internal spaces. These spaces were designed to lift our minds towards that second world beyond the real, as a direct link with gods, and various heavenly realms. From the ancient Greeks onwards secular buildings, such as theatres and stadia, were also constructed, separate spaces for drama and sport. The theatre eventually gave rise to the cinema and concert hall; stadia became modern sports arenas. In education, the agoras and small classrooms of ancient civilizations have been transformed into huge, modern schools and university campuses.

One cannot deny that, even in the real world, there is ample and universal evidence that we want places to escape, for whatever reason, from the real world. These also give us clues about some of the human needs and cultural activities that are likely to take place in the metaverse.

Cave metaverses

To enter the cave at Altamira in Spain is to experience a metaverse from tens of thousands of years ago. There are other examples, such as Chauvet in France, and all show a remarkable spectacle. The walls are covered in animals, predators and prey. It is more than a spectacle, as this is a specially created world, deliberately painted to create a sense of instruction and wonder. It has all the hallmarks of a metaverse; a completely immersive and enclosed space, deliberately rendered in colour, its interior designed for groups of people to enter, cutting off perception of the outside world.

Clark (2023) argued that these were the first places or halls for social instruction, where one would learn in the flickering light how to spot the animals you needed to kill to survive or evade so as not to be killed; instructive simulations. Chauvet had been accidentally sealed by a rockfall, so perfectly preserved a world of animals that are not only exquisitely painted but use the natural forms and contours of the cave to create realism. This is a metaverse of sorts, partly in 3D, illustrated caves, created with purpose, executed with great skill, evidence of a cognitive revolution that saw imagination as the driver of our ability to plan and create future other worlds for learning.

These are not art galleries, but accurate depictions of colour, even seasonal colouring, shape and movement. Recent evidence even points towards a form of proto-writing, representing their reproductive seasons. A herd of bison and pride of hunting lions are shown as they would stand and hunt in real life. We know that the audience for these images included the young as silhouettes of their hands are plentiful, made by blowing ochre from the mouths. They wanted to mark their attendance, show that they were there and had experienced this wonder.

Like a modern metaverse, these are simulations within which you can move around. A large group of people could experience awe, fear, exhilaration and wonder in these impressive places, explore to find hidden niches, where some of the images had been placed. It was a social learning experience where one could experience potential future encounters or explain to others useful experiences you had in the past.

Wherever possible the 3D features of the animals were emphasized and used across tens of thousands of years. Sculptures of animals have also been found in these caves, as well as Palaeolithic Venus figures, such as the Venus of Willendorf, and enigmatic figures such as the Lion Man, perhaps a bear, along with many 3D carved images of bison, deer, horses and other mammals. They speak of our urge to represent ourselves and the animals we lived alongside, as predators and prey, as tangible, sculpted objects.

These caves are perhaps our first monumental metaverses, places of learning, products of our blossoming imaginations and our need to pass on cultural knowledge.

Architectural metaverses

Architecture is a realization of our imagination and ideas, often with a purpose and that purpose is often to allow us to pivot to separate, second worlds. Many buildings, especially those praised as our greatest architectural achievements, are essentially ideas in stone.

As building emerged in the Neolithic, it was not long before megalithic structures, requiring huge communal effort, began to appear on the landscape. As our species settled, we made our mark by creating and building special, enclosed 3D spaces and worlds. Huge passage tombs, henges and dolmens were created, many as places for the deposition of bones, houses for the dead. To step inside these megalithic structures is to step into a place that is deathly quiet and deliberately designed to impress. They were certainly communal, social places where low-density populations came for social exchange, as feast remains have been found at their entrances. Being inside such monuments would have been a really special social experience, as there were very few places like them. There is also evidence for alignment with the cosmos.

Ancient Egypt excelled in creating monumental 3D structures that literally represent the creation and conservation of the world, also continuity into the afterlife. There are many chambers deep inside the pyramids of Egypt at both Giza and Sakkara, spaces that once contained sarcophagi, mummies and physical goods for use in the afterlife. Something about these massive entities and their purpose as mausoleums show our deep urge to create spaces to satisfy both worldly power and heavenly ambition. Just as impressive are the tombs in the Valley of the Kings and Queens. Their mineral colours are still fresh, every wall and ceiling covered with images and writing. To enter from the dazzling sun of the desert into their aisled structures is to enter as the builders and officials did, before they were sealed, deep into passages to the afterlife, funereal metaverses designed to last for eternity.

The Egyptians also created temples on an astonishing scale. One cannot enter Karnak, with its forest of 134 gargantuan papyrus columns, and not be impressed by the creative urge and effort that led to their construction. Up and down the Nile are temples built over thousands of years, protected by the desert sand until their rediscovery centuries later, a 3,000-year culture devoted to monumental architecture, designed to embody virtually imagined worlds.

In the first millennium, out of the eastern Roman Empire, Christianity emerged from the catacombs, themselves sacred spaces, to build the largest buildings in the world. The Hagia Sofia, built in the 5th century CE, remains one of the most impressive structures and internal spaces in the world. Its architectural innovations, arches and pendentives support a dome that remained the largest in the world for nearly a thousand years. The walls were covered in glistening mosaics, of gold, blue, green and every other colour, a fully rendered space to create a sense of sacred wonder and humility. It still does.

Out of this Byzantine tradition came huge basilicas, square and cross churches and octagonal structures that rose to create some of the most beautiful churches on earth. Despite bouts of iconoclasm, their aim was to celebrate what is otherworldly and Godly. These are not utilitarian and secular spaces, they are artificial places to morally engage the mind and contemplate one's fate. The great cathedrals of Europe took Gothic innovations, the pointed arch and flying buttress in particular, to build even higher, with huge windows of glass, as colourful as their precursor Byzantine mosaics. They are soaring metaverses.

In Istanbul, these Byzantine innovations were adopted and adapted to the needs of another religion of the book, Islam. Sinan's mosques are second to none in creating wide and open spaces, free from figurative decoration but covered with geometrically tiled colour. They do more than rival the spaces created within the basilica tradition that carried over into the great cathedrals of Europe; they surpassed them. Being inside these mosques is to be in as open a metaverse as one can imagine.

We have the illusion in many European churches of undecorated spaces that sometimes lack colour but this is post-Reformation iconoclasm. Even the smallest of parish churches, such as those that still sit in their thousands in England, some going back 1,300 years, would have been a riot of colour on the inside, painted with frescoes to instruct the largely illiterate parishioners. Doom frescoes were common, to envelop and threaten worshippers with hell and damnation if their behaviour faltered. The Sistine Chapel is perhaps the most famous of these decorated spaces, encasing the viewer in an entire worldview, with God's creation of the world, man and woman, then humanity's fall from grace up until the birth of Jesus. It is arguably the most perfect example of a building expressing a whole metaphysics as a metaverse.

Over millennia, we have created these huge spaces, alternative worlds, from brick, stone and mortar, places separate from the ordinary world, spaces of worship and contemplation. They required a huge communal, social and collective effort and were seen as public places. These are among the greatest achievements in civilization and seen by us as such. Within these buildings we extend their physical reality through frescoes and paintings to give the illusion of reaching up to heaven or down to hell, trompes l'oeil to give depth and the illusion of 3D, false skies and perspective to make the spaces look larger.

Sacred buildings are therefore truly representative of ideas. Their scale shows the status of religious power, their height upwardly aspirational. It is only when you enter a Neolithic tomb, Egyptian pyramid or temple, Byzantine church, Sinan mosque or European cathedral, that their real purpose is revealed. They demand a feeling of reverence. As metaverses in themselves they are often fully rendered, with windows that are not meant to be looked through but looked at or to act as light sources for stained glass, all designed to cut the mind off from the outside world, to turn our thoughts inwards and towards the metaverse that is the afterlife.

Churches, mosques and temples are therefore proto-metaverses, which illustrate and prepare one for a more perfect metaverse – the afterlife. Yet they also serve the purpose of reflecting and learning about being better moral beings in the real world. We go to such places for metaphysical reflection and solace and come back to the real world having learnt to become better people. Images within these spaces take on deep religious significance, as 3D relics, statues of saints, even icons, where the laity can commune with God through the objects themselves.

So we have decorated and built spaces to escape from the real world, places where we perform rituals, access other worlds, place ourselves within these worlds. We crave the excitement of a social experience that is beyond the norm. Tens of thousands can congregate to worship, support, sing, dance and believe that there is an afterlife. We do not see these worlds as unreal, rather they seem more real, more intense, more revelatory, more exciting, more moral and better than the real world. They therefore give us an idea of what we require of the metaverse.

Modern monumental metaverses

Church and temple building has continued, even in this more secular age. La Sagrada Familia in Barcelona, a Gaudi building, like some medieval cathedrals, not complete but Barcelona's most famous building. The Lotus Temple is New Delhi's Bahá'í house of worship, a lotus-shaped wonder, built from the same white marble as the Parthenon in Athens, which has attracted over 100 million visitors.

The wrought-iron Eiffel Tower in Paris remains one of the most iconic towers in the world. It is the most visited monument in the world and was the highest building in the world until topped by the Chrysler building in New York. The biggest is now the Burj Khalifa in Dubai, at a massive 2,717 feet. But it is not just height that matters. Some buildings really do define a city, like the double Petronas Towers, that resemble a giant M for Malaysia, in Kuala Lumpur, an aspirational idea manifested in these monumental towers. Some of these towers are literally vertical villages, such as the Shard in London, the tallest building in Western Europe, inspired by church steeples. Towers and skyscrapers can define a city and the race to build the highest, most spectacular tower shows no signs of waning.

These are all undoubtedly representations of power in large global centres but they also become common, cultural icons within a city, country and culture. They show a need for metaverse-like physical, but also cultural and psychological, 3D spaces and symbols, on a global scale across all cultures.

Workplace metaverses

The chief architect of the metaverse, Marc Zuckerberg, built Hacker's Way in Menlo Park. Look at it from above on Google Maps, itself a sort of global metaverse, and you see lots of rectangular buildings which are open-plan offices, surrounded by acres of car parking. Frank Gehry designed it to be open, walkable and social. Its Disney-inspired Main Street is a bit twee, with tree-filled public squares, but inside there are huge windows and lots of space. This is a social community that somewhat reflects the designers' vision for a social metaverse, a place for work and play. It is a flat, physical, social network design.

About 30 minutes away by car is Apple Park, a perfect four-storey ring or donut shape, a futuristic, Platonically perfect, non-hierarchical, configurable circle, the perfect metaverse. It reflected Steve Job's idea that design matters and innovation matters more.

A further 15-minute drive and you are at Google's Mountain View HQ, a vast sprawling Googleplex that looks like a circuit board from above. Inside it is open, full of whiteboards and lots of glass, a social space but also with lots of pod hideaways for more solitary work.

These are the antithesis of the old skyscrapers, representing hierarchical structures and power. These physical metaverses are far more likely to represent the open, decentralized, communal and social spirit in which the metaverse will be built.

Of course, even though these physical places were built to embody and stimulate abstract ideas, to be tangible places in the real world, as work changed technologically from the mechanical to the electronic age, we moved out of large factories into offices and, as the knowledge economy grew, entire clusters of skyscrapers housed knowledge workers, doing virtual work in the virtual digital economy. Covid forced all to work at home and many realized that being in a physical office made little difference, so blended working emerged as the new norm. Many in work now meet in virtual spaces, create virtual documents and manage virtually.

Spectacle metaverse

In these secular times, the largest buildings with vast internal spaces tend to be sports stadia. They have their origins in the Ancient Greek Olympics, and you can still run in the oldest stadium in the world at Olympia. The games lasted, astoundingly, for over 1,000 years. There are coliseums and hippodromes across the Roman Empire, revived with the rise of mass spectator sports in the late 19th century, with football stadia in the UK and baseball stadia in the USA. For football world cups, for example, multiple stadia are built, often from scratch, the same for multiple sports in the Olympics. These events are truly global with communal viewing figures in the billions. The 20th century saw the rise of these seated, floodlit and domed stadia and hardly a town now exists without one.

These are fields of dreams, designed as separate spaces, closed off from the outside world to witness the spectacle and drama that is sport. It is easy to forget that sport is the realization of a deep cultural need to practise and display conflict and achievement. They are social spaces on a huge scale, where tens of thousands assemble to share intense experiences.

The theatre, again going back to the Greeks, is a specially constructed space to hold the attention of a large number of people in a shared and imagined social experience. These spaces were in the open air, in the sunlight of ancient Greece and Rome but became totally enclosed in theatres of the modern age, in very different climates. Places of extravagant decoration, the whole point was to lose oneself in the artificially created virtual world of the play or performance. Some of these became cinemas when the recording of film was invented, showing that it is often a technological change that determines our shift in desire for metaverse-like experiences.

Secular buildings that house spectacles continue to be built. The Sydney Opera House is the best-known building in Sydney and one of the most important pieces of architecture in the 20th century, now a UNESCO heritage site. More recently the Staatsoper Opera in Hamburg and Guangzhou Opera House in Guangzhou, China, have become towering presences in their respective cities.

Stadium events and music concerts attract huge numbers to experience spectacular performances. Festivals, enclosed to provide their own metaverse worlds, now exist on a vast scale, over several days, where tens, even hundreds, of thousands pay to enter a world that is deliberately cut off from the real world, a few days of forgetting and reverie. The appeal of large immersive art experiences, such as recent Van Gogh and Dali exhibitions, show there is an endless thirst for scale and immersion in spectacle.

Avatar performance

Millions, over many generations, have loved, even adored fictional characters, such as Winnie the Pooh; also hundreds of Hanna & Barbera and Disney characters, mere 2D cartoons. Artificially produced, if not exactly wholly virtual, pop groups have also been around since the 1950s, with groups such as Alvin and the Chipmunks, their big hit 'Sugar, Sugar' still popular. The Archies, a fictional US group had a TV series in the 1960s; their fictional personas shown as 2D cartoons, the music composed and played by session musicians. And if you think today's audiences wouldn't be fooled by such artifice, think of Gorillaz, a cartoon group created by Damon Albarn with artist Jamie Hewlett. They were The Archies of the 90s.

A more direct example of the virtual was 'Not Easy', a song produced by Alex da Kid in 2016, which saw the direct application of AI in music to aid the creative process and provide data-led guidance on the writing of the song. His hit used IBM Watson to provide data from years of hit songs, movies and articles to inform the lyrics and melody of the virtually created song.

What launched virtual artists onto another plane was the increased quality of motion capture and AI and it was in Japan that truly virtual music artists were first created from scratch. Kyoko Date was born through motion-capture and 3D technology in 1991 but the first real success was in 2007 when Hatsune Miku became a 'Vocaloid' star. Vocaloid is an open-source service and has spawned a whole genre of virtual artists, with tours and loyal fans. The rise of 3D games has also allowed 3D artists to flourish. A marketing campaign in 2018 for the massively successful game *League of Legends* launched K/DA, a four-member K-Pop group. Voiced by real singers, they appeared within the game but became a successful music entity in themselves.

Aesepa, a K-pop girl group, launched a digital twin group in 2020 for each of the four real members of the group. K-pop went one stage further when Etern!ty was launched as a purely virtual group. This appeals, of course, to the record companies, who then have complete control over the group, available 24/7 for global marketing and performances. The technology is now so good that the avatars really do look, move and speak like humans.

Launched in early 2021, Etern!ty has 11 members, all avatars created by AI. The AI company that created the group, Pulse9, recognized that the Covid lockdown was the perfect window of opportunity to launch such a group and the creation process was intriguing. Pulse9 deliberately created their realistic pop stars through an online competition process where fans voted for their favourite potential members of the group from 101 candidates. These candidates were built from a 20-year database of past K-pop stars, from which the 11 were selected. Traits reflecting deliberately different and contrasting appearances and personalities were present. The final 11 were very different with different skills: singing, dancing and rapping. They even created virtual goods, such as concert tickets, jewellery and bags. In a remarkably honest TV interview, one member, Jane, accepted that her facial expressions were a bit crude in the early days but have got a lot better. She went on convincingly to explain her role as a singer, fashion influencer and actress.

This proved to be an interesting juncture, a sort of Turing test for music. Would audiences take to virtual groups? This takes us beyond the normal expectation that our heroes need to be human. It is a sign that the metaverse may well one day be populated by all sorts of famous virtual characters and phenomena by virtue of their virtuality. We already accept that music can be delivered via 3D artists, captured on body-motion cameras, rather than real life. Avatar pop is clearly here to stay.

Unfinished classical works by Dvořák were completed by AI in 2019, 115 years after his death, the work performed by the Prague Philharmonic. In addition to creating works by dead composers, avatars could be the performers for living composers who either do not have those skills or no longer want to perform live. If you think this is outlandish, then consider ABBAtars.

ABBA went on tour in 2022, 40 years after their last performances. Well not exactly, as it was 3D ABBAtars performing live with a 10-piece live band, appearing as their younger selves. This allows music stars to perform well into their dotage, even after death. The idea is not new as Elvis Presley, Buddy Holly, Whitney Houston, Tupac Shakur and Roy Orbison have all appeared as 3D images in shows. What was different was the four original members, along with body doubles, spending five weeks in virtual motion capture, performing their greatest hits. The promise, of course, is that any amount of demand can be satisfied and money made.

Will virtual music and stars overtake real people? Whatever the outcome, one thing is certain: the future of art and performance will be different because of 3D technology and AI. 3D virtual performers, real or imagined, inside real and imagined performance spaces are all platforms for artists, brands and businesses to hold live virtual events.

Iconoclasm

Curiously, 3D representations of reality were often the first to be destroyed in iconoclastic periods. Sculpture, embraced by most ancient civilizations, such as China, Egypt, Persia, Greece, Rome and Mesoamerica, was revered. Only Islam and Judaism rejected figurative sculpture and saw the representation of animal and human forms as idolatrous.

The Romans produced enormous numbers of statues, from public statues of emperors and other known figures to 3D tombstones. From Augustus onwards the imperial image was imposed through statues and relief heads on coins. Emperors could be condemned by their successors or the Senate and their statues defaced or destroyed. Heads were resculpted into the new emperor's image and political erasure was carried out across the empire.

Statues of pharaohs were often reused and reworked by their successors, including the dismantling and reuse of mortuary temples. The nose of a statue was often targeted as it was the place that the breath of life entered the body and would prevent survival into the afterlife. The most extreme example was the Pharoah Akenhaten, who chiselled out the name of the god Amun when he came up with his own religion of the sun. He tried to introduce monotheism but was also subjected to iconoclasm when all trace of his reign was erased and the culture returned to its polytheism. One must remember that these 3D statues were seen as real, not stone representations. They had avatar-like presence and power. Later monotheistic Christian and Islamic periods also destroyed ancient Egyptian images, where pagan gods were often chiselled out and erased, such was the power of representation.

Yet even in cultures and religions where 3D physical representations of people were accepted, they have often become objects of dynastic, idolatrous or sexual suspicion. Many religions have periodically purged themselves of statuary. Even large-scale political movements, such as communism and capitalism, have destroyed each others' statuary. Both sides used destruction as a form of ideological erasure. The symbolic toppling of Saddam Hussein's statue was a memorable moment in the Gulf War, as was the recent bout of statue toppling during Black Lives Matter demonstrations.

The metaverse, under attack from those who see it as unnatural, distractive and ethically dubious, has already attracted iconoclastic sentiment. A common reaction to the metaverse has been a visceral and sometimes hostile reaction to the rebranding of Facebook to Meta, as well as frequent denials of its utility and worth. It may be the only example of an iconoclastic movement to have emerged before it was even built!

Digital Twins

The use of physical spaces in the natural world and monumental architecture, along with 3D representations of ourselves and others in statuary, seems to have been persistent across time and cultures. Technological advances in design, from the lintel to the arch, dome, pointed arch, penditive and even lifts that allowed skyscrapers and towers to soar, allowed wider and taller buildings to create more internal space. Barely a town or city exists without evidence of our desire to create 3D representations of ourselves or 3D places which both represent and allow us to practise abstract ideas and beliefs, some also functional, such as airports and factories. Colossal spaces now exist in many places to satisfy our need to manufacture, play, spectate and worship.

All of these buildings can be seen in the digital twin that is Google Earth, where we can see our entire planet as a single metaverse. We can swoop down and see the Eiffel Tower, indeed the entire city of Paris in 3D. For years, Google has been adding 3D images of monuments, buildings, towns and cities.

Meanwhile, detailed digital twins of airports, buildings and other places are being built for practical design, planning and maintenance. Indeed, no building of this size is now built without being first created as a virtual 3D entity. Almost everything we design as a physical object is designed first as a virtual object. Anything real is creating its own digital twin with endless creative possibilities. In addition, AR is creating 3D objects and layers on top of the real world, with VR allowing us to be totally immersed in virtual worlds.

Metaversities are also being built to deliver real learning, with labs and digital twins of objects where the 3D nature of the entity aids learning. We do, after all, live and work in a 3D world, so it makes sense to learn many things in a 3D world. To learn by doing in context with the ability to apply one's learning is coming ever closer, freeing learning, teachers and learners from the constraints of the 2D world.

Many people have also created themselves as digital twin avatars to move around in such worlds. We all have a large dataset that represents us outside our own bodies and many of us have several avatars in games and virtual worlds used inside 3D worlds.

Conclusion

These thousands of years of building physical, monumental metaverses betray a long-standing need to build on a similar scale in the virtual metaverse. The one is a natural extension of the other. From the technology that built the physical we have moved to the technology that builds the virtual. Patrik Stephenson, architect at Zaha Hadid Architects, has written an influential article on how architects, not graphic designers, will design the metaverse. This is because it needs to be seen as a set of related private, public and social spaces, where navigation has to deal with discovery and serendipity. Architects, he argues, have these skills. We shall meet Patrik again in the final chapter.

Is there much difference between monument building and virtual monument building? They both have their roots in our needs for alternative worlds brought to life by our imaginations. We have seen how architecture, a 3D endeavour, over the last 6,000 years has created ever bigger and more functionally diverse spaces. These served basic human needs for work and play, physical and psychological. We adorned these internal spaces with art and eventually placed virtual artists as avatars within them. A natural progression was to create 3D virtual worlds in themselves. The physical and virtual are becoming paired and entwined in ways we never imagined possible. We are at the start of a creative process that has already twinned but will also create new offspring and entire families and new species of 3D worlds, objects and people, both representations of ourselves and new autonomous agents.

Bibliography

ABBAtars (2023) abbavoyage.com (archived at https://perma.cc/WY5S-S4C9)

Bacon, B, Khatiri, A, Palmer, J, Freeth, T, Pettitt, P and Kentridge, R (2023) An upper Palaeolithic proto-writing system and phenological calendar, *Cambridge Archaeological Journal*, 1–19

Clark, D (2023) *Learning Technology: A complete guide for learning professionals*, Kogan Page, London

Etern!ty (2023) eternity-official.imweb.me (archived at https://perma.cc/JV3Z-WMQ3)

Schumacher, P (2022) Schumacher's 12 Theses on the metaverse, patrikschumacher. substack.com/p/12-theses-on-the-metaverse?r=izzlx&s=w&utm_campaign=-post&utm_medium=web (archived at https://perma.cc/Z3GS-GRWN)

04

Media metaverses

We induce various forms of deliberate daydreaming by willingly submitting ourselves to metaverses invented by others. Reading a book can be hugely immersive, as reading encourages your own imagination to interpret the text as a personal, created world. You are not only pulled into the world created by the author but create mental images and models of that world in your own mind. Radio is an aural medium, as is its most recent manifestation, the podcast, in which we can lose ourselves for considerable periods of time; again, with our faculty of the imagination we build on the words it creates in the metaverse of our minds. Movies and television build visual and aural virtual worlds and can 'show' the metaverse.

As these consumer media developed, the thirst grew for more realism, more immersive experiences. Film, influenced by the games industry, began to use 3D graphics technology and weave 3D graphics, CGI (computer-generated imagery) seamlessly into their offerings, so successfully that audiences are now barely aware of what is real and not real. Entire movies were then made in 3D graphics, now a genre in itself.

Novels, films and television imagined the metaverse long before it started to be realized, but as we chart the story of media metaverses, we see technology push the dial relentlessly from 2D towards 3D experiences.

Novel metaverses

Novels are metaverses in themselves and can take us inside those worlds in our imaginations, and explore the rights and wrongs of virtual worlds, as anything can be built, described and manipulated in simple words. For centuries, since the *Iliad* and *Odyssey*, we have escaped into other worlds in stories and prose. In one sense, all fiction creates other worlds, which we willingly enter and learn from. Text can create complex and varied virtual worlds, explore depths of experience and feelings, as well as moral consequences. That the medium is words does not make them any less rich, indeed some would argue that the richness of language allows the author to create deeper and subtler worlds and narratives that the reader feels with an intensity that can be richer than the merely sensory world of TV and movies. These electronic media often have their origins in the very richness of published books or written scripts. Huge, expansive and imagined worlds in books such as *The Lord of the Rings* and *Game of Thrones* have created global media metaverses that have captured the minds of global audiences, realized both in books and on film. Even narratives for children, such as *The Chronicles of Narnia*, take us through doors into alternative worlds.

Stories and novels have also been prophetic on the metaverse. Specific stories about imagined virtual metaverses are common. Stanley W. Weinbaum's *Pygmalion's Spectacles* (1935) describe goggles that place you inside the movie. Ray Bradbury's *The Veldt* (1950) replaces parents with a dystopian, virtual nursery. Philip K Dick's *The Trouble With Bubbles* (1953) is a short story where, to discover new lifeforms through space exploration, people can buy bubbles, individual metaverses called Worldcrafts, where they set all the rules, but the immense power of individuals over their newly created metaverse domains led Dick to suggest they need to be controlled. It is a warning about unleashing new worlds without governance. Isaac Asimov's *The Naked Sun* (1956) has another planet, hostile to the earth, where people are repulsed by reality and prefer holographic 'seeing'. Vernon Vinge's *True Names* (1981) had VR hackers operate in the 'Other Plane', where 'warlocks' operate in a virtual world, interacting with events in the real world. It has several ingredients that are now familiar themes – the singularity, autonomously dangerous AI and bot generation – but it is the mutual suspicion and sabotage in a metaverse where nothing is real and anything is possible, along with the role that government and bad actors could play in such a world, that makes *True Names* relevant to the metaverse debate. Then there is oft-mentioned *Neuromancer* by William Gibson (1984) who coined the term 'cyberspace', a mass hallucinatory experience separate from the real world.

Then there are those novels that are more singularly and explicitly about the metaverse. *Hyperion* (1989) is a science fiction novel by Dan Simmons. The novel is set in a distant future in which humanity has spread out across the galaxy, and follows a group of pilgrims who travel to the planet Hyperion to meet with a mysterious and powerful being called the Shrike. Along the way, the pilgrims each tell their own stories, which reveal the complex and interconnected histories of the different worlds and characters in the novel. While *Hyperion* does not explicitly use the term 'metaverse,' the novel does deal with many of the same themes and ideas. These worlds are connected by a network of artificial intelligences and advanced technologies, which allow people to travel between them and interact with each other in virtual environments. In this way, the novel presents a vision of a complex and interconnected virtual world that could be seen as a precursor to the concept of the metaverse.

The most quoted luminary, however, is Neal Stephenson, who first used the word 'metaverse' in *Snow Crash* (1992), a dystopian thought experiment – snow crash being the white noise one used to get on televisions when they lost their signal. Your avatars can be anything you want them to be in *Snow Crash:* 'You can look like a gorilla or a dragon or a giant talking penis in the metaverse. Spend five minutes walking down the Street and you will see all of these... The user can select three breast sizes: improbable, impossible, and ludicrous.' There is also a hierarchy of avatars; variations range from cheaper, grainy, black-and-white avatars to boring businessmen exquisitely rendered in suits, up to glitzy rock stars. There are also daemons that are not humans but software agents with specific roles. You can't just pop in anywhere, as that would be confusing, disruptive and would break the idea that this is a consistent world. You enter via ports, like airports, where you arrive then use a monorail or start to walk downtown. You can only have one avatar and it can't be in two places at once and there is some interesting speculation about what happens when you or your avatar gets murdered or dies.

It is not some geeky, utopian, decentralized, duplicate world. It is an oddball world, full of odd people, doing silly, even venal things, a virtual night-time Las Vegas, with a strip (the Street), only worse. There are amusement parks that are really embedded video games and lots of dystopian behaviour with fantasy stalking, stabbing and dismemberment. But, hey, 'there are no gnats in the metaverse.' Stephenson has since admitted he got most of the speculation wrong.

Another novel, often mentioned in the same breath as *Snow Crash*, is *Ready Player One* (2011) by Ernest Cline, a more games-like version of the metaverse. This time, the cultural influence of computer gaming is clear. The whole metaverse is framed as a computer game, with competing teams, the huge corporation versus the little guys, the gamification of virtual life. It is a full-on VR spectacle, with gloves, bodysuits and omnidirectional treadmills.

Reality is a dirty, degraded, trailer-trash world where people live in squalor and pizzas are delivered by drones. Their version of the metaverse is a high-adrenaline games world, its inhabitants largely gamer-types, who can do anything and go anywhere 'but stay because of all the things they can be.'

In an interesting little educational aside, there's an exchange in the film about schools. 'You're not a John Hughes fan' says the baddie, 'because first thing I'd do is convert all the schools on Ludus to replicas from The Breakfast Club and Ferris Bueller.' It is a pop-culture test and *Animal House* is also mentioned. Learning in the metaverse is clearly a clichéd movie version of fun. 'You don't live in the real world' is said as a clever quip that sums up the *Ready Player One* vision of the metaverse. It is a one-dimensional mission game, where teams of gamers compete for the grand prize – cash and control. Halliday, the fictional creator of Oasis, says as much. In Cline's second novel, *Armada* (2015), the game's world and its gamers turns out to be a vast training exercise, so that gamers can save the planet from alien invaders.

Oddly, *Ready Player One*, set in 2045, with Oasis (Ontologically Anthropocentric Sensory Immersive Simulation), is really a revamp of Jekyll and Hyde, of good and evil, the uber-geek James Halliday and Ogden Morrow of Gregarious Games. As a thought experiment, it poses a vision of the metaverse as pure escape and entertainment. If it is prescient at all, it is in seeing the metaverse as controlled by one company. Meta may think of itself as Jekyll but many see it as Hyde.

Most hail sci-fi in literature as prophetic but it is partial. *Snow Crash* in 1992 is clumsy, mechanical, with its main street and a few aperçus about life in the coming metaverse but little in the way of deep reflection and vision. Was it that prophetic? Lanier had started the first VR company in 1985 and the games industry was well underway with a range of alternative worlds which one could actually try in the early 1990s, such as *Wolfenstein 3D*, *Doom* and *Quake*. *Ready Player One* in 2011 was also a reaction to an already mature and thriving games culture, not prophetic of that culture.

The mistake is to see sci-fi as the sole prophetic source of the metaverse, while more relevant written works are ignored. Two thousand years earlier, Ovid's *Metamorphoses* (8 CE) describes 250 acts of metamorphosis that are more fantastical yet far closer to our human concerns than many of these sci-fi takes. In being transformed, Ovid describes human passions, frailty and follies. 'Now I am ready to tell you how bodies are changed into other bodies,' he starts. We see the creation of the world and ourselves transformed into many alternative selves, like avatars in the metaverse. Prometheus appears, the first great myth about the dangers of us falling too readily into the use of technology. There is the tragedy of Narcissus falling in love with his own image, which presages the obvious worries around online narcissism. Erysichthon fells a sacred oak and becomes a starving merchant selling his own daughter to survive, while Midas, offered great power, is turned into an ass by greed, a tale eerily similar to crypto mania. Pygmalion becomes besotted with his created statue, falling in love with his virtual creation, which is a warning to us all about the allure of other worlds. To read *Metamorphosis* is to get to the heart of the matter, which is how we as people are changed by technology and how we become something else, as avatars that consume us with avarice, narcissism and greed.

This is also the stuff of Kafka's *Metamorphosis* (1915). VR and the metaverse can turn us, like Gregor Samsa, into things as yet unknown, its transformative ability quite wondrous but frightening. The story is a dystopian take on transformation, as Gregor starves to death, with the rest of his family relieved at being released from the burden. McLuhan, Lanier and many others point towards this feature of technology, that in creating tools, the tools start to shape us.

And who knows, the fate and folly of the metaverse may already have been written by Jorge Luis Borges in *A Universal History of Infamy* (1954) where he wrote of an empire where overzealous cartographers made a map exactly the same size as the actual empire, its analogue twin: 'In the western Deserts, tattered fragments of the map still are to be found... no other relic is found of the Discipline of Geography.' Will the metaverse suffer the same fate?

Movie metaverses

Despite the reverence around sci-fi novels, it was not the novel but movies that paved the path towards a 3D metaverse. Film as a medium marked a cultural shift away from 2D print to 3D viewing for entertainment and learning. From its inception, even though projected or viewed on 2D screens, it was the 3D illusion that created a vast, global movie industry. It was not just the content but the underlying appeal of 3D moving images and sound that saw the world flock to cinemas, then almost universally watch its even more powerful child, television.

When technology enables a shift from 2D to 3D, it happens at scale. In that sense, as McLuhan claimed, it is not just the content that matters but the way a technology changes the culture. Film changed our culture by bringing realism, moving images, eventually sound and wide field of view. It became a dominant medium but also raised expectations around what it is to have a shared experience in a cinema. It brought 3D experiences to the masses and in that sense it is evidence that we have a deep thirst for the affordances of 3D worlds.

Movies were a vital step towards popularizing the metaverse. A movie is a metaverse in itself; a self-contained, created world in which suspension of disbelief is almost immediate and sustainable over an hour or so. The use of special effects can also simulate the impression of imagined metaverses, as can sound. Films are, in themselves, visual worlds in which we deliberately lose ourselves.

From their inception, movies have also imagined future tech, with narratives that explored not-yet-built technology and worlds. It had several major landmarks, moving from mechanical robots to other planets, then back to earth with movies about threats from future worlds with *Terminator*. With our immediate and total suspension of disbelief, movies grab us and place us inside their created world, whatever those worlds may be. As a medium, film is a series of created metaverses that keep us entranced, albeit with a dystopian bias.

Film was, for most of its history when dealing with future technology, obsessed with *robots*. Understandable, as it is a medium of 'characterization' and virtual worlds were beyond both the imagination and graphic capabilities of the medium. The robots tended to be replays of the Frankenstein myth. Romantic writers, such as Goethe and Shelley, had written poems on the subject but it was through Mary Shelley's *Frankenstein: The Modern Prometheus* that the Promethean creation took hold in the popular imagination, although the creator, not the monster is called Frankenstein. *Frankenstein* had created its own monster, and subsequent films moved the name across to the monster. The story was inspired by the dystopian Prometheus myth that lies deep in Western culture. It goes back to Hesiod, and in the drama *Prometheus Bound* by Aeschylus, where Zeus had Prometheus chained to a rock while an eagle pecks at his liver, which grows again for eternity. His crime was to give mankind fire, but also writing, mathematics, metallurgy, agriculture, astronomy and architecture – what we now call technology. The play prophetically sets up the tension between our autonomy and God, still relevant to the metaverse debate.

Film, with its narrative need for conflict and action, tends to present metaverse ideas as dystopian visions, often the same dystopian ideas that were present in the original novels from which many are taken. Technology represented in film, over the last 100 years, has therefore reflected our fears, often the fear of technology itself but also of the 'other', whatever that 'other' was at the time – the Cold War, crime, violence, helplessness, corporate greed, totalitarianism, climate change and so on. There have been glimpses of a more sophisticated and subtler dynamic, as in *Blade Runner*, the *Alien* series and more recently a rush of movies around AI, as it takes hold on our lives and culture. And as virtual worlds have risen in prominence, and film can now create entirely believable graphic environments, metaverses have appeared in various forms over the last 40 years.

The first sci-fi movie showed a trip to the moon – *Le Voyage dans la Lune* (1902) by George Méliès imagined the future. It has a wonderfully fantastic virtual set but the moon is populated by insect-like creatures which we began to slaughter, bringing one back to earth as a captive. The moon was seen as a hostile place! The art-deco-inspired *Metropolis* (1927) gave us the first robot movie star as the iconic Maria, a highly sexualized, fetishized female representation. It set the dystopian tone for decades to come, as Maria causes death, drowning and destruction. The communist threat was looming and the underlying threat was the mechanization of labour.

The Cold War brought with it the chilling fear that the earth may be doomed and other worlds sought as refuge with *The Day the Earth Stood Still* (1951) and the groundbreaking *Forbidden Planet* (1956), the first film set on 'another world', first to have an electronic score and first to feature space travel that was faster than light. It was to be some time before technology revealed itself again, as the 1960s took hold and tech took a back seat. As the movies tussled with a rising tide of computer technology, the dystopian view came back, literally with a vengeance, with a slew of robot movies.

Total Recall (1990), based on a short story *We Can Remember It for You Wholesale* (1966) by Philip K Dick, takes the idea of implanted memories but its ambiguous ending also plays with the idea that the main character may be in a virtual world. *The Lawnmower Man* (1992) is a virtual reality plot, but more relevant to the metaverse was *The Truman Show* (1998), which had a TV producer controlling the life of the main character, more a manipulated metaverse.

But it was with *The Matrix* (1999) that movies finally unfolded complex ideas of alternative realities and the metaverse. *The Matrix* creates an altogether more philosophical vision and introduces the metaverse idea, or at least the idea that the world we see is a simulated world. It introduces the idea of a simulated reality, created to fool and entrap humans. Once again, a dystopian vision, but with a dose of philosophy, with references to Plato and Baudrillard, it poses a more general proposition that reality is actually a simulation created by machines that echo Descartes' evil demon. *The Matrix* brings Descartes into the 20th century with the 'brain in a vat' hypothesis, variously describing the idea that we may be the subject of deliberately induced hallucinations. Neo thinks he has a body and is in 1999 but he does not; he is in 2199 and his brain is in a vat while he is fed hallucinations. Call the metaverse a 'Matrix' and you get the point. Simulated bodies are avatars and it is a world of induced hallucination.

We now see the rise of movies that have the invisible internet, rather than mechanical and visible machines and robots, as their inspiration. Entirely created worlds become possible as the technology of film evolves into the use of 3D graphics and starts to cope with the ideas around simulated worlds. This is an important point. Graphics creation took great leaps, as advances in both hardware and software gave us ever more realistic worlds and characters on our screens. It was technology that enabled our imaginations to create these new worlds.

3D graphics

A quite separate story needs to be told about the role of 3D graphics in film that leads us in the direction of the metaverse. Claymation had been around for a century but it was at Boeing where the computer graphic 'Boeman' was created in the 1960s to show how people would fit and move inside the cockpit of a plane. Its creator, William Fetter, is seen as the father of 3D computer animation. The 1970s saw further advances on faces and body parts, such as hands by Catmull and Parke in what is seen as the first movie to feature 3D computer-generated graphics, *Futureworld* (1976). This was a key moment in the movie industry, as well as a long pedigree of advances in 3D graphics that lead inevitably to the idea of the metaverse.

One particular genre of film using virtual worlds that was to presage the metaverse and stimulate debate was Disney's *Tron* (1982). It has a programmer, Kevin Flynn, who gets sucked into the Grid, the movie's metaverse, a computer game. It is a stunning piece of cinematic design that shows both the advances and limitations of early 1980s computer graphics. It was the first to use computer-generated animation as a primary method of image production. Much of the Grid is black, stylishly minimalist, as it was not possible to do the full rendering necessary for anything else, yet the result is regarded as an innovative example of art direction and design. That each real-life character had a digital twin inside the Grid was also novel. It became a cult movie with a sequel in 2010 and computer game and comic franchises.

Industrial Light and Magic, driven by George Lucas in the 1980s, used 3D graphics in *Star Wars* but it was tools like AutoCAD from Autodesk and powerful Silicon Graphics hardware that gave us movies with groundbreaking morphing graphics, such as James Cameron's *Terminator 2: Judgment Day* (1991), followed by *Jurassic Park* (1993), but one film stands out as a turning point – *Toy Story* (1995). Its endearing animation of an entire set of characters won hearts and minds and set in motion a new genre of 3D animated movies. All of this takes place as computer games such as *Doom* (1993) and *Quake* (1996) are created, where 2D platform games are suddenly supplemented by full 3D graphic games. It was therefore in the 1990s that the virtual worlds really did become 3D. The deep roots of all this were rapid advances in technology, both for the creation of 3D worlds and characters.

Further *Star Wars* films relied heavily on 3D graphics and *Avatar* (2009) brought levels of character animation never seen before. *Avatar* was released as a 2D and 3D movie and one does have to ask why 3D in the cinema has not really taken off. The answer is that the viewer sits in a fixed position looking at the 3D world, not as in a computer game, moving through that 3D world. The additional value is therefore marginal. The illusion of 3D is already there in cinema, but 3D spectacles are awkward and do not add enough value to make it compelling.

Movies from that point onwards blended real shots and 3D graphics so seamlessly that it is now often difficult, even impossible, to tell what is real and virtual, not just in children's cartoons, but in all other genres, especially sci-fi and action. In truth, 3D animation is everywhere. Film and television use it as a matter of course.

What about the films of the two oft-quoted metaverse novels? Stephenson's *Snow Crash*, although developed as a script, has yet to enter production, as even the scriptwriter sees it as an enormously complex task to convert the ideas of the novel into a film. Spielberg's *Ready Player One* (2018), based on the novel discussed earlier by Ernest Cline, is a film version about that imagined metaverse. Once again dystopian, it is relevant in seeing one medium, film, being heavily influenced by another, games. The film is notable for its vision of the metaverse being a high-octane game. What is more interesting is that the cultural influence of computer games is clear in the film; the whole metaverse framed as a game, with competing teams, the huge corporation versus the little guys, the gamification of virtual life. It is the full-on gamer and VR spectacle, with gloves, bodysuits and omnidirectional treadmills. Reality is a dirty, degraded, trailer-trash world where people live in squalor and pizzas are delivered by drones. This metaverse is the geeks' revenge on the rest of us to lure us away from the harsh reality of the real world into their dreamworld.

As we will see next, it was the computer games industry that allowed us to enter, not just watch, 3D worlds. The move towards the metaverse has been happening for some time as we now live in a world where the real and virtual are often indistinguishable in terms of realism. In this sense, the metaverse has been here for decades – we just couldn't tell the difference.

TV metaverses

Television has also featured lots of series featuring metaverse worlds, VR and AR. From *VR.5* in 1995, where the subconscious minds of other people were explored, to the many practical applications of VR shown in *Harsh Realm* (1999), then into the new millennium, *Caprica* (2009) had VR headsets and any surface could be a digital device. But it was *Black Mirror*, with a series of episodes – 'Playtest', 'San Junipero', 'Men Against Fire', 'Hang the DJ' and 'Striking Vipers' – that raised the game. *Altered Carbon* (2018–2020) has a range of VR tech, also *Kiss Me First* (2018), *Reverie* (2018) and the taking of your mind to the afterlife in *Uploaded* (2020). This gathering momentum tracked the development of the technology of AR, VR and the metaverse over a similar period, acting as a prophetic medium, playing with the possibilities.

Social media

A similar shift from 2D text to 3D has taken place on the internet, which quickly became more of a video-based medium when bandwidth allowed video to be streamed. YouTube led the way and almost all social media platforms adopted the medium. Facebook, Twitter and Instagram all folded video into their services. Some, such as TikTok, have emerged as a purely video form of social media. Streaming video on smartphones, computers and domestic TVs has never been bigger, a recognition that 2D text was never enough.

The technology, especially smartphones with high-end cameras, where one can both shoot and edit videos on the device, led to an explosion of user-generated content. This followed our need to express ourselves not just in flat text but, as we are in the real world, in 3D. Video, especially short-format clips, were found to increase engagement. Long-form content is still largely the domain of TV, computers and tablets; the smartphone is with you everywhere, filling in those gaps when one is bored.

Future of movie metaverses

We do have video content and streaming from within virtual worlds. This happens in the gaming world but is also common from within virtual worlds such as VRChat. But future movies may well be experiences within the metaverse, as 3D experiences in themselves, where we take part, seamlessly, in the narratives. This will require a new type of writer and different production skills. A film is a 2D fiction that represents 3D worlds. The future will almost certainly include 3D art forms that put the viewer inside that experience. This is already true of gaming and almost certain to happen in the new medium of the metaverse. It requires massive bandwidth for fully rendered, seamless branching and such storytelling will have a different set of creative rules but it will happen.

Conclusion

Novels, movies and TV have prepared us well for the metaverse. As thought experiments they give us visceral experiences of what future metaverses may look like, what it is to be in them and the issues around their impact on us as a species.

Psychological evidence in oral stories, writing, movies, radio, TV and video over the last five millennia show an insatiable need to create, from our imaginations, sophisticated and shared worlds. But today's is also the gaming generation. Actual 3D worlds, especially 3D computer games, have become the main rival to 2D linear film and TV, taking away revenue and eyeballs, moving audiences towards actual participation within 3D worlds. That the games industry is now larger than the film industry is telling. What film does not do is provide 3D movement and interaction within 3D worlds. It is a passive, single-viewer, seated perspective. This has its place, largely in entertainment, but other 3D places are clearly more enticing if one wants more user autonomy and active experiences.

In the same way, learning will also shift from 2D media such as text and video on paper and flat screens to 3D, as we have a specific need for learners to participate. Learning is not entertainment, it is about knowledge and skills. 3D worlds offer an additional layer of participation, practice and assessment that is superior to 2D worlds. The future had been televised, then virtualized in 2D. It is about to be virtualized further in 3D.

Bibliography

Asimov, I (1956) *The Naked Sun*, Michael Joseph, London

Borges, J L (2001) *A Universal History of Iniquity*, Penguin, London

Bradbury, R (1950) *The Veldt, The Saturday Evening Post, Periodical*

Cline, E (2011) *Ready Player One: A novel*, Broadway Books, New York

Dick, P K (1953) *The Trouble with Bubbles. The Collected Stories of Philip K. Dick: We Can Remember it for You Wholesale*, Volume 2, Doubleday, New York

Gilchrist, T (2023) Joe Cornish Explains Why A Snow Crash Movie Crashed, Says it Could be Revived, *SYFY Wire*, www.syfy.com/syfy-wire/joe-cornish-explains-why-a-snow-crash-movie-crashed-says-it-could-be-revived (archived at https://perma.cc/79HP-NMG7)

McLuhan, M (1964) *Understanding Media: The extensions of man*, McGraw-Hill, New York

Schwartz, J (2011) *Out of a Writer's Imagination Came an Interactive World, New York Times*

Simmons, D (2004) *Hyperion*, Doubleday, New York

Spielberg, S, Silvestri, A, Penn, Z et al (2018) *Ready Player One*, USA, Warner Bros

Stephenson, N (1992) *Snow Crash: A novel*, Bantam Books, New York

Vinge, V (2015) *Armada*, Penguin Random House, London

Vinge, V (2015) *True Names and the Opening of the Cyberspace Frontier*, Tor Books, New York

Weinbaum, S G (1974) (1935) *Pygmalion's Spectacles*, Ballantine Books, New York

05

Virtual metaverses

In 2022, John Helmer and I recorded a podcast, one episode in our *Great Minds in Learning* series, about the metaverse. We have done these in the same room, over Zoom, also in front of live audiences in Berlin and Dem Bosch in the Netherlands. This time, we spoke to each other as avatars from within a virtual world, in AltspaceVR. The point was to discuss AR, VR and the metaverse from within that virtual world, so we met there to discuss the philosophical, pedagogic and practical issues around learning in virtual 3D environments. In the future, we may do this in a fully fledged metaverse with an invited virtual audience; all avatars together in one virtual space.

Traditionally, we would have published our interview in print, recorded it on radio, even filmed it on television. In books, radio, TV and film, even podcasts, you take the bus and go where the driver takes you; in virtual worlds you drive a car. In virtual computer games we actively enter and take part in metaverses, where our actions determine whether we succeed in a sport or virtually live or die. When we invented these active media, we could not only participate as agents in such worlds, we could team up with other people. These gaming metaverses did not just divorce us as individuals from reality, but allowed us to share that experience with many others. This is why computer games pave the way towards the invention of the metaverse.

The enormous amount of time we now spend on social media is yet another example of us immersing ourselves in spaces that are not real. Twitter is not a place, as Dave Chapelle famously said, and social media marks another form of Metaversian activity that is markedly social. The scale of this activity is astounding with over half the world's population using such virtual spaces, from Facebook, Twitter, Instagram and LinkedIn to TikTok.

Virtual worlds

Second Life

About the same time as Google Earth, Second Life started, in 2003, as an open 3D platform, open in the sense of having no stated goals, so entirely user driven. Aided by good publicity, it grew precipitously but then suffered a slow decline, as interest waned. Nevertheless, it is a useful precursor for the metaverse as it was a real, large-scale service that grew to around a million active users and matches a vision of the metaverse that many express today.

What we learnt was that the social and creative agency of users in a multi-user 3D environment can surprise and excite participants. Also, the whole issue of multiple personas, changes in appearance of avatars and other persistence issues were played out in Second Life. *Our Digital Selves: My Avatar is Me!* (2018) is a documentary that tracked 13 disabled people and their Second Life avatars. Some have disabled avatars, others don't. That they saw their avatar representations as quite real or at least augmentations of themselves was revealing. Avatars that take on your real-life persona or a wonderful array of creative forms were popular but, in the end, Second Life lacked the social affordances that social media provided. We also have much to learn from that world about moving around in the metaverse, as it had walking, running, use of vehicles, flying and teleportation. There was also an attempt at a more democratic version of Second Life with *OpenSim*.

Of course, Second Life has also become the go-to example of why the metaverse will not work. The Second Life fallacy is to take one failure, ignoring all other examples, and use it to dismiss a new vision. Second Life was not VR and arose in a much more primitive hardware and software environment. There are hundreds of millions of players and users in 3D games' worlds – *Fortnite*, Roblox, *Minecraft*, then VRChat and dozens of others. The fact that Second Life did not succeed 20 years ago, doesn't negate what has been achieved by this generation. Almost everyone in current 3D worlds was born after Second Life started; almost everyone who teaches was born before Second Life was launched. The world has moved on but we are still stuck in the 'what about Second Life' argument. We tend to forget that even Second Life, in an era of low bandwidth and simpler technology, was at one point worth half a billion dollars, with $55 million converted in into real world currencies. Like early phones, computers, games, social media, whatever – things evolve.

We still have much to learn from Second Life, including some of its educational experiments. There was the virtual economy, selling virtually created objects, from shoes to avatars, which thrived in Second Life. Communication at various levels was also implemented from private one-to-one chat to global. Lessons were learnt and literature emerged, such as Boellstorff's *Coming of Age in Second Life: An Anthropologist Explores the Virtually Human* (2015), which explored the concept of personal identity in virtual worlds. Castronova's book *Synthetic Worlds: The Business and Culture of Online Games* (2008) dealt more widely with parallel worlds online – what it is like to enter, inhabit and meet others, as well as a detailed examination of their economies.

Second Life was also the nearest we have seen in learning to a metaverse. What happened there, in its use as a learning technology, was at times creative but often disappointing. In learning, it attracted particular attention from higher education, largely rebuilding existing or imaginary campuses online, often with traditional buildings and lecture theatres. We can see this being repeated again with Meta's recent funding of campuses in the metaverse, the so-called Metaversities. History has a habit of repeating itself. It was a classic case of old analogue practices and pedagogy being rebuilt in new digital worlds.

Harvard Law School even began to offer courses. These experiments are still relevant to current discussions around learning in the metaverse, with lots of lessons learnt on what did and did not work. Charles R Nesson and his daughter Rebecca Nesson, who taught Harvard's first class in Second Life 'CyberOne: Law in the Public Court of Opinion', rightly wanted to bring students from different physical places to learn in a digital world. Classes were held on Berkman Island, a virtual place that vaguely resembled Harvard Law School, specifically in an open, amphitheatre-like lecture space with students standing and sitting with their names attached to their avatars. The lectures were at fixed times for two hours and recordings available on the course's website, along with the syllabus and a wiki.

Rebecca Nesson's experience was positive, with students coming together to meet socially, which she thought helped students to stay engaged in the class. The problem of introverted students and those with English as a second language remaining silent 'just totally disappeared'. She noted that text contributions did not attract the unwanted attention that face-to-face interactions did, reducing anxiety. Neither did normally dominant students take over discussions. The second course on virtual law in virtual worlds was fascinating, in that she saw the delivery of the course in a virtual world as entirely appropriate and relevant, the right medium to convey the content of the course. There were hundreds of other learning experiments on Second Life and despite its detractors and ultimate drop off, we still have lots to learn from those pioneers.

At its peak, participation in Second Life was hugely popular. Yet, as Philip Rosedale, the chief architect of Second Life, who gave up on High Fidelity, a VR version of Second Life, to focus on spatial audio technology, says, 'it didn't break out, it didn't become a billion people. And the hope that Facebook has is that there'll be a billion people using a metaverse.'

Google Earth

Google Maps started as an acquisition in 2004, and has developed into a service that over a billion people use every month. With its various representations of reality, photographic, schematic, with layers of information plotted and superimposed, this is an enormous 3D global metaverse. It literally changed the world, and our view of the world, forever. To go anywhere was a revelation, to use it while walking or in one's car with voiced instructions; even more astonishing, it gets us back on course when lost. Combined with search, it is a world which we willingly enter and use practically to preview, get to, identify and explore the world. The direction of travel for Google Maps is to use AI to combine billions of images to produce a realistic model of the world, so that you can seamlessly soar over, then move down into street view. Our progress from printed maps to personal printouts of specific routes, to 2D maps on smartphones, then 3D street views and full 3D rendering, shows the progress that technology combining imagery and AI has made. It is truly becoming a global digital twin or metaverse.

Many of us can still remember when we opened up Google Earth for the first time. The experience of picking anywhere on earth and zooming down to that place sticks with you as a pivotal moment, as great as that famous image of the earth taken from the moon. We now had a more God-like vision of our own planet and could explore it at will.

We take this for granted now but it was the result of many different forms of technology from satellite photography to image compression and the smart delivery of data to the internet. It is one of the great combinatorial technologies of the age. When we use GPS (satnav) systems in our cars, we forget that this is a triumph of spatial technology, tapping into and triangulating from a network of satellites, to deliver an optimal route from any one place to another, meeting our cognitive needs and recalculating when necessary.

The switches in perspective from more figurative maps to a photographic or topographic view is also astonishing, as is the layering of useful things such as hotels, restaurants, museums and things of interest. We have a lot more to learn from Google Earth than many imagine, in terms of user needs, navigation and beautiful simplicity.

Its evolution from a rather clunky service to its smooth and useful delivery was gradual but the next leap is quite wonderful. Google Earth is taking billions of images, doing some neat data crunching and AI, to allow you to glide down into real-world locations. It is, in a sense, creating a true 3D digital twin of the entire world, which you can fly over but also descend into and explore. It does not have the sensors and data feeds of a true digital twin but does link the sensors in smartphones with your experience.

Planet Labs are in the same space using satellite data to create digital twin replicas of real-world buildings and landscapes, schools, universities and company locations. These will be used for training, from factory floors to nuclear reactors. Emergency-service simulations could be held by avatars in digital twin locations. Selected only moments before, battles can be planned minutes before action.

We can learn from Google Earth as its usefulness is beyond doubt. In simply representing the world we actually live in, there is no other geographical resource that better reflects, with all its layers, terrain, places and routes, the entirety of our world. It has also developed into a place where one can explore and discover the many wonders of the world, architectural and historical, a preview tool for actual visits. Its next iteration and links to other data sources will make it a door to exposition on art, history and many other subjects. It is this breadth of possibilities coming together with other sources of knowledge that point towards the usefulness of digital twins as learning experiences.

The experience economy has grown dramatically, so it is natural that these experiences will also become wholly immersive. Travel is a common form of escape from our existing world into a new and different world. We yearn for the sun, snow or sea, places that are markedly different from where we live. The thrill of being in another land, different language, food, landscape and culture satisfies our need for seeking out the new. Google Earth VR is already available for many of the world's more famous sights. Google Earth points relentlessly towards the metaverse as a destination.

Microsoft's Flight Simulator

Another amazing virtual world, almost unnoticed in discussions of the metaverse, but noted by Mathew Ball in *The metaverse R*, is Microsoft's *Flight Simulator*, something that has grown steadily in size and significance from its launch in 1979, bought by Microsoft in 1981. For over 40 years it has shown how persistent 3D and successful development can be. Other consumer flight simulators include *X-Plane*, launched in 1995, with its focus on realistic graphics and flying experience, using a sophisticated aerodynamic model.

The difference between *Flight Simulator* and most games is that it is so expansive geographically. *Flight Simulator* has realistic 3D scenery for more than 17,000 airports around the world. How does it cope with its 500 million square kilometres of landscapes, with such stunning levels of detail? It keeps most of its stuff in the cloud, with only a tiny portion available at any time on your computer. You even get weather delivered, actual clouds, from the cloud!

Flight Simulator is another good example of a metaverse being created by AI. Covering the entire planet, it has 197 million square miles of terrain. It is quite simply enormous and could never have been achieved without AI. Production studio Blackshark trained a model to create this 3D environment from 2D satellite images.

It also works well for becoming familiar with cockpits, processes and procedures, experiencing different weather conditions and navigation. As there is real-time weather in the simulation, storm chasers take off to fly around and into virtual hurricanes. It is not difficult to make the leap into experiencing existing and predicted changes in weather to experience and study climate change. Future worlds, in terms of climate change, are essentially virtual worlds created from predictive analytics, using models and data. These predictions are metaverses of a sort.

With helicopters and the beautiful, silent experience of flying a glider, along with weather and cloud layers *Flight Simulator* is truly impressive, and with its marketplace where you can purchase planes, games and airports. It can also be used with realistic peripherals, such as real cockpit controls and pedals.

In learning, *Flight Simulator* is used as a useful precursor in courses that teach pilots. There are YouTube tutorials on the fundamentals of flying, even formal online courses, such as Udemy's 'Learn to fly like a real pilot in Microsoft *Flight Simulator*' where you learn to correctly use the cockpit instruments, use flaps, make standard turns and practise for real pilot courses. It is also used when studying in fields related to aviation.

Flight simulation is one of the best examples of why 3D training works, proof of its effectiveness as well as its limitations. It is not wise to train in dangerous weather conditions or for some potentially catastrophic failures. Cost can also be prohibitive, so the more you can do on the simulator the better. A pilot's flight hours in an FAA-certified simulator can, within limits, count towards flight time if an instructor or inspector is present.

This is a virtual world in which a specific set of knowledge and skills can be acquired. It raises issues in learning and training that have been researched for decades: how far virtual training can go, how congruent with the real world it has to be and how much transfer to the real world can be achieved. We shall explore this in later chapters, once we have visited a few more virtual worlds.

Virtual hangouts

There is a range of places one can visit and hang out to get different flavours of the immersive metaverse. The web now teems with spaces that have emerged for games, cinema or various forms of social events.

Rec Room

Rec Room is a cross-platform, multiplayer, VR games environment but is more than just games. These virtual spaces have games at their core but they are really creative and social spaces where you create your rooms, build play spaces and hang out with people.

Once you have created your avatar, you try out games created by others or by yourself. One of its strongest features is the 'Maker Pen', a 3D pen that squeezes out shapes and objects. Just open up your watch to see the floating menu then select shapes, colours and a ton of tools for created objects, gadgets, props and inventions which can be rotated and manipulated. What makes Rec Room special is an extra level of functionality, the 'circuit' layer, the ability to use a programming language, using 3D objects to create networks that execute actual programs to control objects, lights, other effects and games. You use chips, boards, components and wires to connect them all.

This is heading towards a model of learning by doing that is well researched and productive for tasks that require actual performance, bringing knowledge and skills together in electronics, lab work, engineering tasks and other practical skills. It is proof that an intuitive interface, the Maker Pen, with lots of tutorials, often on YouTube, allows young people to learn and acquire skills. It is a good example of holding attention within a virtual world then allowing simple educational tools to be made available that allow complex tasks to be created and performed with feedback.

Rec Room, as a generative creative and learning world, is undoubtedly a great example of the type of user-generated, multiplayer, social and immersive worlds that will form part of the metaverse.

Bigscreen

A different sort of space is Bigscreen, more of a social hangout where you can watch movies, 3D movies, TV series and games, which can all be streamed into the platform. The advantage is that you can watch movies with your friends, even though you live in different locations. The social side shows that there is more than just shareable content; there are good communications within VR with spatial audio and a choice between public and private rooms.

A Bigscreen Classroom environment has also been built that gives a teacher the ability to live-stream their computer, show YouTube videos and so on. This is another form of learning, possible in virtual worlds, where learners and teachers from anywhere in the world can come together to learn formally in a traditional but virtual classroom environment. A shared learning experience, with the social and spatial audio features, shows what can be done within this format.

VR spaces

AltspaceVR is a solid introduction for those who want to use or build existing environments for events. Another significant environment has been Facebook's Horizon Worlds, Meta's collaborative space, aimed at the Oculus VR headset market.

I have already mentioned a podcast on 'VR and the metaverse' from inside AltspaceVR. We talked for an hour, on the history, research and philosophical issues around the metaverse, discussing individuals covered in this book: Lanier, Makransky, Chalmers, Zuckerberg, Baudrillard and Nozick. Using set camera perspectives we could create a final video, using cuts from the real to virtual world as well as wholly within the virtual world. It gives a glimpse into the many possibilities of the metaverse.

Microsoft already has an impressive metaverse ecosystem with Azure, HoloLens and Xbox. Real intent towards the metaverse came in buying Activison Blizzard in 2022. Microsoft Mesh, which unifies holographic virtual collaboration across multiple devices, be they VR headsets, AR (HoloLens), laptops or smartphones, shows the intent. But the public face of the VR vision is still the 3D playground, AltspaceVR. You can bring people together, from anywhere, in its full set of templated VR environments for virtual events: live concerts, conferences, comedy shows, festivals, tech talks, team meetings or remote collaborations. The avatar design feature gives you choices where you can design your body, head, face and clothing. Once in a chosen environment, many built by the community, or in one you have built yourself using the World Builder, which you can edit, you are ready to go. How you operate within a world is device specific but in general you can do lots of VR stuff – walk, run, turn, shuffle and look around. You can grip, grab and even throw things like basketballs.

Personal presence you control through a small menu, where you can create a bubble around you to protect your personal space. Invasion of that space causes the other user's head, arms, whatever, to disappear. You can also mute yourself. These bubbles can be useful in formal learning environments to prevent any nuisance, awkward, even unintentional interactions. Social presence comes with nametags: just select a person and that person will appear. You send requests and if they agree, their nametag turns blue. You can silence, even block, so they disappear. All sorts of meetings from church events to corporate events are held here.

Expressing yourself is by voice, although you can pop out floating emojis and, if you want to remember the moment, take a snap or selfie. Selfies are strangely satisfying in terms of reinforcing presence and snaps are fun when encouraging a group of students to interact and get to know each other.

The learning opportunities are obvious. One can do the obvious, such as talk, teach, lecture or deliver a podcast, such as the one I did on the metaverse. Raising the stakes, small group seminars are possible with a group of students, no matter where they are located. Specific tasks can be set for practical training and group work or exploring built worlds. Connections are cemented with friends' lists, messaging, invitations and replies. You can also chat with fellow Altspacers on Discord.

One advantage of these spaces are the specialist learning groups and professionals who come together in the world to discuss learning. You can schedule events and classes and there is an 'Educators in VR' group, which holds hundreds of events a year.

VRChat

A nice bridge between movie metaverses and future virtual words is the documentary *We Met in Virtual Reality* (2022). It follows several real users as they explore, find friendship and love in AltspaceVR, showing just how deep the social experiences can be, especially for people who genuinely experience isolation and loneliness in the real world. A sign language teacher finds it a place where people who are deaf or hard of hearing can find companionship; others take real-world activities, such as dance and make a life for themselves as teachers. The documentary reveals a rich world with people finding things they could not find in the real world. Their experiences are rich and full of accidental encounters, fun, humour, disappointment – all the ups and downs that come with social interaction.

What it shows are levels of friendship and intimacy that reflect, but in some ways transcend, the real world. This may be true for some forms of learning, social or otherwise. Those who feel a little shy or nervous of social interaction in the real world may find solace in the virtual. The metaverse may well open up possibilities for deep learning beyond the 2D world of books, classrooms and lecture theatres. We may, paradoxically, feel less alone than in the real world, where social and physical constraints limit the number and diversity of people we are likely to encounter. It may revive a vision of discovery and learning beyond the limitations of institutions. People teach and learn in VRChat, not because it is an institution but because real needs are being met, when a sign language teacher can help others to acquire that skill or a dance teacher teaches steps.

Digital Twins

Another way of looking into virtual worlds is through the rapidly expanding world of digital twins. A digital twin is a virtual copy of an entity in the real world, a digital double that can be used in any way you want, without putting people at risk or harm; similarly with environments and objects, where no real damage can occur.

Imagine digital twins of workplaces, indeed any complex environments. This twin can be a digital representation, a simulation not only of the physical infrastructure but also the processes, systems and their dynamics over time, a data rich counterpart. The idea is to use the digital twin like a mirror, not just to replicate or mimic the real but to allow you to do things that are difficult in large physical environments, such as design, integration, monitoring, testing and maintenance. A digital layout can be shown altered, experimented with and tested. This eliminates more errors, reduces expensive iterations, saves resources and keeps projects to timelines.

This holistic view of design and planning rises above the usual siloed nature of problem solving. Suddenly, you have a risk-free way of designing or redesigning new additions to the facility, predicting what will happen, optimizing and visualizing designs. You can play and amend, to optimize decision making.

Digital Twin buildings also use BIM (building information modelling), which has become the norm in construction, where 3D design and modelling software is used to speed up and optimize building projects. It needs an up-front investment, but when the 3D model is built, you can realize all sorts of returns on investment, including training.

Digital Twin airports

Digital Twin airports are taking off. The designers of the digital twin for Hong Kong International Airport are aiming for what they call 'a single source of truth'. The entire airport will be digitized into a twin to streamline and optimize new projects. Ideas will be realized through a natural, visual interface which is data rich, so that predictions on use can be tested and visualized, along with any unintended consequences. All stakeholders in the airport will be able to use the digital twin to design, experiment, run trials and redesign.

Schiphol, in Amsterdam, is using a digital twin to optimize operational decisions and overcome capacity problems, such as rerouting passengers when maintenance or operational failures happen. It is also being used to enhance the passenger experience. Hamad International Airport (HIA) in Qatar has a digital twin with an analytic engine used to optimize operations. The 3D model, data and AI driven decision making is used for everything from aircraft stand conflicts to emergencies. Vancouver Airport in Canada, Aeroporti di Roma in Italy and many others are taking this path. The point is to reflect the real airport in its digital mirror, to see not just what you have but what you could or will have.

Airports are complex places, with complex learning needs: everything from security, dangerous goods and engineering to passenger safety briefings in the aircraft. Training is everywhere and highly regulated. Digital Twins are therefore useful as they are holistic, natural interfaces for people running large facilities. This makes them ideal for training. You can train people not only in existing contexts but also future contexts, so that the new facility is ready to be used immediately. The fact that you are training in the actual context also makes the transfer of training more probable. It is also risk free, allowing for mistakes and failure, no matter how catastrophic.

At the high-end of the spectrum you have simulations for pilots, yet much of the training in the airline industry is still delivered via PowerPoint in classrooms. IATA are changing this with more 3D simulations in areas such as dangerous goods. Imagine, however, a complete 3D airport as a smart training environment, in which you can place and integrate all of that training, smart airports with digital twins that can deliver smart digital training inside those digital models. Everything related to training to enhance the passenger experience can be covered, from parking, handling virtual queues, going through security to passport inspection and boarding. Operational excellence in security and safety, along with processes and procedures, from baggage handlers and load controllers to cabin crew, even air traffic control, through to visualizing future training needs through future expansion are all possible.

The multi-user aspect of metaverse learning also helps. Security and passport control involve teams, as do operations in getting baggage from passenger to plane. The aircraft itself is run by a highly trained team, starting with ground crew through to pilots and cabin crew. To get the best out of these teams, simulation training in virtual environments will be a boon.

Digital Twin networks

Deutsche Bahn, Germany's national rail company, is the largest railway company in the world. It is on track with its digital twin. What makes this different from airports are the size and scale of the operation, with 5700 stations and 33,000 kilometres of track. Omniverse, Nvidia's 3D platform, created photorealistic and physically accurate doppelgangers of trains, tracks, stations and infrastructure in one single model. The digital twin uses AI to predict, identify and optimize responses to incidents, along with rescheduling. Simulations can be run but the ultimate aim is to automate responses, especially rescheduling in response to real incidents. Linked to the real network through sensors, 5G communications and edge technology, it attempts ambitiously to see the entire network as one entity. Data gathered from the virtual digital twin will be used to train the AI models to further improve the network and services.

DIGITAL TWIN CITIES

Cities are complex ecosystems, interrelated places that need to be governed and managed. Like any complex system, they suffer from congestion, pollution, inefficient energy consumption, waste problems, flooding, emergency incidents and planning problems. Huge cities, from Singapore, Shanghai and Seoul to smaller cities such as Tallinn and Des Moines, already have digital twins. A digital twin city allows the use of simulations to monitor, plan and simulate ideas to keep its dwellers safe and plan for sustainability. Once created, they start to be used for more and more tasks.

The visualization of the city to solve problems is especially useful for the public. New buildings can be visualized by citizens to show shade, sightlines and views. The effect of new buildings on street signs, road markings and outdoor advertisements can be identified. Sensors produce data to measure traffic and pedestrian flow, useful for retail businesses, along with data from underground utilities and transport systems. Planning in general can be made more efficient through visualization but the key to a successful digital twin is its use of data to feed evidence-based decisions.

Digital Twins for learning

The metaverse can host learning in several ways, digital twins being one of the most promising. Digital Twins of institutions, such as Metaversities, can place traditional learning into the metaverse, as can other twinned places, such as museums, art galleries, archaeological sites or other real places to situate learning. Why conduct workplace learning in a classroom when the workplace is available as your classroom? Once digital twins are built, for whatever purpose, they can also be used for learning. Digital Twins are the education and training world's best friend, opening up opportunities to deliver realistic, low-risk, high-transfer learning experiences.

Beyond just learning in a realistic, virtual place, there is also the opportunity to interact with others within that space. Multi-user learning is important in general but also when teams deliver services, and that is almost always the case in large organizations and complex facilities. To get the best out of these cohorts of learners, teams and groups, simulation training in virtual environments will be a boon.

A good starting point would be onboarding. Everyone has to join a school, university or workplace at some time. We are at our most curious before actually turning up; often nervous, but keen to learn. So the best time to deliver onboarding is before we arrive. Open up your digital twin school, university, office or workplace to your new learners or employees with an introduction and induction to their new place of learning, study or work. Even when they arrive, virtual tours of other sites and places relevant to their job would be welcome.

The University of Manchester uses a digital twin to onboard students. Music students are given access to a 3D immersive environment of the music school, its rehearsal and performance spaces. So, before they arrive on the real campus, first-year students could move freely or take prescribed paths and learning could be layered onto that experience with other media, such as video. You become familiar with the space and facilities and much more: the damage caused by coffee cups left on expensive instruments and the general misuse of equipment and musical instruments, and how to store instruments safely. This was supplemented by a quiz that students could take as many times as required, with feedback and repeated access to the digital twin. Once they had successfully completed the quiz, they were given access to the performance rooms. More than just getting students to comply with a code of conduct, the 3D immersive learning experience was designed to raise excitement and motivation about their studies and their use of these spaces. For students who could not attend the open days, it provided a useful alternative. Staff also reported that it saved them invaluable time in answering emails. These are learning principles that can be applied to any educational institution, workplace or building that humans intend to visit and use.

Digital Twins are not just places, they are also objects. Almost all designed objects are now designed in 3D digital forms. Digital Twin objects can be designed, tested and updated. They can also generate useful data before, during and after the release of a product. Continuing the music theme, you can learn to play musical instruments in VR, such as the drums or piano. VRtuos teaches you piano, where you use a real piano or keyboard and get lessons via the VR headset.

Lastly, assessment will also be possible. We already have sophisticated assessment for pilots on 3D flight simulators; this will start to be applied in other areas. Your actual performance can be assessed formally as you learn, but also in a final assessment that allows you to practise in the workplace.

DIGITAL TWIN CAMPUSES

Meta funded a series of digital twin campus learning projects, with an initial $150 million for educational metaverse projects in schools and universities. It chose historically Black colleges and several land-grant universities founded in the late 19th century to encourage the teaching of practical subjects, often located in rural communities. This is an interesting selection, as they are not the big Ivy League and other names, but rather smaller, more vocationally inclined schools. Many of these schools already had remote or rural-based learners and others have a strong track record in online delivery, with a focus on diversity and vocational subjects, avoiding the wealthier end of the US educational spectrum. Many also have a strong track record in VR. They share resources, problems and solutions.

These digital twin metaversities are being built, each with a virtual meta-campus mirroring the real campus. This is good in the sense of playing to the actual institution's brand and sense of place. The buildings gleam, shadows are cast from a few clouds in blue skies as we glide along tree-lined paths. To be fair, the metaversities look fabulous, but is this the best way to use that space? We went through this in Second Life, with lots of dull lecture rooms and lectures. Building exact copies of buildings, some no longer fit for purpose, seems odd, as they may add nothing to the learning experiences. One would have thought that they would reimagine or re-envision learning and build anew, not port existing architecture into the metaverse.

This may well be exactly how the metaverse plays out, with almost exact replicas of real buildings. The problem is the carryover of old, offline, analogue pedagogies into the new, online, digital world. Dozens of lecture rooms are being built, meaning the delivery of avatar lectures. When tried in Second Life, it did not turn out well. Replicating a university campus is one thing; replicating its inefficiencies is another. Campuses were built for completely different pedagogical approaches, with lecture halls, seminar rooms and a library. Why not do something better by using new pedagogical techniques more suited to an environment where you are free from the constraints of the real world? We may look back and see that porting the old world into the new was like early movies when theatre performances were filmed.

An interesting model did emerge from these projects, where digital twins were created not from scratch but from templated rooms, then branded for use with students, potential students, faculty and alumni. Virtual models of standard classrooms, labs and other locations could be bought individually, and customized at low cost. The first lab made generally available was the 'cadaver' lab for medical and healthcare students.

Although the digital twin campus is the current focus, where a number of 'metaversities' have been created as part of an exploratory push into the $77 billion global higher-education market, that market has yet to mature. Those universities and schools that already have a long and strong track record in online delivery seem set to gain the most, such as the University of Maryland Global Campus, which has long delivered distance learning to the military. Early reports suggest that social interaction keeps vulnerable and unmotivated students from dropping out. New Mexico State University, which largely serves Hispanic American students, is raising the stakes, planning for an entire degree within the metaverse.

To be fair, the projects are imaginative and teachers and students have been encouraged not to simply mimic what was done in lecture rooms and normal campus environments. The point was to learn and create new experiences and opportunities as they go. Morehouse College used its 3D environments to study physiology and the Napoleonic campaign in history. Dr Muhsinah Morris at Morehouse College, who taught a course in inorganic chemistry inside the metaverse, reports positively about the ability to examine and manipulate 3D atoms and molecules within a 3D world. The pedagogic advantages are immediately obvious as chemistry is very much a 3D subject. The haptic side, in particular, cannot be replicated on Zoom and that matters in many stem subjects.

University of Kansas School of Nursing has built examination rooms and a hospital ward and simulates exercises in clinical judgement. Healthcare is an obvious example for virtual learning, as it takes place in clearly defined physical spaces with lots of specialist equipment. South Dakota State University's digital twin has, of course, lecture theatres but also social spaces and an organic chemistry lab and promises an anatomy course with a cadaver and model experience lab. In the University of Maryland Global Campus, students will study speech, human resources, education, biology, journalism, astronomy and criminal justice. In two courses that teach crime scene investigation and examination, a virtual crime scene will be used by students to investigate crime scenes, examine, and come to conclusions either individually or as teams.

There are, of course, concerns about repeating the mistake in Second Life of simply building spaces with not enough effort put into the deliberate design for learning, along with concerns about student data. However, there is commitment to experiment and to allow faculties to do what they want without interference.

Conclusion

Many virtual worlds can be described as digital twins. *Flight Simulator* is an astonishing achievement, a global digital twin with a specific function. Google Earth is perhaps the most used and well known of all digital twins, as it envelops the whole planet with innumerable layers of information, used for navigation and a useful 3D window into our world.

We have innumerable other examples of things on this earth that have digital twins. It is not that the metaverse will be built then people invited to come into some freshly built city of dreams, with its ready-to-buy-or-let real estate. It will be built dynamically, by users, institutions and businesses. There are already spaces, such as Microsoft's AltspaceVR, Bigscreen and VRChat, where people can socialize, see live shows, have meet-ups, do classes, hold conferences, all the while sharing documents, spreadsheets and so on. These spaces are proliferating as we read.

More specific digital twins are already having an impact in factories, airports, cities and rail networks, and in learning. Virtual worlds are now everywhere, used for work and play, evidence of the shift from what were 2D worlds of screens and social media to 3D worlds and avatar chat. Digital Twins are a move from 2D plans and processes to 3D design, visualization, simulation and decision making. The world is being digitized in 3D.

We have yet to see how metaversities will unfold but developments have certainly stimulated debate on how learning will manifest itself in the metaverse. There may well be good applications, where VR brings motivation, attention, context and the ability to do things, to create new 3D learning experiences. That is already underway in VR (Clark, 2022). Beyond this, new forms of education and learning are likely to emerge from the metaverse, new models of access, payment, even pedagogy.

Bibliography

Boellstorff, T (2015) *Coming of Age in Second Life*, Princeton University Press, New Jersey

Case Study: Hong Kong International Airport Terminal 1, scottbrownrigg.b-cdn.net/media/4742/hong-kong-international-airport-case-study.pdf (archived at https://perma.cc/4R7L-UUHC)

Castronova, E (2008) *Synthetic Worlds*, University of Chicago Press, Chicago

Chapelle, D, Twitter is not a Real Place, LaughPlanet, 9 October 2021, www.youtube.com/watch?v=kS-E6VtD_rE (archived at https://perma.cc/DC8T-BBJ6)

Clark, D (2022) *Learning Experience Design: How to create effective learning that works*, Kogan Page, London

Computerworld, Harvard virtual education experiment in Second Life, 27 May 2007, www.computerworld.com/article/2477054/harvard-s-virtual-education-experiment-in-second-life.html (archived at https://perma.cc/V8F3-CH5M)

Creator Philip Rosedale says a virtual reality internet is still some way off, *IEEE Spectrum*, 7 November 2021, spectrum.ieee.org/metaverse-second-life (archived at https://perma.cc/57LY-7JEF)

Digital Engineering 247, Deutsche Bahn on Track with Country-Scale digital twin, 14 October 2022, www.digitalengineering247.com/article/deutsche-bahn-on-track-with-country-scale-digital-twin (archived at https://perma.cc/B44D-LMU7)

Gent, E, What can the metaverse learn from Second Life?

Great Minds on Learning, VR & metaverse [podcast], Series 3, Episode 13, 26 September 2022, greatmindsonlearning.libsyn.com/gmols3e14-vr-metaverse-with-donald-clark (archived at https://perma.cc/EGX6-T6R3)

Hunting, J and HBO (2022) *We Met in Virtual Reality* [documentary]

Manchester University, Using Matterport to create a virtual student induction at the University of Manchester, 2022, media-and-learning.eu/type/featured-articles/using-matterport-to-create-a-virtual-student-induction-at-the-university-of-manchester/?fbclid=IwAR0c8iOEfnlsBtL8Aaepvku5ppZlyG3k3iZtM8bZkkgmIPmIYIB_PvcmUFQ (archived at https://perma.cc/F6QJ-79MR)

Our Digital Selves: My Avatar is Me! [documentary] (2018)

06

Gaming metaverses

The games world is by far the most important origin story for the metaverse. It is a huge and significant part of our culture and many of the features discussed in relation to the metaverse have their origins in games. We can track its evolution straight into the metaverse proposition, as a lot of what is now being imagined within the proposed metaverse has been tried in games: 3D worlds, avatars, multi-user, manipulation of objects, virtual economies, AR, VR and AI.

Games also provide insights into how the 'fourth wall', the assumed wall separating viewers from created worlds, was demolished, something that happened occasionally in traditional media, but the dam burst in computer games, where the wall all but disappeared, as viewers became players and entered these new virtual 3D worlds. This 'breakthrough' changed the very notion of media, from passive to active, from being presented to being co-created. Once that dam had been demolished, the way was open towards entering and creating new worlds and the metaverse as an idea was born.

Culture and play

Homo Ludens: A study of the 'play' element in culture (1938), written by Johan Huizinga, the Dutch cultural historian and theorist, stresses the cultural role of play throughout the history of our species; the word 'ludens' having a broad meaning in Latin, of play, sport, school and practice. His definition of play is similar to the vision of the metaverse:

> Summing up the formal characteristics of play we might call it a free activity standing quite consciously outside 'ordinary' life as being 'not serious' but at the same time absorbing the player intensely and utterly... It proceeds within its own proper boundaries of time and space according to fixed rules and in an orderly manner.

For Huizinga, play is part of our cultural development as a species and has five features:

1 Free and freeing, an expression of a human need
2 Not ordinary or real life
3 Separate from ordinary life
4 Creates and demands absolute order
5 No material interest or profit.

This is close to some descriptions of the vision of the metaverse, where you can be free to play and learn. You will be able to use 3D worlds to learn precisely because the metaverse is not subject to the constraints of the real world such as time and place. The metaverse is separate but provides the order, structure and support which is necessary for contextualized and social learning. Lastly, we would hope that the metaverse's online accessibility and scalability frees playing and learning from its existing, and at times horrifically expensive, costs.

Coming back to Huizinga, play is not serious but played seriously. It encourages the freedom to play but within the bounds of strict rules, where breaking the rules is a serious matter. Along with a recognition that 'teams' matter, dressing up to play is part of its ritual, as it fosters a sense of community. This is eerily similar to multi-user, avatar-populated, virtual spaces. Even though play lies outside life, and its goal is not material gain, it is a serious and intense activity, yet this activity is also joyful and exhilarating. This is exactly what we see in 3D computer games: rich, separate spaces where users play individually or in teams to a set of rules, where autonomy, becoming competent and social dimensions are compelling.

For Huizinga, play is also a part of culture, yet sits side by side with culture, as almost all societies seem to demand play. Western civilization, in particular, especially in its earlier stage, was rooted in play. Culture did not emerge and add play, it is entwined with play; play being both in and part of culture. We saw how many of our most monumental built 3D spaces in ancient Greece were entertainment and sports arenas. We explored this same cultural drive to create monumental virtual spaces played by hundreds of millions of games players. This cultural drive to play lies at the root of what drives us towards being in separately defined spaces such as the metaverse.

Huizinga disliked the idea that playful activities become all too serious or that serious occupations become too playful and saw play as being in decline. He saw us as losing something valuable, the ability to 'play' and not be 'played', where it loses its real function in culture, subsumed under the complexity of society, rather than something separate. He wrote his book just after the Berlin Olympics, where play became used as part of the tyranny of an ideology. The metaverse, as currently imagined, as an open environment, like the internet, moves us further away from that form of tyranny.

He could not have foreseen the rise of virtual games on computers, consoles and smartphones. These too he would have welcomed as fitting his wider definition of play as a cultural phenomenon. And he would surely have welcomed the rise of computer games and the metaverse as the latest flowering of *Homo ludens*.

2D to 3D in games

The first use of the word *Avatar* (1979) was in a game of the same name created on the University of Illinois' PLATO system, an early learning technology platform. But multiplayer games go back much further to *Tennis for Two*, which ran on an oscilloscope, designed in 1958. We then had *Pong* and a rack of shooter and racing games that emerged in the 1960s and 70s. The 1970s also saw the appearance of MUD (multi-user dungeons) text-based command games.

Home computers came on sale in the 1980s and games like *Habitat* (1986) were launched by Lucasfilm Games, an open-world game where you could choose your own avatar and speak to other people, albeit via speech bubbles. It was all a bit blocky but was an early example of an open virtual world, a graphical MUD or MMORPG (massively multiplayer online role-playing game). Virtual worlds, at this time, largely took the form of flat 2D platforms, hence the term 'platform games' such as *Super Mario Bros*.

The breakthrough from 2D to 3D came later. In painting, central linear perspective happened only once in human history. This radical shift in art took place in the Italian Renaissance in the 15th century, first attributed to the architect Filippo Brunelleschi in 1415. Perspectival art in northern Europe was then imported by artists who had travelled to Italy, notably Jan Goessart. It changed visual art forever. Something similar happened in the computer games world with *Quake* and *Doom* in the early 1990s. Suddenly, virtual 3D worlds with a modicum of realism were everywhere and the games world was never the same again. John Carmack, college dropout and the brain behind *Wolfenstein 3D*, *Doom*, *Quake* and ex-CTO at Oculus, literally took games from 2D to 3D. With *Wolfenstein 3D* (1992) he took his 2D game code for the block map and characters and brought the viewpoint down from the vertical god-like view of 2D games, to the horizontal, human perspective of moving through a 3D world. At that moment, Carmack saw games as becoming more playable and intrinsically personal, as it matched human perception and action to move horizontally through a world. This move was seminal. Games suddenly matched human cognition and expectations, and the shift has continued to this day through decades of successful games, eventually into VR and the imagined metaverse.

Virtual worlds in the games world had their Cambrian explosion; freed from the technical and imaginative constraints of 2D and platform games, 3D worlds exploded into action. And not just shoot-'em-ups, there was everything from sport sims to the huge, sedate galaxies and universe of *Eve Online*. This volcano of early 3D games exploded out in all directions and just like those plumes of billowing ash that attract attention then fall to earth, 3D games now cover much of the planet. Hundreds of millions are familiar with such worlds and that is the future audience for the metaverse

Doom (1993) was the real design and programming breakthrough, as its increased graphic fidelity led Carmack to develop a new 3D games engine. In this engine you could change (mod) the media but not the game. Then *Quake* (1996), with better lighting and even better graphics, allowed deeper game mods and, crucially, became a multiplayer game on the internet. At that point, the road towards the metaverse was open.

A generation or two then grew up in more recent 3D environments with *Runescape* (2001), *World of Warcraft* (2004) and dozens of other avatar-driven, multi-user games. In a sense, the metaverse is literally playing to that games generation, one that is comfortable in mass, multi-user, 3D environments. The games world is perhaps the nearest we have to the metaverse, with its myriad of genres, degrees of openness, multi-user variations, economies and highly developed grammar of avatars who acquire skills, respawn, teleport and so on. It is a huge, rich, complex and wonderful universe of innovation and complexity.

Another foundational moment in the evolution towards the metaverse are user-generated worlds and games and custom servers, where you create and host your games. This goes back to *Counter-Strike* in 2003; *Gary's Mod* was another from Valve. These were open enough to allow modifications to games by users, even new genres of games, such as racing or zombie games. Games were no longer fixed worlds but user created and this unleashed a frenzy of innovation that resulted in specific companies, worth tens of billions of dollars, operating in this 'user-generated' space.

Battle Royale games, such as *Fortnite*, came from a mod to a military simulation game called *Armour 2*. This mod was called *DayZ*, a zombie survival game. This, in turn, was modified to create *Battlegrounds*. So, a mod of a mod created this new genre, Battle Royale, which has gone on to massive participation in *Call of Duty: Warzone* and *Fortnite*. The games world had turned into mini-metaverses, through user innovation. Games culture and genres morphed and evolved, as will the metaverse, not because large tech companies determined that future but because innovation lay in the hands of users in the form of both creation and demand.

Games have developed out of hardcore gaming into a wider more inclusive and diverse world of playing at various levels of commitment, from hardcore gamers to casual players on smartphones, and the viewing games played by others on video, with rich social activity and e-sports. It is a vast, expanding virtual ecosystem.

So in computer games we already have a massive Multiverse, made up of many separate metaverses with many genres of games that already reflect the shape of possible metaverses to come. This history of mods, evolving worlds and internal digital economies has been a feature of gaming for decades. The real place to find the embryonic metaverse is, it has been argued, in *Minecraft*, *Fortnite* and Roblox, where hundreds of millions already play, engage in activities and just hang out. The scale of these proto-metaverses is staggering and they do have specific lessons to teach us about the user-generated metaverse. The metaverse as interconnected worlds can build on the proven, global successes of *Fortnite*, Roblox and *Minecraft*. It also confirms the idea that there is a massive audience ready for the metaverse.

Fortnite

Fortnite, owned by Epic Games, was released in 2017. It has three versions: *Fortnite Battle Royale*, a game where up to 100 players fight to the death, last player standing; *Fortnite: Save the World*, a tower game where up to four players fight and defend; and *Fortnite Creative*, where you can create new worlds. With an astonishing tens of billions of dollars in revenues from its launch in 2017, it has become the biggest fashion vendor in the world, outgunning all the luxury brands, selling virtual avatars, backpacks and emotes. If this is not proof of the reality of a virtual economy, what is?

Open to deals with film, music, sports companies and other products, marketing events are frequently held in the *Fortnite* world, an interplay between the real and digital. The Ariana Grande tour in *Fortnite* lasted three days and attracted over 27.7 million unique users, with 1.3 million concurrent viewers at its peak and over 11 million live hours streamed on Twitch and YouTube. Physical concerts are no longer enough, with new audiences clearly eager to consume virtual events. This is what keeps *Fortnite* relevant. This interplay between the virtual and real also exists in its in-person *Fortnite Champion Series* (FNCS), started in 2019, with $1 million in prize money.

Epic Games also owns the Unreal engine, a hugely successful games and virtual world tool and engine (first released in 1998). Many varieties of virtual worlds are made real with Unreal, which means it is likely to play a significant role in building the metaverse. What emerged on *Fortnite* was something that had been growing in the games industry since its inception: the thirst for user-created content. Users started by playing games, then want to make them and can even progress into using the Unreal engine. In this sense, it is a rich learning environment where users learn serious skills that fuel their own content creation, supported by formal tutorials.

Fortnite has been able to capitalize on young users' needs to both consume and create. Its format of chapters and seasons also refreshes the brand, with the release of new features. This is one lesson that metaverse builders have to realize, that it is kept alive by new compelling experiences.

Another feature of *Fortnite* that is relevant to shaping the metaverse is its social dimension. You can play solo, giving you complete freedom to play as you wish but many play in a duo, trio or squad, as you can play with your friend or friends. These huge gaming platforms actually become social platforms as the huge numbers of users talk and play with each other. They create an ecosystem of social activity both within and around the platform on YouTube, Twitch and other social platforms. It is this ecosystem growth and development, using one tool as its core creative tool but linking out to other platforms, that gives us some idea as to how the metaverse may evolve and develop.

Roblox

Another hugely successful games environment is Roblox. Its founders David Baszucki and Erik Cassel ran an educational software company Knowledge Revolution, with a physics simulator called *Interactive Physics*, which simulated physics experiments. Praised for its accuracy and liked by students, it gave them the background and platform to add 3D modeling and create Roblox.

Papert's constructionism, the idea that one creates and builds to learn by doing, had been the inspiration for a 3D approach to learning physics and projects in Roblox have included virtual robots, maths, STEM content, playing piano, history and astronomy. Indeed, the creators' background in ed-tech led them to create a $10 million Roblox Community Refund that encouraged the use of Roblox in learning.

Created in 2004, released in 2006, Roblox is a games platform where you create your own avatar which you can use across different games, as well as create your own games. As a creative platform with free tools, it has over 20 million games (they call them 'experiences' after a spat with Apple). The most popular is *Adopt Me!*, where you raise and trade pets. Developers earn a cut of everything created (albeit small) in their own internal currency Robux. Floated at a value of $41 billion in 2021, tools and hosting are free, and it is users that create their own games. It is estimated that over half of all under 16s in the USA have played in Roblox.

Roblox is not an individual game; rather you have a Roblox character that can be put into Roblox games (experiences). It is therefore not so much a game as an entry point to millions of games. It is the entry point that matters here, where you define your character, and this is what makes Roblox an interesting prototype for entry into the metaverse. It has already hosted film events, virtual concerts, promotional parties, even huge product promotions, again pointing to the versatility of these spaces beyond game playing.

Much is made of the creation, buying and selling of its virtual products and revenue generation for its users but Roblox only makes money for a tiny number of developers of their games. Like many supposedly open systems, it is a tiny minority that get to the top of the hierarchy and it is they who are supported and become influencers. The organization takes 30 per cent and pays the rest in Robux (the internal currency) which has a high withdrawal threshold and has been targeted by scammers; another lesson that the metaverse must learn is the opportunity for deception. There is also a Roblox education area on the site, showing you how to make money, which most don't. We can see here the explosion of creativity but also an exploitative and manipulative transaction economy, with marketing that targets children. We have many positive things to learn from Roblox but also some negatives.

Despite these early problems, what young people find in these worlds is not just gaming but the opportunity to create their own worlds, their own bit of the metaverse. These are places where huge amounts of creative activity have emerged and evolved by users. They also experience a rich social world, far from the limited opportunities in real life. It is this fusion of consuming, creating, learning new skills and socializing that make these fascinating places to find clues as to how the metaverse will evolve.

Minecraft

By far the most interesting 3D games world, in terms of relevance for learning, is *Minecraft*, around since 2009, a sandbox game where it is easy to make your worlds (servers) then mods attached to them. It is an open, creative environment, a multiverse and metaverse of sorts.

One interesting feature of *Minecraft* and some other immersive 3D worlds is the low-fi nature of those worlds. This is commensurate with available technology and bandwidth and shows, interestingly, that high-fidelity graphics do not seem to be a necessary condition for immersive, virtual and social success in 3D worlds. This has not held back creativity. One teenager, Christopher Slayton, has built the universe in *Minecraft*: Earth, other planets, galaxies and so on, with immersive lighting gradients and effects. He was able to block-build the Sun, complete with solar flares, then a galaxy and universe of galaxies. He even built a black hole. His universe, as a proto-metaverse, is impressive.

But it is in education that *Minecraft* has shown innovation relevant to the future of learning in the metaverse. *Minecraft Education*, available since 2016, is a version of the service that focuses on schools, for teachers, parents and other groups closely related to education. You can learn to code and there is advice for teachers on how to use *Minecraft* in lessons on history, chemistry (with experiments), financial literacy, STEM skills, collaboration, problem solving, literacy – hundreds of subjects and topics. With a lot of support for teachers, some have mapped *Minecraft* resources on to their national curricula. It has also proved useful as a way for parents to get involved in the education of their children, with introductions available on YouTube. This gives us interesting insights into how education could use the metaverse for real-world teaching in schools, as a form of blended learning.

An interesting observation from *Minecraft* educators is how independent and autonomous learners become. This is a consistent theme in these 3D environments, where users are given the tools and skills to create and build on their own. Autonomy releases a willingness to learn new competencies and skills and allows users to learn how to create their own worlds. This is a new form of digital literacy, one that allows learners to build 3D worlds and participate with others within and outside those worlds, a combination of autonomy, competence acquisition and collaborative and social efforts that propel them forward.

The social side of *Minecraft*, with its forums, messaging and chat, shows that this is the glue that really holds it all together. The sociology of a future metaverse is likely to be similar to the existing sociology of *Minecraft* and similar worlds. *Minecraft* does show that a sandbox world can support all sorts of participation, from building and game playing to social activity and learning.

Evidence for the metaverse

These three virtual-world platforms already have enormous levels of engagement with hundreds of millions of monthly users; that figure will rise to billions. The metaverse in this sense is already here. These hundreds of millions of young people, some very young, will mature into online adults. They are used to hanging out in virtual environments, in places where they express themselves, create stuff, buy and sell stuff, and be in social groups. They spend time in these worlds because it is *not* the real world and they can find what they cannot find in the real world, a switch-on/switch-off world of fun, social contact and ready friendships. This is the audience that is cued up and ready for the metaverse.

We should ask ourselves if this mass, global participation in games playing has had any significant effect on the wellbeing of the players, as it is often assumed that it does, the assumption being that it is negative. Governments have issued edicts trying to limit time playing games, such as China's attempt to limit young people's game play to one hour per day. With around 3 billion gamers, and growing, 2.8 billion have played on a mobile device, 1.4 billion on a PC and 0.9 billion on a console; it is an enormous, global industry. So studies looking at the impact of this immense amount of human activity are certainly worthwhile. The largest of such studies, by Vuorre et al (2022), took place over six weeks with three waves of self-reported and behavioural data from 38,935 players' game-playing, provided by seven global game publishers. The conclusion was that time spent playing video games is unlikely to impact wellbeing.

One question still hangs over this evidence for the success of the metaverse. These are all, fundamentally, games worlds. Will these astonishing figures for users and engagement carry over into other areas in the metaverse?

Games and technology

What this evidence shows is that when compelling experiences are created, motivated users not only have a sense of autonomy in themselves or in the context of small teams, they are also driven and motivated to learn new skills and create, in other words to learn and learn by doing. The glue that holds them together is the network of social connections made within these worlds and on other social platforms. We shall see later how the psychology of learning has drawn from this evidence and can be used to shape future learning in the metaverse. The computer-game world has therefore advanced 3D worlds enormously.

The sophistication of the global business, online distribution, genres and compelling experience is unparalleled. Games have transcended TV and movies and show no signs of slowing down. From e-sports and serious gamers down through to huge numbers of casual gamers on smartphones, game playing has broadened out into every demographic.

Games have also pushed technical boundaries in their use of available computing resources in graphics, animation and sound. The computer-games industry capitalized on a wave of hardware and software innovations that gave it a continual, evolving edge over film, TV and other traditional media. It matured from a hobbyist movement into a multi-billion dollar steamroller that still drives strong growth towards an industry of over $300 billion by 2025. No other media industry has grasped the opportunities that technology offers in the way that the creative forces in the computer games industry have.

Technological advances since the 1990s have allowed the games industry to design and deliver compelling games, more conveniently, across platforms for a wide range of audiences. At the heart of this is increased processing power and graphics cards, also known as GPUs (graphics processing units). More energy efficient, multiple GPUs acting in unison, with more processing speed, memory and specialized 3D design have driven the industry forward. Shader technology, using specific processors, calculates shading, reflections, refractions, lighting and other graphics effects that throw the right shade and lighting as one moves through the 3D world. Ray tracing, as opposed to the older rasterization methods, replicates how light behaves in the real world, as it bounces across objects, and has revolutionized effects and animation. High resolution textures give more detailed and realistic appearances. These graphics engines drove the video gaming world hard and fast.

Another innovation was cloud gaming. Subscription services, streamed on demand also expanded the market allowing players to access high-end games, with controlled data management, on inexpensive devices. This expanded the reach of games into new audiences.

Mobile gaming, on the back of the ubiquity of smartphones and tablets has also exploded. Games from puzzle and strategy to action and adventure are convenient playable anywhere, at any time. The freemium model, where players only pay for additional features, has also made this form of casual gaming popular. Additional features, such as GPS, accelerometers and touchscreens added to their appeal and popularity, along with social features.

Another sign of their success has been the rise of e-sports, short for electronic sports, organized video games played by professional players and teams, online or offline. The cash prizes are substantial with millions attending live or watching the live streams on YouTube or Twitch. Universities are even offering e-sports scholarships.

The next big area for expansion is into AR and VR games. With AR, games are played partially in the real world with layers as digital overlays. VR games take this one step further in fully immersive 3D worlds. Some of these games are quite innovative, like the addictive lightsaber-slashing of blocks coming at you, to high-octane music, in *Beat Saber* (2018). *Beat Saber* is one of the most popular VR games; simple, super-easy to pick up, quirky, no moving around, the slicing works well in graphics and it has great audio and music. It also keeps you fit! It was bought by Facebook in 2019. We can see how the games industry has always moved steadily towards more levels of immersion. This does not mean that everything will end up as fully immersive VR but the metaverse promises much more in the way of 3D immersion and new opportunities for a wider range of compelling games. New technology spawns new opportunities for richer gaming experiences.

But what really drives games is the placing of the player into a compelling 3D world where they have agency and presence, improve their skills and have social experiences.

Breaking the wall

In addition to the creation of sophisticated 3D worlds in which incredible personal control and skills can be learnt and employed, the games world did something groundbreaking in media. Something that is often overlooked. It broke the fourth wall.

The fourth wall, an imaginary wall or convention that separates the actors from the audience is, when one reflects, a rather odd convention. It assumes the actors cannot see us but that we can see them. Ever since theatre began in ancient Greece, writers have assumed but also broken through the fourth wall. Shakespeare did it often and Woody Allen in *The Purple Rose of Cairo* (1985) has a character turn to the audience and exit the film. This is known as 'metatheatrical' when drawing attention to the conventions or 'metareference' in cinema, when actors address the camera.

It also applies to other media such as books, where it is called 'metalepsis', deliberately taking the reader outside the main narrative, used extensively in 'metafiction', where a character is deliberately revealed as being fictional. *The Canterbury Tales* and *Don Quixote* are two famous examples.

With computer games, this is the norm, the very premise of the medium, where the player is invited to enter the game, see scores and other features. You can be the active player in having a god-like view of a game or be a recognized participant inside the game. In video games the whole concept of a fourth wall dissolves as there is no longer any wall to be broken. The player is immersed in the game and becomes an autonomous agent within that virtual world.

One can see how the fourth-wall convention of traditional media has been expanded to the degree that it disappears by degrees in mixed reality until it disappears almost completely in wholly immersive VR experiences and the metaverse. Once the fourth wall has been well and truly broken, dissolved or melted away, as in games, virtual worlds, and especially VR, it leaves a new borderless medium. The metaverse, in that sense, becomes something quite new and different, a genuinely new place where old conventions no longer apply. That is its promise, an exciting new frontier for innovation around the design, development and delivery of learning.

This is a fundamental shift from 2D to 3D, a shift that frees us from the tyranny of time, place and passivity. Learning can take place at any time, in designed places that are always available 24/7 to do things in context. Breaking the wall is to break through into learning by doing, not in a classroom or lecture theatre but in 3D environments which more accurately represent the world in which we live, learn and work.

Conclusion

We can see how gaming has already built innumerable 3D worlds that have pushed the technology of user engagement, 3D graphics, avatar creation, navigation in 3D, user-created content, muti-user functionality and sophisticated social interest and collaboration, all in usable and stable environments.

The magic dust of games and gamification has already been used in learning and gives us the best signals yet as to how the metaverse will evolve. We have seen how learning in the metaverse can build upon the motivational and pedagogic lessons learnt in these worlds, not to produce simplistic, behaviourist games, with extrinsic motivation of scores and collecting virtual objects, but sophisticated 3D environments where learners are motivated to learn and collaborate, driven by curiosity and intrinsic motivation.

The games industry has, to date, shaped the development of 3D worlds. It was the first to make a wholesale shift from 2D to 3D and it will play a significant role in the development of the metaverse. The remaining task is to bring these separate worlds together so that the social dimension allows us to become independent, individual, autonomous agents, in control of our own destiny, who can explore one metaverse and the gifts it will bring.

Bibliography

GlobalData (2019) Video games market set to become a $300bn-plus industry by 2025, www.globaldata.com/media/technology/video-games-market-set-to-become-a-300bn-plus-industry-by-2025 (archived at https://perma.cc/5K74-G67E)

Huizinga, J (1949, 1980) *Homo Ludens: A study of the play element in culture*, translated by R F C Hull, Routledge and Kegan Paul, London

Minecraft Education, education.minecraft.net/en-us (archived at https://perma.cc/K7ZC-VBBB)

Wikipedia (2023) Avatar (1979 video game), en.wikipedia.org/wiki/Avatar_(1979_video_game) (archived at https://perma.cc/8F8J-Z4MB)

Vuorre, M, Johannes, N, Magnusson, K and Przybylski, A K, (2022) Time spent playing video games is unlikely to impact well-being, *Royal Society Open Science*, 9 (7)

PART TWO

Shape of the metaverse

07

Shape of the metaverse

Meta-verse's shape?

Meta implies *above, more* or *beyond*, as in metaphysics, metadata or metamorphosis, in contrast to -verse, meaning *everything*, a *totality*, as in universe, multiverse and diverse. The meta-verse is therefore not a fully formed concept, it is both beyond and everything! Yet we need some idea of the form of the metaverse in terms of what lies between these two ideas. What shape will the metaverse take?

The definition game often results in something becoming what people want it to be and that is to be expected when there are various institutions all jostling for a trajectory into that one space. At the moment there is no fixed definition as the metaverse has yet to be defined and built. To avoid the pitfalls of this game, we should sit back and remain *de minimus* on definition. My simple definition of a radical shift from 2D to 3D preserves what is done in 2D but sees 3D as a major shift in activity, especially in learning. This happened with the internet, as text, audio and video began to migrate online. The metaverse will slowly take over, as the web did, but there will be no exact tipping point. If we follow the users, we find they have abandoned the real world and 2D representation of that world, and continue to do so, increasingly looking for 3D virtual worlds in their many manifestations.

Let's first focus on the 'meta', the future vision of the metaverse network, the degree to which it will in an abstract sense be centralized or decentralized.

Metaverse as a network

Will metaverse technology open up a new world of decentralized autonomy for users? Or will it remain owned and controlled by corporations and governments? A curious feature of decentralization is that there is something in it for everyone politically. The 'left' see it as freedom from capitalism, banks and corporations; the 'right' as a world without state interference; libertarians a haven for freedom of expression and activity.

Various degrees along the centralized-decentralized spectrum have been proposed for the metaverse. The debate often reflects the explicitly political perspectives, from centralist planners through to a single organization, then centrists with a balance between governance and open markets, through to libertarians and even anarchists. As usual, the practical implementation is somewhere in between top-down and bottom up, centralized and decentralized.

Let's start with a network. Whatever structure emerges will be a network and networks are complex. A network has nodes (dots), edges (lines), hubs with the most centrality and clusters which are high-density areas of the network (Figure 7.1). In a totally random network, nodes would have roughly similar numbers of edges, much like road networks. A less random network, and more common, would be more like airports, where you have a few major hubs with lots of edges feeding into it and a large number of smaller node airports with varying numbers of edges.

FIGURE 7.1 Network

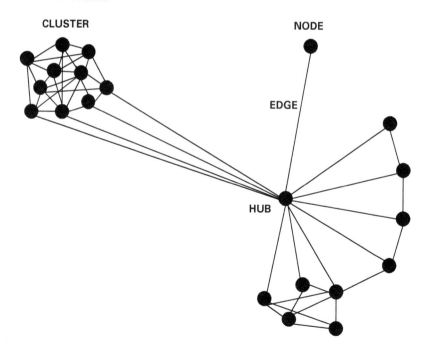

A hub has lots of edges. Degrees of association lead to clusters with a strong set of edges across a tightly situated set of nodes.

We can see that even in the physical learning world there are hubs like government departments and organizations set up to quality-assure institutions, with institutions having necessary edges to and from those hubs. Institutions are nodes, often in clusters nationally, regionally or with some educational purpose. Nodes can also be people, teachers, lecturers, trainers, instructors, learners and experts in a formal context with edges out to each other. Nodes can also be content such as recorded books, academic papers, online courses and tools such as Wikipedia, Duolingo or AI-driven chatbots. Nodes can therefore be organizations, institutions, users, learners or learning content. The sheer complexity of a network as a single metaverse, even a learning network within the metaverse, gives you some idea of the issues that building the metaverse involves.

To take just one example, looking at a learner as a node in networks of learners, a student may be relatively isolated, knowing only one or two other students or in a group where a larger number know many of the others in the group or part of a degree or year group or all studying in one institution. They also have connections to learning sources and people outside of the institution. Learning in this important sense has become more democratized as learners access more online content and services. Individuals are never alone in a network but all nodes are not created equal. In learning, a node could also be an institution related to only one, two or a very small number of other institutions, or an institution within a cluster of institutions that all know each other. Again they are not all equal. There are also connections across hyperlinks and cited content. Wikipedia is a good example or papers with citations.

A network is also a dynamic entity, which gains its potency not just from the number of nodes but use. Layered upon any network are other relationships, such as the flows of payment, likes, comments, shares, shared interests, repeated connections, use, branding and so on. You build power and influence by increasing your position as a node.

Networks also change constantly, with lots of other emergent qualities. They can very quickly change from lots of hubs to a small number of very powerful hubs, as the tech companies have done. The addition of a new hub can radically alter the whole network, like Amazon entering the book and retail market.

So what is the likely networked structure of the metaverse?

Centralized

Our species has certainly evolved to 'network' and our brains are adapted towards social interaction and groups. We, the co-operative apes, have distributed cognition and this has increased massively as technology has allowed us to network more widely. Technologies, as we have seen, have been the primary catalysts. Nevertheless, much human social behaviour has been tempered with chiefs, kings, lords, emperors and so on, hierarchical structures that lead and control, even the web is now spun by hierarchical and rapacious spiders – the giant tech companies. Organizations and governments are also highly centralized and do not fit readily into decentralized models.

All roads may lead to the metaverse but not all organizations have the time, money and strategic intent to get there. When Facebook, one of the biggest brands and companies on the planet, used by billions of people, rebranded to Meta Platforms, Zuckerberg also announced his moonshot – the metaverse. Facebook is already bigger than any single country and is likely to be a major player. Could it be the single player? Unlikely, as many players are already investing considerable sums of money and time in building their presence in the metaverse. If we were to identify a dominant hub, however, it is likely to be Facebook. It would have to double-down on its intent and pour a huge amount of money and resources into the build, but that is possible.

It may decide to act as a 'road tax' entity making money, as it does from advertising, but not interfering with the landscape in terms of entities. Facebook's stated intent to encourage an open network may be treated with suspicion but this could be its genuine intention, as it would mean rapid growth through extension not exclusion. This was the model for most social media, where the service was free and growth fast and furious.

Decentralized

Another model is a decentralized network, where there is no overall control by a single or even oligarchical group of companies. This is often touted by those who see the metaverse as a counterpoint to the way the internet has turned out, with a few large companies controlling most of the traffic and revenues. So what sort of decentralized models can we call upon?

Decentralized deschooling

One radical, decentralized vision of education, put forward to free us from our obsession with 'schooling', is Ivan Illich's idea of open interaction and exchange. In his seminal text *Deschooling Society* (1971), 'schooling', he claims, confuses teaching with learning, grades with education, diplomas with competence, attendance with attainment. Schools are separated, unworldly places that lead to psychological impotence and we become hooked on their role in society to the extent that other institutions are discouraged from assuming educational tasks and roles.

For Illich, we are 'schooled' in institutions run by technocrats that take responsibility away from other institutions for social responsibility and learning. It is all based on an illusion, he claims, that most learning is the result of teaching. Most people acquire most of their knowledge outside school. Most learning happens casually and even most intentional learning is not the result of programmed instruction, mostly a by-product of some other activity defined as work or leisure.

Adults tend to romanticize their schooling, yet most, when pushed, recognize the smothering atmosphere of the classroom and feeling of incarceration in school. Even supporters of schools and schooling recognize that the school has remained largely unchanged since Victorian times with age grouping, classrooms, desks, terms, prefects, rituals, curricula, corridors, timetables, prize givings and reports.

Illich sees alternatives in skills centres, educational credits and the use of technology to create institutions which serve personal, creative and autonomous interactions. Well before the age of the internet, he foresaw its power in education and knowledge, as an alternative to schooling through a decentralized network or service which gave each person the same opportunity to share their interests with others, motivated by the same cares and concerns. His core idea was that education for all means education by all. He sees us providing the learner with new links to the world instead of continuing to funnel all education through the teacher. In this sense, the inverse of school is possible, with different types of educational experiences, skills' exchanges, peer-matching and access to the services of educators.

Informal learning

One could argue that this has been happening for some time with the advent of technology in learning, through search, free content in Wikipedia, OERs,

MOOCs, social media, learning services such as Duolingo and Khan Academy and now generative AI tools. There is a tendency to see everything in terms of entities and organizations, yet what fuelled growth on the internet was not content but 'search'. This fuelled a swing towards informal learning as knowledge became freely available and quick to access by anyone on the web. The arrival of generative AI has made this even more powerful, as it identifies the 'intents' of the user through prompts, thereby identifying and generating more powerful targets. These informal networks are very different. We could well see the emergence of new, AI-driven entities that reshape learning, truly decentralizing and disintermediating institutions and formal learning. The metaverse could eliminate more of that worldly fixation with formal learning and institutions to provide a people-rich environment where this vision is possible.

DECENTRALIZED THROUGH WEB 3.0

On the other hand, the danger is that a massively decentralized Web 3.0 has actually manifested itself as 3.0 scams: NFTs, cryptocurrencies and blockchain; not decentralization, just greedy speculation and rug-pulls adding nothing to human progress. Unregulated, decentralized cryptocurrencies and NFTs seemed to suck in a curious mixture of the greedy and gullible.

Hopelessly utopian visions of a 3D internet completely replacing everything else has led to the rightful criticism that this is not how technology evolves. A more sensible vision is not the Web 3.0 version that sees the metaverse dominated by NFTs, cryptocurrencies, decentralized autonomous organizations (DAOs) and blockchain. That vision is presented in a number of books, including *Navigating the metaverse: A guide to limitless possibilities in a Web 3.0 world* (Hackl et al, 2022). With the collapse of the NFT, crypto and virtual real estate markets, this vision looks less and less likely. The failure of unregulated, decentralized finance led to massive fraud, volatility and ultimately the collapse of these markets. Cryptocurrencies turned out to be speculative assets, not real currencies. It was a bubble de-anchored from regulation, physical assets and reality. The promise of blockchain was also severely damaged as the entry points, exchanges and brands collapsed. This vision of a future internet – a utopian, unregulated, supranational, virtual economy – has been shattered. It may rise again but only when safeguards are in place to prevent the predictable anarchy that prevailed. We have run that experiment and it failed.

Commentary on tech swings from utopian to dystopian, from hype to horror in a flash. But the metaverse could turn out to be a crime-ridden scamfest, full of fakery, rug-pulls, NFT frauds and cryptocurrency. The real world has plenty of crime and scams, as does the existing online world, but the metaverse may actually create worlds where this is made so much easier. No one can hear you scream in cyberspace. We may all have our digital twin in the metaverse but there will be swarms of Jekyll and Hyde twins to deal with, where you may not know the difference.

A more likely outcome is a blend of governance and capitalism as, since the 1990s, the mixed economy has emerged as the dominant political environment around the world, even in communist China.

Squares and towers

A more likely vision for the metaverse, one that is more of a compromise, and one which history suggests always arises, is examined in *The Square and the Tower* (2017) by Niall Ferguson, who takes the public square in Sienna and the tall tower that looms above, as a metaphor for flat, open networks and the inevitable, accompanying hierarchical structures.

Ferguson's point is that history shows that both squares and towers have been around for a very long time. He sees history through the lens of networks, the main distinction being between the disruptive networks we have been looking at, often fuelled by technology, sitting below the pressures of institutional hierarchies, such as families, political parties, companies, institutions, governments and so on.

He regards the Renaissance as the first of the truly networked ages. Then the age of discovery, the catalysts being navigational technology and trade networks. But the big disruptive network was the Reformation, partially caused by printing. Whether Luther did or did not nail his 95 theses to the door is beside the point. What matters is that the printing press allowed the spread of these ideas to challenge the hierarchy of the church. The control of language through Latin and of knowledge through scripture was blown wide open. From the Reformation came revolutions, again fuelled by print and networks. Financial networks flourished, sometimes ruled by family hierarchies. Scientific and industrial networks expanded, giving us industrial revolutions but controlled by the wealthy.

In truth, complex systems always end up being compromises as global technologies need some semblance of centralized or generally agreed governance, with checks and balances to keep everyone honest. Ferguson shows how most networks lie somewhere between a purely decentralized and purely centralized model. Every agora is metaphorically overseen by a regulatory tower.

It seems clear that the metaverse, ultimately, will have centralized governance over technical issues such as interoperability, regulatory rules and standards. On the other hand, the metaverse will clearly contain micro, medium and megaworlds, with ownership likely to be across a range of small, medium and large organizations. This will be reflected in learning with different types and sizes of services.

Metaverse as multiverse

The vision of a monolithic tower-only metaverse is far less likely than a Multiverse of multiple worlds, with variety in aims, size and look. In the highly differentiated and genre-driven games world, there is everything from high-fidelity graphic worlds to low simple block and polygon worlds, with everything in between. It is unlikely to be the product of a single-vendor, centralized world. It may well turn out to include thousands of little metaverses, like small theme parks, all competing for your attention. Multiple sizes will emerge, with mega, medium and microworlds, some very large, expansive and open; others of moderate size; others specific, precise and small. Multiple build strategies will also emerge, with some created centrally, others by professional designers, others by users.

The likely model for the metaverse is therefore an open, overseen, decentralized metaverse as a multiverse held together by common standards and overseers. This is similar to today's internet, with a few large hubs, run by large existing players and likely new entrants, with a strong track record in 3D worlds. Beyond this maybe other hubs and clusters would form a large and varied landscape. Hubs are likely to be large well-known tech and games companies, with clusters forming around smaller players and groups of common practice, self-built worlds and so on.

Multiverse of learning

The state and the market are to a large degree separate; the state defining and overseeing the laws within which the market operates. Similarly in education, the state defines what is to happen in schools and universities but leaves them fairly autonomous in what they teach and how it is taught. The same 'square and tower' distinction is likely to survive for learning in the metaverse, although, just like the real world where the ivory towers have been under siege from other market providers, this is likely to increase in the virtual world.

University enrolment has been falling in the USA for over a decade and universities have been losing their share of adult learning as other entities such as Coursera, Google, Microsoft and other educational providers have entered the market, some with their own accreditation. This has been particularly true with courses in vocational subjects such as business, IT and healthcare. Sophisticated AI-driven tutors may accelerate this process. What may make a huge difference is that the large online tech companies are creating these worlds and have expertise way beyond that of the ivory towers. It may even topple some of them, if not alter the learning landscape into a more diverse ecosystem.

The metaverse may provide a new and unique environment in which learning technologies and techniques, some known, some yet unknown, may flourish. This may turn into a new gold rush, creating a wonderful new educational market. What makes this different from previous proto-metaverses, such as Second Life, is that the underlying technologies and standards inside a ubiquitous, high-bandwidth, cloud-based internet can make it a much more sophisticated world. As we spend more time in such places, we may well be willing to spend money on learning in the places we inhabit. This is the economy of experiences, perhaps valuable learning experiences.

Metaverse players

All the major tech companies then have an eye on the mountain that is the metaverse and all have climbing teams that have set off to climb. In base camp, we already have some big names, notably Facebook, Microsoft, Google, Apple, Nvidia and Amazon. No doubt the major Chinese tech companies will be in their tents, working away on their own routes to the summit.

AR is also likely to be a feature of the metaverse, worked on by several of these companies, especially Apple. Rather than being locked into a purely VR world, mixed reality is likely to be a huge feature, as a bridge between the real world and the metaverse.

Facebook's land grab of the virtual world through its 'Meta' branding is slick PR. It is as if just naming something makes it real. The brand alone acted as a new centre of gravity. Metaverses have been around for decades, but what is different is the branding and financial commitment, in the billions of dollars. Billions have already been spent by Meta to build a full-stack platform, and other tech giants have been active. Facebook's acquisition of Oculus in 2014 for $2.3 billion was a landmark acquisition and it has continued to release headsets with ever better specs and functionality. The focus on the Oculus headsets, now rebranded under Meta, has pushed their education trial in newly created metaversities and they have the advantage of having hardware being used in virtual worlds and in many educational contexts.

Microsoft buying Activision in 2022 was a massive signal, as it pointed directly at the heart of the metaverse. These are the suits sitting at the back of the room doing deals, while watching the tech kids eat pizza. Microsoft already had an impressive metaverse ecosystem with Azure, Teams, HoloLens and Xbox and showed further intent towards the metaverse in buying Activison. It has stuck to AR and the HoloLens but its ambitions will be, as always, global, but with a virtual playground in AltspaceVR, Halo and the mighty *Minecraft*, Microsoft is in this race. Its strategy is likely to focus just as much on work than play and one can see it expanding Teams into the metaverse as working virtually becomes a virtual reality.

Google was stronger on AR with Google Glass in 2013, which has receded but not gone away, as the company continues to spend billions on AR companies such as North and Raxium. It released Google Cardboard, a great idea, in 2014, which had an educational platform offering VR field trips but this, oddly, has been discontinued. Daydream was its headset, launched in 2016, also discontinued. As the research in VR for learning shows, novelty and just showing 3D places is not enough in learning; you must have strong, deliberate pedagogy that people are likely to learn from and retain learning from these experiences. Confusing the consumer with the education market is a mistake. Google recognized this lack of focus and Google Labs is now bringing all VR and AR into one space.

Amazon had a brief foray into AR with Echo Frames glasses but is otherwise quiet. Silence, however, does not mean inactivity. It bought a games engine and had a games streaming service but this is not its natural habitat. One would expect that, behind the scenes, it has its retail eye on buying and selling within the metaverse. So, although all is still quiet on the Amazon front, where the focus is on the real-world economy, when the shift to 3D happens, it will be there. AWS is a significant cloud provider and its cashless stores show every sign of having the technology that could be used in virtual worlds.

Apple has been strangely quiet. It has never been one for launching products prematurely but in typical Apple fashion it is racking up patents and acquisitions. When the Apple drops from the metaverse tree, it will drop hard.

Tool owners will also have a great deal of power here, as they already hold the key to a big problem – how will the metaverse be built and who will build it? Tools from the games world, such as Unreal and Unity, are already dominant and have emerged as the constructive force behind the metaverse, as they have already created many of the minor metaverses, especially games. Epic Games own *Fortnite* as well as the Unreal engine and their CEO, Tom Sweeney, has strong views on the metaverse, seeing it as being games-driven. Beyond being in games, both tool developers are also players in virtual concerts and entertainment events, business spaces, prototyping for architects and product design.

Sony has the PlayStation empire and VR headsets but is proving to be aloof on standards. Disney celebrated its 100th anniversary in 2023 and has shifted from largely 2D animation to the real world of its theme parks, as well as 3D animation. Created 32 years into the company's life, the 3D theme parks now represent a huge portion of its profits. It will undoubtedly move into mixed-reality experiences. Even dating companies have expressed an interest through the Match Group.

In China, ByteDance (TikTok), Alibaba and Tencent have stated metaverse intent. The question is whether people outside China would trust a government-controlled entity or group of entities, with a bent towards surveillance, being part of the unified metaverse. We may therefore end up with two or three huge geographically separate metaverses.

Business of the metaverse

All of the global tech companies have missed huge growth opportunities in the past and are scared of doing so in the future, as they have share prices and investors on their backs. They could and can afford to lose a major battle or two; what they cannot afford to lose is the whole war. This means that they must work with each other to realize the metaverse. There will be many such skirmishes in the usual struggle over influence and ownership, the metaverse being the overall prize.

Beyond standards and protocols we also need to ask whether there is a viable business model. Interoperability is important but yet to happen. We now expect free online platforms, driven by ads. Is that enough, or what would replace that business model? This is where the big tech companies have the advantage.

Facebook has talked about the metaverse as an open platform. It seems, for the moment, to be open to open standards and practices. Yet, as its primary source of revenue is ads, it will want to take that model into the metaverse. Just as the internet thrived on common standards, so the metaverse must be a connected world with interoperability, open standards, protocols and common file formats.

It is unlikely that the metaverse will follow the route of apps, where Apple takes 30 per cent of the revenue and Google dominates the other half of the apps market. To allow the smartphone OS owners (iOS and Android) to own the gateway, and therefore revenues, would be a mistake. There has to be a fair and open marketplace. A peremptory challenge from Epic Games on Apple has already begun. It would seem that the metaverse is already bringing some of the contradictions in the market to a head.

Open protocols are needed but if the metaverse is built by users, then it is likely to be open but a mess. If it is built by tech companies, it is likely to be usable with a working business model. On the other hand, there are a lot of people working in crypto, NFT and blockchain businesses telling us the metaverse should be a free-for-all. A new model is likely to emerge. Of one thing we can be sure: without a developed business model or actual certainty around how this will evolve, it could still end up as the white noise of *Snow Crash*.

Metaverse monopoly

Hearteningly, the pull of the metaverse is already forcing regulatory action. There is a sort of Battle Royale in the metaverse, before it has even been realized. Many, for example, see Apple's restrictions on apps and payment through the iPhone as unfair. They argue that Apple should not use its hardware to restrict open-market software, an idea which has become a premise of the metaverse. Platform lock-ins, from the OS owners such as Google with Android to hardware blocks from Apple, could restrict the metaverse. The tech giants have been building their power bases on the internet and one of the forces that attract people to the metaverse is the need to bring them back to earth, closer to the needs of real people and their social goals. The metaverse is already forcing them out of their proprietary pens into a serious room where standards, protocols and interoperability are on the table. No one has a veto and if they do play that card, they may be out in the cold.

There seems to be general agreement and intent that whatever emerges has to be different, democratized and more decentralized. This is positive and progressive.

Metaverse experiences

Remember that 3D movies and 3D TV bombed. Sure, we like 3D, but desirable experiences are not all about 3D fidelity. Even stereo is no longer such a big deal in listening to music. You are reading this as text, as media rich is not always mind rich and it is not clear that the metaverse will be the learning environment some think it will be, as it does not cope well with low-fidelity 2D media such as text.

Podcasts are popular precisely because they are simple, stripped down, single-media experiences. They feel intimate, like eavesdropping into a conversation. It turns out that for entertainment and much else, we like just enough to do the job well. Even with immersion, for most, that means a large 2D TV and no more. The metaverse may be piling on the pixels but it is not clear that this is what consumers and learners need or want.

In practice, all new media technologies vector across into other media. The internet vectors back into print through Amazon; film and television through YouTube, podcast platforms and streaming. The same will be true of the metaverse. Brands and franchises cross over all platforms and the metaverse will be no different.

Reality

We should also remember that learning often needs to be real. Is learning helped by another layer of representation – avatars? Maybe not. We may want to hear real voices and see real faces. The key is not actually the learning technology but how the learning is set up and run. It needs a good teacher, clear learning goals and focused learning, along with a movement towards competency. Having a cartoon avatar layer may not help one bit. In fact, it may distance you from others, introduce awkwardness or smother the learning.

Appearance

Avatars are critical in the metaverse. It is you that is represented out there and it is important that you have the option to be who you want to be. It also needs continuity across different virtual spaces. An avatar is a form of representation and expression. The digital representation of self is more than just appearance, it is what you think of yourself and what others think of you, your friends and followers and your context. In the digital world, this expanded version of self is only limited by your imagination.

In most virtual worlds, strange and wonderful avatars are therefore the norm, as many people, for example, don't really want to show their true age, weight and looks online. How people represent themselves online can be far from what they look like in the real world. It is all colour, costumes, animal features, weirdness and cartoon fun. Will we have a parallel world where people are perennially young, good looking and thin or look like oddballs to mask their ordinariness? It promotes exaggeration of social norms around what one should look like on one hand and freakshows on the other.

Communications

The metaverse could also have problems with communications. It may therefore have a worse group dynamic than Zoom, a lot worse. In a fascinating piece of research by Carnegie Mellon, it turns out that turn taking and problem solving went better when learners turned *off* their video cameras. It would appear that not seeing others in a group is sometimes a lot better than full visibility, as one can focus on the task, not the people. The Carnegie Mellon learning study surprised a lot of people who had turned to teaching online during Covid, where the general advice was to keep students' webcams *on*. Counterintuitive though this may be, it seems that students are concerned about how they and their home environments look online. This says something about being careful about true needs in full-blown online environments. That is why most existing metaverses are chock full of bizarre avatars.

Build, but will they come?

Active user figures for virtual worlds like Altspace and Horizon Worlds have been disappointing. Then again they do depend on VR headset sales. Until VR headset sales reach some sort of critical mass and are used in social environments, the very idea of a metaverse is under question.

Misfires give us a clue as to what the metaverse is likely to be and it is not big corporate or government brands building a huge space and hoping that we will just turn up to be subjected to their condescending largesse. An example of this was a magnificent failure by the EU, where only five people turned up to an event designed to excite young people about the EU. In a bizarre setting with avatars dancing beneath palm trees, the few people who turned up were genuinely bemused. The €387,000 spent on the platform is clearly a disaster and shows exactly why this should not be a top-down effort, especially when the people at the top are unimaginative bureaucrats.

The metaverse may be proven in games environments and we have seen how the evidence, investments and intentions point towards its eventual existence but until then it remains an unproven proposition.

Deepfakes

Nina Schick, in *Deep Fakes and the Infocalypse* (2020), presents a worrying picture where the real and virtual blur and dissolve, so that we are left de-anchored from reality. This was the concern that started to look all too real when a video of President Obama in the Oval Office appeared on social media. It was an AI-generated fake.

Generative AI is now capable of creating faked text, images, audio and video that looks real. Without knowing the provenance, you would have no way of knowing whether it was real or fake. From presidents to films stars in fake sex tapes, along with AI-generated photographs winning photography competitions and fake, conspiracy, posts on social media, there is a real danger that the metaverse could end up in bad shape.

When an unreal piece of media is deliberately used to misinform, that is a deepfake. Many states, especially Russia, have used these techniques, and the danger of bad actors, even individuals, as these tools are readily available, far from being fake news, is the reality. Video is now the medium of choice with fake, photorealistic 3D avatars reading fake news. That will all be possible in the metaverse, where you may well encounter fake avatars, with fake identities, saying and doing fake things, with fake behaviours.

In education, fake coursework and essays, long a problem from essay mills, was made easy through ChatGPT, where the output could pass exams and was credible text that could not be detected by plagiarism software as fake. It raised issues around weaknesses in current teaching and assessment, as well as fresh thinking around learning and assessment. The prospect of creating a toxic environment around teachers and learners, as one side hunts down the other, gave way to new ideas and the use of the tool in more positive ways in writing and research. We would hope that the latter is the route taken in the emerging metaverse.

Conclusion

The metaverse is a concept that has been discussed and explored by many, and as such, its eventual shape is still very much open to interpretation. However, there are some general ideas and predictions about what the metaverse might look like.

It will be an immersive and interactive virtual world that allows users to engage with digital content and each other in a realistic and intuitive way. As a multi-dimensional space, it will combine augmented reality, virtual reality and other emerging technologies to create a seamless experience that blurs the lines between the physical and digital worlds. A wholly decentralized Web 3.0 model is unlikely but there will be no single company or organization controlling it. As a social space, it will allow users to connect and interact with each other in new and meaningful ways. It will also include features like virtual economies and marketplaces, where users can buy and sell digital assets and services. It will certainly be accessible to anyone with an internet connection and the necessary hardware, such as a VR headset or smartphone. This could make it a truly global phenomenon, accessible to people from all walks of life and all corners of the world.

Of course, these are just some general predictions, and the shape of the metaverse could still be very different from what we currently imagine. The development of the metaverse is still in its early stages, and it will be interesting to see how it evolves.

Bibliography

Ferguson, N (2017) *The square and the Tower: Networks, hierarchies and the struggle for global power*, Penguin, London

Hackl, C, Lueth, D and Di Bartolo, T (2022) *Navigating the Metaverse: A guide to limitless possibilities in a Web 3.0 world*, John Wiley & Sons, New Jersey

Illich, I (1971) *Deschooling Society*, Harper & Row, New York

Nikolaj, N, EU spends €387k on a metaverse, throws low-attendance gala, EU Observer, 27 December 2022, euobserver.com/digital/156503 (archived at https://perma.cc/D7D8-XRDV)

Schick, N (2020) *DeepFakes and the Infocalypse: What you urgently need to know*, Hachette UK, London

Tomprou, M, Kim, Y J, Chikersal, P, Woolley, A W and Dabbish, L A (2021) Speaking out of turn: How video conferencing reduces vocal synchrony and collective intelligence, *PLoS ONE*, 16(3), e0247655

08

Metatech

Immanuel Kant once said that 'Out of the crooked timber of humanity, no straight thing was ever made.' The metaverse is no exception. Still ill-formed, we have gathered the evidence for its trajectory from 2D to 3D. We also have to be honest about potential problems and risks. Without descending into largely irrelevant lists of past failures in technology, a feature of almost all technological progress, or nimbyism, 'What's with that photography thing, we have been able to paint for ages', there are issues that demand serious attention.

The idea of the metaverse as a single technical entity is hard to imagine, never mind realize. It is difficult to see how even the existing virtual worlds can be brought together. They all seem like different galaxies in a universe, completely separate and unrelated. The software stacks in, say *Minecraft*, bear little resemblance to *Fortnite*, which in turn is very different from Roblox. This is an interoperability problem but it goes much deeper, as there are different tools and a range of different approaches to the build and maintenance of these worlds.

These proto-metaverses are still separate, self-contained virtual worlds with their own separate internal economies. What we have now is a bunch of metaverse precursors that are disconnected from each other, many with increasingly self-contained economies. The metaverse is unlikely to be a success if this model continues. Connection and persistence across platforms are fundamental to the vision of the metaverse with open standards, network protocols and file formats. The solution to this problem, and what will make it accessible and compelling to users, is a single gateway or metaverse browser that allows entry into multiple metaverses. An entire ecosystem of hardware and software is then needed to create, access and operate within the metaverse.

Metatech

The internet came together after a lot of heads got together and protocols were finally agreed. Like the postal system, there had to be a postal service (TCP/IP), addresses (IP addresses and URLs) and letters (HTML). File standards took longer to sort out, with awkward proprietary formats, like Flash from Adobe, holding out until they were so hated and impractical they were unsustainable. It took time but it did happen. A similar evolution is likely with the metaverse.

Although the metaverse does not yet exist, there are several technologies that suggest how the shift from 2D to 3D will evolve, as well as technical conditions for a more substantial 3D world with common protocols and standards. This shift is a long process, not an event, with a number of steps in between.

Mixed reality

The metaverse is not an immediate leap into a wholly immersive virtual world. It is the move towards various forms of 3D experiences – mixed reality. Neither is this a simple spectrum going from real at one end to virtual at the other. There are lots of mixed modes in between where varying degrees of sensory access and interaction with the real and virtual worlds are possible. It is more like a constellation than a spectrum.

We already exist in our own metaverse – consciousness. It re-creates what we receive through sensory input and re-creates that world in a stereoscopically 3D version of that real world. Consciousness is not 'real', even in the sense of being a full and exact copy, it is a selected approximation, influenced by the predictive and powerful analytic ability of our brains. Any simple optical illusion, such as the Necker cube, shows this in action.

If you wear glasses, you are already enhancing or augmenting the real with magnification technology. Your lenses are dealing with deficiencies in your sight. They solve a cognitive problem. I have worn glasses since I was five years old, so my entire education and career depended upon them. And that is just one simple enhancement. Our environment is full of virtual extensions and worlds – glasses, cochineal implants, televisions, radios, computers and smartphones.

Similarly, technology now delivers various forms of mixed reality and immersion, from the real, as presented in consciousness, through to fully immersive VR experiences, with varying levels of mixed reality in between, such as interfaces into other virtual experiences, see-through AR and semi-immersive VR. Even full VR immersion is partial; in spite of haptic and body sensors, one cannot escape the basic feeling of embodiment in the world. Gravity, feet on the ground, temperature – there is always a grounding in the real world.

Mixed reality in learning

Mixed reality in its many forms is not just toys and gadgets. It signals a future where AR and VR are new media in themselves. Just as online learning brought us the democratization of knowledge, so mixed reality brings us the democratization of virtual learning and blended 'experiences'. We will see online learning emerge from the flat screen to its placement in the real 3D world.

Much in learning is basic concepts, explanations, rules, processes, procedures, often presented as text, which falls short, as we need to show and do, as well as just tell. Even the addition of images and diagrams falls short as there is often a dynamic, causal, temporal process involved, as well as context. There is almost nothing in chemistry, biology, physics, geometry, geography, engineering, hydraulics, pneumatics and almost all vocational subjects that would not be enhanced through 3D augmentation. We are stuck, not in death by PowerPoint, but death by 2D attempts to show 3D phenomena.

Problem solving, the application of knowledge and skills, often involves real people with real objects and takes place in real places. A strong example is language learning, where learning and practising a new language benefits hugely from immersion in the context in which the language is actually used. It makes little sense to teach practical skills from a lecture or PowerPoint or in the classroom, yet this remains all too common. This loyalty to 2D slide decks has meant the squeezing out of practical skills from schools and universities, where practical work is well-nigh impossible. The hope is that, after being pushed back and out of sight in education, practical learning will be given a cool kudos, through technology, placing it on the same pedestal as academic learning.

What makes this shift different is the 3D nature of these new virtual worlds, accurate representations of the real world, which, as we know, is 3D.

Augmented reality (AR)

AR places 3D objects into the real world. It allows anything to be added to the existing world. What was once the domain of the imagination can now be realized as real 2D and 3D images in context.

Pokémon Go, AR's first global success, was a work of genius. Its use of AR became a global reality in weeks, a unique melding of the real and non-real through addictive gaming and it did what most 'research' projects failed to do – capture the imagination. AR is also common on smartphones, enhancing photographs and videos. Its appeal was its presentation of layers of reality; smartphone maps (idealized mapped representation of reality), camera view (photographic representation of reality), Pokémon and the other imagery (superimposed upon the other realities), all finally framed within a single conscious view of these different realities. That is before mentioning the layers of the internet (itself a created reality) and GPS (a created dynamic co-ordination path within both the virtual and real). Then there is the social reality, something that binds this together across peer groups and the entire community of *Pokémon* players. It was heady stuff.

AR games that use real-world environments had a huge hit with *Pokémon Go* and they will be much more common with new consumer AR devices. Its use to assist visually impaired people with overlaid words and highlighting of objects will certainly be useful; its use for people as a way of accessing information in the flow of work and life has the potential to reach everyone, but it is its use in learning that interests us most in this book.

This basic idea of making the real word come alive with augmented possibilities will eventually be available through glasses, other devices or straight to your retina. One vision for AR is having a screen anywhere on glasses, so that you can watch video and the typical content you currently get on a smartphone. It allows hands-free access when walking and trying to find somewhere, call up answers in situ, learn in situ.

Miniaturization, down to a few millimetres, allows for high-resolution images and a usable battery life inside the frames of normal-sized spectacles. High-resolution images, with ever increasing fields of view, can be displayed, including video, games, readable text and computer displays. Reading in bed without disturbing your partner is another interesting advantage. Such glasses can combine real-world and created images, delivering 3D stereoscopic images. This move from smartphone to the eyes, with contextualized experiences in the real 3D world, will be yet another move in the shift from 2D to 3D that is part of the evolution towards living and learning in the metaverse.

AR in learning

Retailers, for example, are already experimenting with AR as a customer experience. As retail has shifted online, there is a far greater, global need to experience products virtually, from dream kitchens and bedrooms, to individual pieces of furniture and artwork in a room, to clothes, customized shoes, glasses, watches and make-up. Brands that allow customers to try before they buy will have a competitive advantage.

Yet, one of the most reported advantages of AR is that it promotes enhanced learning achievement (Akçayır, 2017). The learning possibilities include increasing attention by both cutting out real-world distractions and increasing focus on the learning process. Immediately available means learning anywhere, at any time. Learning in situ is also possible, in the office, on the factory floor, on the construction site, in the hospital ward. One can also see immediate applications in language learning and tasks that require constant practice.

If we take some of this AR 'magic dust' and sprinkle it on learning, we can lift and augment tasks that were traditionally passive, static and 2D into activities that are active, dynamic and 3D. Why is this useful? The world we live, learn and work in is active, dynamic and 3D. Once you can superimpose or place virtual artifacts anywhere on anything for anyone, you bring personalized learning opportunities into education and work. Blending realities takes AR into mainstream learning.

Another form of AR technology is holograms. MIT has been creating holograms using AI in what it calls 'tensor holography'. A model was trained using 4,000 generated images. The trained model can create a 3D hologram, almost instantly, from almost any 2D image. Holograms are now feasible from the technology built into a smartphone. 3D holograms look likely to be a cool feature in the future.

Virtual reality (VR)

VR takes us to another level in mixed reality, with partial and full immersion. Presence, autonomy, agency and the ability to navigate, do things and be with others. This makes it a technology like no other.

The technology continues to improve with more comfort, less nausea, adjustable eyepieces and substantial progress in functionality. You experience a wider field of view, eye tracking means less nausea, there is see-through to the real world and more sensors making it more of an embodied experience. This has made it much more acceptable for all sorts of uses from leisure to learning.

As learning normally involves shorter learning experiences, many of the ergonomic problems are less important. The point is not to spend days on end in training, but to provide short learning experiences and shorter times to competence.

VR pass-through

Pass-through in VR is the ability for you to see the real world while wearing a VR headset. This is typically achieved through the use of cameras or other sensors, mounted on the VR headset, which capture your surroundings and display them on your headset's screens. You can then see the real world in front of you, even while you are fully immersed in a virtual environment.

Pass-through is important as it allows you to remain aware of your surroundings while using the VR headset and some VR systems allow you to switch between the virtual environment and the real world at will, using pass-through technology to 'see through' the VR headset.

This can be useful for your safety, as it helps to prevent you from tripping or bumping into objects in the real world. It can also be useful for navigation, as it allows you to see where you are going and avoid obstacles. It gives you control over which reality you want to be in and switch between. It can be used for things as simple as taking a drink from your coffee cup on the table, or briefly checking out of the virtual to see others in the room.

It can also be used in learning to switch out to a live tutor for some feedback during training. Training tasks in VR are often likely to be chunked and short, requiring frequent feedback on performance. This can be in real time from gathered data, but a real person outside of the VR environment may also give you guidance, advice, feedback and review.

You may also want to do something that is more efficient in the real world, like take some notes, type or search on the web.

Scaling the metaverse

Quite simply, as learning technology evolved, its scale and reach increased. With Moore's law, computers, processors, cloud storage and peripheral devices have all got smaller, faster and better. Metcalfe's law saw that the number of potential connections between nodes in a network always outstrips the number of nodes, so connecting networks always create a value greater than the simple sum of the two networks. The value of a network is therefore proportional to the square of the number of connected users of the system, giving the number n^2. We also know that Metcalfe's law fuels Reed's Law that sees, additionally, that the value of large 'social' networks scale, not proportionally but exponentially. The real growth of use on the internet is therefore social use, defined as a network with n members having 2^n possible groups. There are natural, cognitive limits to our ability to cope with this potential but this is still exponentially huge.

What is clear is that it defines the immense learning power of a network and the potential connections, hence the scaling of teaching and learning between brains on the network.

Another sense of scale lies in the scale of the build. Virtual worlds need builders. Many are also skilled in using the two leading development tools for virtual worlds and games, Unreal and Unity. But this is not simply a matter of having 3D tools available. Possessing Word does not make one a novelist; it takes skill, yet tens of millions have mastered simple to professional skills in building virtual worlds in *Fortnite*, Roblox and *Minecraft*. We should therefore expect huge levels of user-generated contributions in the metaverse. AI is also starting to play a significant, generative role in building such worlds.

Metaverse tech stack

What the metaverse does need is a workable tech stack, interoperability standards and business model. Until there is an agreed set of separate standards outside vested interests, there will continue to be lots of teams heading off at different speeds, with different equipment, towards the imaginary mountain. It may get a little crowded up there, some will almost certainly die on the way to the summit, yet unity of purpose is essential.

Although 3D seems like the next step for the internet, we should not underestimate the technical problems associated with this leap. It is easy to design, even build small virtual worlds and games, but quite another thing to build a persistent, social, scalable 3D world. The history of programming is the history of trade-offs and this is still true; optimization is always needed to make things work faster and better, with massive bandwidth, storage and computation needs. Delivering the metaverse to mobile is also a huge challenge as it is a restricted environment.

Hardware is, as always, the bridge between our real selves and the metaverse. It is hoped that the metaverse, as we stated, would be hardware independent, yet this is the bottleneck that may prove most challenging. The metaverse needs an array of hardware and devices that allow the development and design of the metaverse, as well as access to that virtual world. The major tech companies have made serious moves on this front but it is not easy to see any commonality of approach. It remains an area where device fetish seems to reign supreme.

Technology

Networks have technical constraints when one tries to scale. Our current methods of routing traffic on the internet were designed for asynchronous delivery, not real-time, persistent 3D interaction. Rendering and generating 3D worlds in real time is a massive constraint and requires computing power magnitudes greater than is necessary for 2D. This is why persistence is such a mind-numbing problem.

Gaming is the most advanced playground for 3D build development as it is in games that users require synchronous experiences and reliable connectivity. Without these, games would be patently and latently unplayable. Yet existing virtual games and worlds do not work by having a huge, persistent world through which players and users move. It is important to understand that 3D virtual games' worlds do not really exist as 3D worlds. They are, in real time, destroyed and created as you move through them. They present the illusion of persistence using all sorts of clever tricks. You are in a bubble created on the fly and lots of technical tricks keep that bubble afloat.

The internet was never built for continuous presentation and streaming. It uses discrete packages of data, optimally routed to deliver and update static pages. These have to be delivered to make you feel as though what you are watching and doing is smooth and in real time. It is all a bit messy but data is usually discarded after use, or weighted towards relatively small groups at any one time and wallpapered. Nor are most synchronous experiences actually synchronous. You may imagine that Netflix is streaming but it is desperately trying to do things behind the scenes to keep the show on the road, such as preloading data and context compression to reduce file sizes if the bandwidth changes. Delayed streaming is another trick, sending stuff with a delay so that things can be corrected.

Most games therefore limit the number of players. *Fortnite* limits that number to 100; *Call of Duty* to 150. Multiplayer games do not often support more than these numbers, as the technology can't handle it. 'Sharding', placing copies of the same game onto different servers, allows the games provider to increase player numbers, without the problems of having too many players and their actions to process.

The Metaverse will need continuous, real-time rendered worlds that are persistent, which needs very high bandwidth and low latency. It is a wholly shared environment, not the world of Zoom, Teams and Google Meets. In the metaverse, large numbers of people will be in the same place interacting in a fully rendered world.

Governorship

The rise of technology in the 21st century has meant that governments per se are losing control. That is not to say that 'governance' is absent. There are international bodies, such as W3C (World Wide Web Consortium) and the UN and so on, that govern standards, even behaviours. There is also the need to reconcile various national metaverse initiatives. The USA is leading the way, with China in hot pursuit and Japan has created an 'open metaverse infrastructure from a role-playing game perspective', so it is hard to see that a single, international entity will emerge unless global standards are in place, such as happened with the internet.

Open networks, such as the internet and proposed metaverse have been shown to be vulnerable to crime. Mutual legal assistance treaties between countries are common but catching large-scale criminal fraud is difficult and rare, simply because it requires too many resources and too much time. Ransomeware may turn into actual kidnap and avatar ransom in the metaverse and, of course, ransoming pieces of the network. Finance, commerce and crime have all drifted into that other world that is the internet, yet these supranational initiatives have their problems, as they lift entities above and beyond national legal systems.

The idea of multi-stakeholderism, where no one entity is in charge, has become normalized through the internet. This is the likely governance model for the metaverse. Communal agreement on protocols is the beating heart of the internet and so it must be with the metaverse.

Standards

It is easy to wax lyrical about a future metaverse but innovation is easier than implementation, which is why we need standards for interoperability.

A multitude of technical standards bodies exist, deliberately separate from the entities that use the technology. This is because the metaverse is a combination of several layers of technology from devices to cloud delivery. There are also several large companies, with successful business models that rely on proprietary, unique or closed systems. The companies also compete against each other for market share and revenues.

To create a set of open standards, and discuss how those standards should be governed, a place must be found where they leave their weapons at the door and get talking. That place emerged out of an organization called the Khronos Group, whose 150 members have, since 2000, a strong track record in creating usable and used standards in 3D graphics, 3D assets, XR, VR and AR in games and have long used these standards for cross-platform goals. Khronos has experience in segmenting markets, creating working groups, agreeing standards and adoption programmes. Named after the Greek god of time, who emerged at the moment of creation, it is a suitable place of origin, as it has a track record and integrity.

The emerged entity is the metaverse Standards Forum, which sees '*cooperation and coordination between a constellation of international standards organizations*' as a necessary condition for success and already includes the Khronos Group, IEEE, W3C, Open Geospatial Consortium, OpenAR Cloud, Spatial Web Foundation, Adobe, Alibaba, Epic, Mete, Nvidia, Unity and many others. They hope to get agreement through patient discussion, to define virtual objects and characters in such a way that their qualities, such as shape, textures and physics, can move through the metaverse. This all comes down to the interoperability of data. It is not a standards organization in itself, and has no intention of creating or policing those standards, but it has brought many of the major players together. This may be the second time, the internet being the first, that technologies converge and combine, so the sum is greater than the whole.

If these new protocols are agreed, it may unleash the next-generation internet. It is not that they need to be perfect, even right, but a necessary condition for success is agreement. Robert Couilli and Tim Berners Lee, the originators of the World Wide Web, had some regrets about the agreed protocols for the internet, and both thought the protocols had become outdated. The point is that nothing is perfect but nothing gets done without agreement. If these protocols and technical solutions are agreed at the start, you create a new, future platform with massive opportunities, just like the original internet.

Although success came in time, the internet operated like a black hole as it sucked other networks towards it and into it, establishing common sets of protocols, file standards and conventions. File formats started off as varied but were whittled down as time passed, as developers or consumers did not want to handle file format problems. This is not uncommon in finance where common payment and transaction systems emerge. To use another analogy, across time, it acted as a Darwinian survival of the fittest model, natural selection being user demand and adoption. We can expect a similar process in the shaping of the metaverse.

Metaverse as Web 3.0

Some see the metaverse as part of a much bigger shift in tech, redefining itself as Web 3.0 with an open, permissionless, decentralized world of block-chain, cryptocurrencies and NFTs. Why? They argue that if you are locked into the clearly unsatisfactory world of the current internet or have regulatory trouble in this world, create a new one. You are then free from those constraints and authorities. The metaverse, as framed through Web 3.0, is where blockchain underpins the new model and cryptocurrencies and NFTs allow people to interact and trade currency, virtual places, agreements and objects. But are we being misled by this decentralized vision?

Most metaverses, even Second Life but mostly large-scale games, create worlds in which people want to buy and sell virtual stuff. That is fine on a small scale. When you have a world that is the size of a small or even a large country, you have an economy. But economies are regulated and do we really want Facebook to be a regulated economy, like a country? There are already serious concerns about Facebook's role as a supranational force. One can see the time when such virtual worlds have the status of a country.

Notice also how Facebook dabbled in cryptocurrency. In 2019, it created Libra, rebranded in 2020 as Diem. This created such a backlash that it has all but disappeared. That doesn't mean it has disappeared. Facebook as a central bank controlling a cryptocurrency is a frightening thought. Allowing it to create a global virtual world with a virtual cryptocurrency and economy is being touted and this is frightening.

Even better, create a system where you make money, and that literally means 'making' money as cryptocurrencies. You create money, then rake in even more money, make virtual stuff, sell it – all of a sudden you have an economy, free from governments and control. Trades happen online, making it difficult to pin down taxable entities such as true sales and profits, then the entities shift to low tax regimes to divert revenues from the actual countries that accrue the sales and profits. They are the masters of illusion, as what they deal in is illusions. This next step could be to create a wholly illusory, controlled world within the metaverse.

The libertarian roots of Silicon Valley have outgrown their teenage years. They are now greedy adults – they want it all. Not content with grabbing all the real money, they may want to destroy the real and make even more money from the unreal. In truth, cryptocurrencies have suffered from a series of catastrophic crashes and are now seen by many as a high-risk asset type, not currencies at all. The NFT market also crashed catastrophically in late 2021. This has led to scepticism about these being the key drivers of the metaverse with Web 3.0 as the vision.

People will have to learn from the mess that is cryptocurrency, so that it doesn't become a Wild West, with the big boys staking claims, volatility that verges on anarchy and a metaverse populated by scammers and ne'er-do-wells. Cryptocurrencies have turned out to be crypto-assets, a very volatile class of assets, with more than its fair share of abuses. Problems with blockchain have also become apparent, as it has failed in its promise to eliminate fraud and is weak on reverse transactions.

Then there are technologies such as blockchain. This has been mooted as the underlying distributed technology and its role in enabling persistence of identity and owned virtual objects in the metaverse, along with micropayments for content creation, has been heavily marketed. For some it is an assumption. Yet there are already problems with this vision of the metaverse. Blockchain has proved to be less useful and fruitful than thought, with alternatives already in place. It has come under attack as the classic 'solution looking for problems'. Indeed the problems with the technology itself have become legion: ransomware, money laundering, scams, theft, financial instability and huge emissions from the inherent 'proof-of-work' model. These concerns were reflected in evidence given to the US government in 2022.

In learning, most blockchain projects have doubled down on credentialism but we don't have a shortage of credentials, we have a shortage of educational opportunities and skills. That is not to say that it will not be the underlying technology of the metaverse, given its power of unhackable encryption, but this is looking increasingly unlikely.

Others have seen the fediverse as the end point. This is a set of decentralized servers, connected on open standards, independently operated, used for web publishing and social media. This also seems unlikely, as it needs computing power many orders of magnitude larger than such federated networks.

In truth, no one yet knows what the underlying technology will be, and it is unwise to nail the flag of interoperability to a single mast.

Metadata

Conformity and control

Jaron Lanier is a computer scientist and writer who has explored the concept of VR and the metaverse in depth, and has expressed both excitement and concern about its potential implications. In his book *Who Owns the Future?* (2014), Lanier discusses the potential for the 3D technology to be used to create new forms of wealth and value, but also warns about the potential for it to be used to reinforce existing power dynamics and inequalities. In an interview with *Wired* magazine, Lanier describes the metaverse as 'a new kind of collective experience' that could 'revolutionize human experience' but also cautions that it could be used to 'enforce conformity' and 'control people.' He warns against 'digital Maoism' (2006), where we drift into slavish followers of large monolithic, almost totalitarian services that present their view of the 'truth'.

In addition to being subjected and controlled by vested interests, Lanier also fears that we may be dehumanized. A consistent theme in *You Are Not a Gadget* (2010) and *Who Owns the Future?* is that we are unwittingly duped into handing our personal data over, without any returns to these organizations. In *Ten Arguments for Deleting Your Social Media Accounts Right Now* (2018), Lanier takes an even more negative position, claiming that social-media users are becoming the tool they use, and are being turned into fractious, tribal addicts losing their sense of wellbeing and place in the real world. Ultimately, Lanier's views on the metaverse are complex and nuanced, reflecting both the potential benefits and potential drawbacks of this emerging technology. These are considerations that must be taken seriously.

PERSONAL SAFETY

If you are in a virtual world, you may feel unsafe, in unfamiliar territory with lots of strangers. Even though avatars are mere digital representations of you as a person, sexual harassment, aggression and many other forms of harm, nuisance and annoyance can happen. The fact that it is a digital world makes it easy for some to assume that they can do what they want and that the norms of social behaviour do not apply. Bad actors may well be a problem, especially as the strong sense of presence in virtual worlds can be powerful and traumatizing.

To be fair, existing virtual worlds have had to deal with these problems and come up with solutions to personal identity, security and safety. Indeed, solutions in the virtual world may be stronger than in the real world. You can set up a safety bubble around you to stop anyone reaching, stepping or encroaching into your personal space. Other avatars you do not want to see or encounter can be muted or blocked and personal identity strengthened.

Just as in real life, there will always be ways in which some people will attempt to interact inappropriately or try to scam or cause harm to others. The good news is that although this is a tough problem to solve in the real world, it becomes a design problem in the metaverse. You can literally create authentication, security and personal safety features that deal with these problems.

DATA PRIVACY

A harder issue to deal with is privacy, as data is in one sense the lifeblood of 3D environments, where sensors track what you do and want. Location data is just one species of data that can cause problems; there are many others. There is also the issue of learning data in these environments.

An additional problem is 'virtual cameras', a bit like CCTV cameras in the real world, but recording activity within virtual worlds. As in real life, could such recorded video be used in law and court cases to detect crime or be used in evidence to prosecute or defend cases? What sort of events in virtual worlds could be classed as harassment or stalking? As always, new technology, especially technology where we exist as entities in an alternative world, will throw up some legal conundrums.

Learning in these environments also involves data and there is no getting away from the fact that mixed reality and the metaverse requires virtual visibility and data and therefore degrees of protection and privacy. The fact that you can be seen and interact with lots of other people means there is ample opportunity for bad actors to cause harm.

Impersonation is another problem and this is not easy to avoid, as it is a matter of degree, from the similar to high-fidelity deepfakes. Authentification is therefore likely to be important. The deepfake problem exists in 2D media with fake text, audio and video. It could be an even bigger problem in the metaverse, where avatars and AI dominate.

Privacy by 'default' seems like a sensible solution, where users are automatically protected and have to unlock permissions and settings, rather than the reverse. The regulation of activity for children and vulnerable people also has to be considered.

Conclusion

Considerable obstacles have to be overcome to manifest the metaverse. Above all, a unity of purpose is needed to bring the big players together and agree that gains for all trump individual rewards. The technology required for the metaverse is expensive and needs agreement from a wide range of stakeholders, so it is unlikely to be a 'build and let them come' investment. Evolution not revolution is therefore the likely process by which the metaverse emerges.

Emerging from a long history of our human need to create second worlds, we have seen how virtual worlds exist in many forms and as the vision gets clearer, standards, protocols and technology will be built, in response to demand. It happened with the internet and happens in other industries from finance to healthcare. Every metaverse needs a 'meta' vision but also a 'verse' as the totality of delivery. We have the vision; we have yet to see the reality of that totality but we are well on the way to discussing, defining and, hopefully, delivering the solutions.

Having established the evidence for this march towards the metaverse, it is time to see how all of this applies to learning.

Bibliography

Akçayır, M and Akçayır, G (2017) Advantages and challenges associated with augmented reality for education: A systematic review of the literature, *Educational Research Review*, 20, 1–11

Houser, K, MIT's new AI can make holograms in real-time, Freethink*, 14 March 2021, freethink.com/hard-tech/make-holograms?utm_source=facebook&utm_medium=social&utm_campaign=BigThinkdotcom&fbclid=IwAR1MwuEjAU-NX_bqXRUGzoJsMfUrZvqf5yDvj45dbRtXBuKkAUyvu1yCHiw (archived at https://perma.cc/ND4Y-75RZ)

Kant, I (2017) *Idea for a Universal History with a Cosmopolitan Purpose* (Vol. 7), Delphi Classics

Lanier, J (2011) *You Are Not a Gadget: A manifesto*, Vintage, New York

Lanier, J (2014) *Who Owns the Future?* Simon and Schuster, New York

Lanier, J (2018) *Ten Arguments for Deleting Your Social Media Accounts Right Now*, Random House, New York

Lanier, J, Digital Maoism: The hazards of the new online collectivism, conversations, 29 May 2006, www.edge.org/conversation/jaron_lanier-digital-maoism-the-hazards-of-the-new-online-collectivism (archived at https://perma.cc/Z9GL-2H38)

US Government, Letter in Support of Responsible Fintech Policy, 1 June 2022, concerned.tech

PART THREE

Learning in the metaverse

09

Learning in the metaverse

To establish a case for learning in mixed reality and the metaverse, we must identify the problems to which this is a solution. There are social arguments for bringing practical and vocational learning back into focus in education and the workplace. These issues have been rising politically as the mismatch between education and the real world causes reflection on what we need to rebalance the system. There are also plenty of arguments from the psychology of learning to support such a rebalance, with more focus on learning by doing in 3D environments.

The case for 3D learning

There is a tendency for learning professionals to imagine that everyone works in an office and can work several days at home. Many working people, with physical jobs, so often get written out of the narrative, yet they are the ones that build our world, make things and keep the world turning. A large majority of the global workforce does not sit at a desk. The world has to produce, construct, manufacture, transport, distribute, sell and deliver goods and services. It also has to deliver social and healthcare, along with many other services, in real places.

Learning technology has failed this vast workforce, the people who had to keep on working during Covid. Look at the revenues of large online learning companies and you find they largely serve knowledge workers, who work in offices. Deskless workers are often left to fend for themselves. They get less training, are often written out of the discourse on learning and are paid less. Text- and graphics-based online learning is often weak and inappropriate for what they actually do.

It is hardly surprising then that we have huge shortages in these areas of employment. Training in competences in deskless jobs have been ignored as budgets have flowed upwards to leadership, DEI and abstract training topics that often seem remote and irrelevant to those who do physical work. Their experience of HR and L&D is also often negative in terms of working conditions and past redundancy. The culture of the factory floor, construction site, street, retail outlet and hospital is often not understood. These are often workers who do not see work as some sort of vocation but as a way to earn money, living from one pay cheque to the next.

The case for learning in 3D and in the metaverse is strong when you realize that this type of training is not well served by lectures, classrooms, text, PowerPoint and flat online learning. These jobs require real hands-on competences, often necessary health and safety and the opportunity to fail safely while learning. Training, increasingly, does not serve them well.

Online learning courses have become the norm in the workplace. Almost all large organizations have enterprise-wide software, a VLE, LMS or LXP that handles large amounts of content, courses and data. These platforms are getting smarter, delivering in the workflow through smart content driven by smart data. Unfortunately, in all of these contexts, learning by doing and practice, to transfer learning to performance, is still largely missing. The learning world has become more rarified, more theoretical, leading to huge labour shortages for practical workers, as vocational learning was sidelined in favour of theoretical graduate education. In parallel, we have also seen continuous, declining enrolment in higher education in the USA for well over a decade. We may already have passed the point of peak enrollment in college, as costs have soared and the benefits are questioned. A rebalancing of the system on academic and vocational is long overdue and will be made easier in 3D virtual worlds.

3D training and the metaverse will be of great benefit, as the problems of soaring costs, limited access and scarce teaching skills mean less practical learning. As a social good it may increase access, reduce costs and accelerate learning. Never have those most in need of learning been so far from it, as resources get sucked up and spent on the few at the expense of the many. We know that innovations in technology beget innovations in pedagogy. It was true of all learning technologies; writing, printing, broadcast media, personal computers, the internet and smartphones. It is proving true of generative AI and will be true of mixed reality and the metaverse, the shift from 2D to 3D. 3D training may revolutionize the supply side of vocational learning.

Goodhart describes the need for more focus on heart and hand and less on head, Caplan describes the vast waste of money spent on signalling, and Sandel thinks change is needed to reinstate the dignity of work. It is also what Schank recommends in training.

Head, heart and hands

David Goodhart strongly believes that education is too often a force not for good, but social division. He calls for reforms away from the too-dominant, academic, knowledge economy, towards caring professionals and vocational skills.

In *The Road to Somewhere* (2017), he was prophetic in seeing the UK split down cultural lines, where the ballooning of higher education and decimation of vocational opportunities has led to a graduate class that looks down upon the other as 'uneducated', something unhealthy in a democracy. His second book, *Head, Heart and Hand: Why intelligence is over-rewarded, manual workers matter, and caregivers deserve more respect* (2021), is a plea for the rebalancing of society, economics and rewards away from the head (cognitive work) towards the hand (making and manual work) and heart (health and care work). Having reached what he calls 'peak head', the funnelling of everyone towards university degrees, he recommends a sharp shift towards heart and hand.

Education, for Goodhart, now drives an economic system that rewards 'head' (knowledge) workers at the expense of all others. Educational stratification has not created a better world. Entire economies in the east, China, South Korea and Taiwan, were built not on a university system (they came later) but by a more rounded approach to development. Goodhart claims that higher education, in particular, has divided us and rewarded people unfairly. These inequalities have stretched societies to political breaking point. What he recommends is policy built around the head, heart and hand triumvirate. He explains how this hostage taking of society, property and money has evolved and backs up his arguments by building on Caplan's work on education, which claims that, economically, too much money is wasted on 'signalling' in universities and that alternatives have to be found, for the general good, but also on the basis of avoiding social unrest. The deification of higher education has been at the expense of the majority who do not go there. The metaverse may either reshape tertiary education or reduce our obsession with its supposed worth.

Signalling

Bryan Caplan, in *The Case Against Education* (2018), asks a bold and uncomfortable question, 'Could it be that we have too much education?' In his deeply researched and comprehensive book, he concludes that education, especially higher education, is around 80 per cent 'signalling', therefore much of it can be seen as of little value to society or even the students themselves. Although there is still some essential value in the 20 per cent, a degree for many has become a sticker on one's forehead saying 'hire me'.

More people are getting 'schooled' for longer and longer and the percentage of one's life being schooled is increasing. But to what end? Lots of people are now being prompted and pushed into academic environments, prolonging their schooling, when the evidence suggests that it 'neither raises their productivity nor enriches their lives'. Caplan's 'signalling' theory explains some odd phenomena, such as prevalence of cheating, the final year being worth more than all previous years, rising graduate underemployment and so on. Signalling, economically, also raises salaries but not necessarily skills, through credential inflation.

Caplan's almost heretical claim is that we should spend less on education, allowing that money to be spent elsewhere, such as healthcare. Lowering education spend tends to be politically unacceptable but 'At what point would education spending be excessive?' His recommendation is that we need to spend less as that will deflate runaway credentialism, without reducing skills.

Why teach so much academic stuff for so long, for almost two decades, when students are going to forget much of it anyway? Reading, writing and functional maths are necessary basic skills but much of the rest of the other-worldly curriculum is, Caplan argues, outdated. Millions are learning a foreign language in the USA, now largely taught for college admission, something students rarely use, and in any case couldn't use, as they don't gain even a basic competence. Schools have the odd and catastrophic result of making almost no one fluent in a language.

Importantly, Caplan thinks we should reboot vocational learning. This, he thinks, is a more worthwhile spend. We have evidence that it works from the success of economies such as Germany, Austria and Switzerland. Rebalancing the system towards vocational raises pay, reduces unemployment and increases school completion. The very fact that it carries a stigma, reinforces his 'signalling' theory, as the fact that middle-class parents and employers rank vocational learners as inferior is proof of this proposition.

We have a system that crowd-pleases the middle classes, while the disaffected and school dropouts become embittered. Credential inflation has been rampant, worse still, to push an academic track on the 'failure prone majority is cruelly misleading'. The answer to not having a good view at a concert may be for the individual to stand up, but if everyone stands up, no one gains.

At the national level, research about the economic benefits of education seem to 'vanish'. The effects, when found, seem 'puny' and do not seem to justify the vast sums spent on education, making it more of an act of faith than evidence-based policy. There is even evidence that reverse causation may be at work here. It is not that schooling creates prosperity, but prosperity leads to more schooling. The richer a country becomes, the more it spends on politically appealing education. Yet Harvard's Lant Pritchett, formerly of the World Bank, did the data crunching and in a now famous article 'Where has all the education gone?' found little evidence between education and higher economic growth. Cambridge economist, Ha-Jon Chang confirms the idea that 'more education in itself is not going to make a country richer'.

Even worse, could education increase inequalities in society? This is a challenging question. Inequalities are certainly rising, especially in countries with large education spends. Caplan argues that massive subsidies for education hurt the poor through credential inflation, which reshapes the job market to their detriment. The economy has not changed, we just have more graduates. Goodhart's *The Road to Somewhere* also unpacks this phenomenon in the UK in terms of the emergence of a powerful 'graduate' class.

His signalling theory also explains why online education that simply apes the current system, MOOCs for example, is bound to fail. No matter how successful these are, they don't provide the 'signal' (the degree) and that is what students are really paying for. Students are buying signals, not human capital. Online learning makes perfect sense in terms of access, flexibility, cost and convenience – yet all of that is irrelevant if the signalling is absent.

Caplan is really a whistleblower. One of the reasons that education doesn't really get put through the economic, sociological, political and pedagogic wringer, is that most of the people responsible for policy have been through highly academic institutions.

Common good

A more general, social and moral case for more focus on vocational learning is put forward by Michael Sandel, Professor of Government at Harvard. He also sees contemporary education, especially higher education, as a force for inequality and social division. In *The Tyranny of Merit: What's become of the common good?* (2020), he diagnoses a relatively recent shift from the common good to a competitive meritocracy in higher education.

The financialization of economies and changes of attitudes towards success have led to a divide between winners and losers. Finance has moved away from the greater good and rewards for all, towards enormous rewards for the few who work in finance, based on speculative finance, not the creation of valuable goods and services. This, for Sandel, has eaten away at the dignity of ordinary work. Rewards have become hopelessly imbalanced, buoyed up by meritocratic hubris and the success ethic. If chances are assumed to be equal or could be made equal, then those that flourish can attribute their success to personal agency; it is all down to their effort. This is what animates the meritocratic ideal. This divide has deepened, aided by higher education, which induces a feeling that the winners, the graduate class, deserve their success and that the rest fail because it is their fault, which has led to one group looking down on the other. A side effect of this is a lack of respect for vocational skills and work.

The 'rhetoric of rising' is wrong-headed and this hierarchy of esteem works to the detriment of other educational institutions, namely vocational colleges. We must recognize that the large majority of people do not have degrees. Sandel calls for a re-evaluation of education and new respect for vocational and other forms of learning and the dignity of work.

Learn by doing

How can 3D and the metaverse solve these problems? Roger Schank has been criticizing the current educational model for decades, with its overreliance on teaching by telling, lectures, memorization and standardized tests. His blunt assessment was that 'There are only two things wrong with education: 1) What we teach; 2) How we teach it.'

He claims that current subjects became fixed into a curriculum designed for testing and to filter students for university. This 1892 curriculum became fossilized and in seeing schooling as a funneling process for universities, other subjects and forms of learning are pushed aside. Higher education distorts education by seeing it as the destination for all, and even within higher education, research-oriented faculties often do not have adequate teaching skills, see teaching as a secondary activity, even a burden, so focus on potential researchers, not undergraduates.

Schank's work in cognitive science led him to see learning by doing and practice as essential, rather than lectures and essays. As the originator of script theory, he recommends a focus on learner autonomy, exposing learners to model scripts while allowing them to build their own. This gives them the internal motivation and competences not to 'know that' but 'know how' to do things. For Schank, there really is no learning without doing. Learning needs to be meaningful to the learner and contextualized so that it can be wedded into their existing schemas. A proponent of doing first, pulling theory in to support that doing, as well as simulations, he sees practical work as allowing the necessary failure and ultimately success. Learning is messy and failure the norm.

Long a supporter of case-based learning, role playing, scenario and simulation training, he sees context and realism as important. You need a designed simulation where the learner plays a role, a story-centred curriculum. This is where the cognitive processes, described in *Teaching Minds: How cognitive science can save our schools* (2015) can be learnt, with high levels of autonomy, leading to real and relevant competences, as well as social skills. Autonomy allows you to fail, learn from that failure to acquire competences, and have that put to the test in a social context. Real cognitive competences, applicable in the real world, come through conscious, analytic and social processes.

As a cognitive scientist, Schank provides a theory and framework for learning by doing, but when considering learning in 3D and the metaverse, what other evidence is there, in terms of cognitive needs for learning in mixed reality and the metaverse?

Thinking and language in 3D

George Philip Lakoff believes that metaphor plays a primary role in language and thinking, that all forms of cognition and reason are grounded in embodiment and that the brain takes its cues from the body, how our bodies are situated physically in the world, how we act and move. This determines how and often what we think. Thinking is therefore shaped and limited by this embodiment. In that sense, ideas are physical.

Evidence for this, for Lakoff, comes from the relative absence of pure logical thinking and reason. When we think, it is common to think spatially, referenced to embodiment. We frequently use figurative language, especially spatial 3D metaphors, across almost all subject domains in an attempt to understand, communicate and explain them.

3D in interface design

One clear example is in digital interfaces where difficult objects and operation on 2D screens use 3D metaphors to make them more usable, showing our deep, cognitive need to relate the abstract to the concrete. Examples on the 'desktop' include files, folders, tabs and stick-on notes, calling upon the language of the real 3D office. Even completely abstract ideas like time and data are represented by real objects as 3D metaphors, a 3D watch, clock or clock face, data as a file within a folder. A file and folder can be seen as both the object and container, an email literally as a letter icon. A bell is used for notifications in social media. A chain represents hyperlinks. A house takes you to the homepage. Even a procedure can be seen as a 3D object, such as scissors for cutting, brushes, pencils and other painting metaphors such as palette boards and paint pots, the magnifying glass for search. A spinning wheel or hourglass shows that the system is busy performing a function. Directions, up and down, right and left, are also used metaphorically, such as fast-forward and rewind for video. This shows our deep-rooted need for metaphorical objects when performing even digital tasks.

Teaching, learning and metaphor

Metaphor allows us to understand one thing by another, making the abstract more concrete. Teachers and learners communicate through language which is deeply metaphorical, with varying layers of metaphor. Typically, we use spatial 3D language to explain and represent non-spatial ideas. This allows us to communicate concepts and processes, especially to those unfamiliar with those ideas. We ground the abstract in the familiar, which is the physical world within which we operate. We therefore learn by relating the abstract to our existing and everyday experience and that experience is of the real 3D world.

3D metaphors, far from being merely ornamental, are fundamental to teaching and learning. Note that they can be used to crystallize the very purpose of education, both positive and negative; learning as lighting a fire, a spark; an investment, as opposed to the banking of knowledge, the filling of a pail. Teachers guide learners, take them on learner pathways or journeys. Positional metaphorical language can also be judgemental and embody values. Our mood is up if we feel happy, down if we feel depressed. Good is generally up, bad is generally down.

Lakoff's point is that metaphors are not in language but thought, and thought itself is rooted in space, time and action metaphors. When we say that students can move up a class, we have used the word 'up' as a direction and 'move' as motion. Learning, like life, has its ups and downs. We have 'higher' education, being marked up or down. We feel these metaphors as embodied, directional acts.

Learners need metaphors to internalize, assimilate ideas, explain things to themselves, generate ideas and help remember them. Learning in imaginary 3D worlds would therefore allow the learner to internalize what they are learning. Fewer linguistic metaphors would need to be used if virtual places, objects, processes and procedures could be taught in any imagined, virtually created place, at any time. The idea that a teacher or learner could literally generate a 3D place, allow a quick experience by the learner, reinforce that experience and form a lasting memory is a very powerful form of learning. Different types and levels of actual metaphorical places and objects could be used to match the learners' needs. This could also use the Von Restorff effect, where items that stand out are more easily remembered, so to place a familiar object in an unfamiliar even bizarre context allows you to trigger the recall of a memory when you see that object again.

Lakoff believed strongly in the use of the arts in education, as a stimulus for creative thinking, as it often uses a more visual, metaphorical approach to communicate ideas. Of course we should not take the idea of language and learning as metaphor too far, as it is not a theory that has total explanatory power, it is clearly partial. However, it is a strong enough element in learning to suggest that the metaverse may offer real opportunities for teaching new ideas to students by allowing them to incorporate those ideas into their existing experiences of the world. This metaphorical evidence is backed up by the fundamental nature of spatial thinking in our brains.

Memory palaces

Imagination, remembering and dreaming use the same part of the brain that sees that same action or movement taking place in the real world, as evidenced by the memory palace (or loci) technique. This has been around for thousands of years and plays to our facility to remember things embedded in an imagined 3D context, to help us remember and recall.

This memory palace idea has even been used in VR to allow students to place their ideas within immersive 3D worlds and has been shown to be effective. The University of Maryland study (Krokos et al, 2018) split 40 people into two groups then showed both groups pictures of famous people. One group experienced the images in imaginary locations in 3D VR; the second group saw the same images but on a 2D desktop screen. Recall was 8.8 per cent better in the VR group and 38 of the 40 said they preferred the VR for that learning task. Questioning revealed that the VR learners reported an increased sense of 'focus'. The researchers concluded that the physical presence within the VR world provided an experiential component that deepened the learning experience.

It would seem that learning experiences within 3D worlds could increase the encoding of episodic memories. How you process that knowledge and skills depends on how you process the experience. This is called encoding and when you encode information you can strengthen the encoding through an elaboration process, linking it back to your own, personal experiences. This is where presence and focus within virtual worlds can support encoding and learning.

Spatial thinking

Spatial thinking is the norm. We think spatially, move around in a 3D world, manipulate objects in a 3D world, and interact with 3D people. Psychology shows we do not socially construct reality but are born with an evolutionary legacy where we already bring to the world a spatial knowledge of that world. Stephen Pinker provides a good summary in *The Blank Slate* (2002). Our evolved spatial capabilities include an intuitive:

- physics about the concept of a 3D object, its persistence, predictable movements and action of forces. It also includes, as Geary (2005) explains, a folk physics of impetus within such objects, found to be false by Newton

- spatial sense of 3D space, which we know how to navigate and place objects within. This is a constantly updated, complex reckoning of our body's position within a set of spatial maps, as we move and turn through the 3D world

- engineering, a sense of 3D tools, which are made for a purpose and used with goals in mind. This is an intuitive understanding not of the body, but things used by the body beyond its boundary

- psychology of other 3D people and animals as having minds, beliefs and intentions which result in their immediate behaviour.

These 3D abilities may seem obvious but many assume we are born with a blank mind and no understanding of the world we are born into. Learning theorists have a heavy weighting towards social constructivism, language, reason and text, meaning they make false assumptions about the absence of our prior knowledge of the 3D world, to assume it is also fully constructed. It also leads to teaching and learning that ignores the real 3D world of doing and actual performance in favour of over-theoretical language and text-heavy courses that fail to relate and transfer skills to the real world. This is why so much training fails: it is far too text and theory driven, decontextualized, disembodied and de-anchored from the real 3D world.

Episodic and semantic memory

Another insight into cognition that helps us understand the spatial and temporal elements of thought is Tulving's (1972) distinction between episodic and semantic memory, the former used to remember experiences, the latter facts. Episodic memory is more autobiographical and allows us to time-travel from the present to the past. This episodic ability to recall specific events from the past from a particular place at a particular time, tells us a lot about how we think and remember. We use this ability almost without thinking, for example in remembering where we parked the car, also for critical events, such as remembering where our life-saving medicine is stored and when to take it. It is a necessary condition for functioning in the world.

Episodic memory also helps you to see yourself in the future. The ability to situate yourself in the past also allows you to imagine and throw yourself into future situations. Our ability to recall episodes from the past therefore allows us to posit, prepare and plan future events.

Episodic memory suggests that 'space' seems to be more primary than 'time', as time itself is represented as a mental timeline into the past, as a linear spatial display. We can place things in order on that timeline. This suggests that spatial and temporal elements play a very important role in learning and memory but are downplayed in education and training, where things are very text-based, playing to semantic words, rather than episodic memory. This is important, as it suggests we often teach performance in the real world the wrong way through the wrong media – 2D text and graphics. We humans are 3D entities that evolved in a 3D world and have 3D perceptual systems to deal with that world, along with powerful 3D episodic memories. Now that we have the technology to mimic this cognitive legacy, it can be used to good effect to teach and learn.

Extended mind

Widening the argument for spatial learning we can see that much learning needs to be done or situated in a 3D context. Roger Barker and James J Gibson are the doyens of ecological psychology. They saw, in their very different ways and methods, behaviour as wholly situated in 3D 'ecological' contexts and systems. These ecological psychologists would ask 'not what's inside your head, but what your head's inside', namely a 3D environment.

Barker set up the Midwest Psychological Field Station in Kansas to study real behaviour and is seen as the founder of embodied psychology. He stayed for most of his life in a tiny town in Kansas – Oskaloosa, population 725, to study ordinary people, free range, in the wild. This was to study human behaviour in real contexts, not the laboratory, as he theorized in *Ecological Psychology* (1968) that our behaviour is situated and shaped by different environments; being in a sports stadium, church, supermarket or workplace. We are radically situated in the sense of being shaped by our ecology or environments, far more coherently than identifiable cognitive traits.

Gibson was a more traditional academic and psychologist whose later work focused on ecological psychology, a direct attack on cognitive psychology. In *The Ecological Approach to Visual Perception* (1979), he saw that we make sense of the world by perceiving and feeling certain behavioural 'affordances'. An affordance is something that has behavioural potential. A door is seen as something you open and close, a doorbell to bring someone to that door. The basis of perception is 3D physics but it is interpreted in terms of potential action. Things like our height and weight also play an important role in the environment but it is the 3D environment that suggests behavioural potential. For Gibson, perception and action are one and the same thing, inseparable. We explore the 3D world as we exist and move through it, which is why we get so frustrated, for example, with lags or lip-synch problems. Perception and action are for us the same thing.

This leads naturally out into embodied cognition, the idea that the whole body is involved, especially the perceptual and motor systems. They reject the static view of cognitive psychology to see the world as a form of active perception, a place where we have opportunities to operate. These more radical views of embodied, ecological psychology push beyond simply adding embodiment to standard cognitive science, seeing embodiment as a few supplementary additions to cognition. They see embodiment as a fundamental and more universal approach to psychology (Chemero, 2009).

Ecological psychology has found a home in sports science, where perception and action lie at the heart of understanding performance, as well as design and ergonomics. Donald Norman, for example, knew and admired Gibson and his work and used his work for the purposes of design in *The Psychology of Everyday Things* (1988).

Embodiment in VR and the metaverse

A more recent application of ecological psychology is in understanding VR and learning in 3D environments. Ecological psychology defines psychology as the relationship between people and their environments. It sees behaviour as being predicted by one's environment and the importance of environmental affordances in behaviour and learning. We have evolved to proactively see and seek in our environment affordances that trigger action. Perception and action are therefore intimately entwined. Affordances are what the environment offers or suggests to us as possible actions.

We can see how this view of psychology reframes learning as something that takes place in a situated environment. If such situated environments can be re-created then the metaverse can become the ecological environment for both embodied and wider ecological learning. It is a place that can mirror ecological contexts, allow for embodiment, even focus on what elements of these really matter for learning. It provides evidence that some forms of learning – even things that are assumed to be wholly cognitive, like maths – other subjects, and of course skills that require bodily movement, may find a receptive home in the metaverse.

This is why learning must be central to the metaverse. Our bodies will always need physical activity, real places and the infrastructure of living in the physical world. This can never be wholly replaced virtually. The delivery of abstract knowledge and skills is something that *can* be delivered virtually, as it is, in essence, the creation of memories in minds, that most virtual of places. Changes in long-term memory lie at the heart of learning and define learning itself, and that can be done in safe, cheap and accessible worlds. Rather than learn in one place, your local school or college, you can learn in any place and in places from history or the present that are more relevant to what you want to learn. You can also learn at any time. But what really matters is being able to learn *anything*. In looking for applications in the metaverse, we should look to the current limitations on learning, the limitations of 2D teaching and learning tools and embrace learning in 3D and the metaverse.

Motivation in the metaverse

Herman Narula, author of *Virtual Society* (2022), the CEO of Improbable and supporter of the metaverse, has been involved in military simulations using VR in multiplayer environments for many years, extending them out to cover entire nations. He is both a theorist and practitioner. Theorists who have a grounding in practice bring both evidence and experience to the table. Narula presents a vision of the metaverse that is based on value, not just the creation of some vast social agora. With a track record in large military simulations, an area few know much about for obvious reasons, he has the credibility to make claims about value.

Military sims and games have been at the forefront of immersive training for a very long time and are another place to find proto-metaverses. War simulations go back to the 19th century, with board games such as *Kriegspiel*, with metal soldiers, designed to play battle scenarios, designed by German general Moltke. The US military has been a pioneer in the modern era in using 3D games for training.

The advantages are obvious: safe training in risk-free virtual environments where no one gets injured or dies, along with realistic contexts and scenarios that prepare soldiers for action. At its most basic we have BOGSATs (bunch of guys sitting around a table) right up to full 3D simulations with huge numbers of virtual participants, friend and foe. Training and instrumentation command (STRICOM) games simulate entire wars (Afghanistan, Iraq). Modern multiplayer games even stretch out to include civilians, press and political interventions.

Games such as *Doom* and *Half life* (redesigned as *DIVE – Dismounted Infantry Virtual Environment*) were quickly adapted for military use, as their first-person perspective, mission and weapon options proved useful for training soldiers on the ground, especially in urban environments. In one large wargame, *Millennium Challenge*, played by the US military prior to the 2003 Iraq war, 13,000 troops played along with their hardware. Blue forces (USA and its allies) fought red forces (Iraq). It took three weeks and would have been shorter if Lieutenant General Paul Van Riper had not used the surprise tactics of mosque prayer calls to sink the US fleet. Van Riper was so successful that the Pentagon had to reboot and start over. Even on the subsequent run, Van Riper had to be asked to ease off to allow the US to win. This, of course, is the whole point of a learning experience – learning through failure.

America's Army was a free, downloadable game produced by the US Department of Defence. You start in bootcamp, become a real soldier and use real weapons in a range of battlezones. It had over 1 million players and 100 million missions played, with regular updates. The US military even raided the largest game conference in the world, E3 in Los Angeles, using a Black Hawk helicopter and real troops, an astonishing example of an organization using learning games to increase recruitment.

So successful was the game that it drew international hackers, so the US military had to fight off hacks such as 'Evilhack', which threatened to destroy the game by making it easy to win, as your guns never missed! The US military employed undercover military players, pretending to be real players to destroy cheats and ban hacker players from the game.

There are many other examples of games and games techniques in simulations that have helped turn the US military into a learning organization. The vision was to have troops who learn before, on the way to, during and after battle. Games and simulations certainly had a major role in this vision.

Narula's multi-user worlds are the latest in this long history of 3D simulations in military training with its natural evolution into large, multiplayer, metaverse-like environments. His starting point, rightly, is motivation.

Intrinsic and extrinsic motivation

Intrinsic and extrinsic motivation are two different types of motivation that can drive people to engage in certain behaviours or activities. Intrinsic motivation refers to the desire to do something because it is personally rewarding or fulfilling. This type of motivation comes from within the individual and is driven by their own interests, values and desires. Examples of intrinsically motivated behaviours might include reading a book for enjoyment, playing a musical instrument for the love of music, or volunteering for a cause that the individual cares about.

Extrinsic motivation, on the other hand, refers to the desire to do something in order to obtain a reward or avoid a punishment. This type of motivation comes from external sources, such as incentives offered by other people or institutions. Examples of extrinsically motivated behaviours might include completing a task in order to receive a cash reward or avoid a penalty, or studying for a test in order to earn a good grade.

Both intrinsic and extrinsic motivation can play a role in people's behaviour, and different individuals may be motivated by different factors in different situations. However, research has shown that intrinsic motivation is often more effective at promoting long-term engagement and learning because it is self-sustaining and does not rely on external rewards or incentives. In contrast, extrinsic motivation may be less effective at promoting long-term engagement and learning, because it can undermine people's intrinsic motivation and can lead to a focus on the rewards or incentives rather than the activity itself.

There is clearly a need to create a metaverse that is more sensitive to intrinsic motivation, personally meaningful experiences that offer long-term fulfilment. This is not to say that extrinsic motivations will play no part, only that they have to be secondary for the metaverse to succeed. Narula is right that motivation really matters if the metaverse is to succeed. He is also right in referencing self-determination theory as the key to unlocking compelling learning in the metaverse.

Self-determination theory

Deci and Ryan see specific, deep, satisfying needs as the path to leading a fulfilling life in general, as they explained in *Self-Determination and Intrinsic Motivation in Human Behavior* (1985). Their self-determination theory has three components:

1 Autonomy – in control, able to take action that results in actual change
2 Competence – learn knowledge and skills to achieve more autonomy
3 Connection or relatedness – feel attached to other people.

Ryan, with Rigby, then saw that self-determination theory also explained the massive global success of gaming, as a three-stage definition of intrinsic motivation. In 'The motivational pull of video games: A self-determination theory approach' (2006), they found that gaming was driven by feelings of autonomy, the satisfaction of learning new competences and that strong sense of connection game players feel with other players.

The following three components are found in gaming.

1 Autonomy

That feeling of being autonomous, that sense of powerful presence and agency, being able to determine one's own actions, was identified as a key component in games. It is the springboard for powerful learning experiences. You play *Fortnite*, *Minecraft* or Roblox games because you may have created those games, confirming a strong sense of autonomy, you succeed in killing, getting somewhere or gaining something, also confirming your autonomy.

2 Competence

One learns to progressively overcome challenges and stretch oneself, up through carefully designed and structured levels in a game by acquiring new competences, through real action and performance, all in virtual environments. This also confirms your learnt competences, to yourself, also in the eyes of others. The trajectory of a game is in the deep game design, in keeping you going with achievable challenges and satisfying primal needs. This, not mere fun, is what makes games so compelling.

3 Connection

Finally, connection is a strong feature in gaming, being in a social environment before, during and after a game, also within a larger community of gamers and the gaming community in general. After a game, fan chat, videos and streaming all show that the social side is confirmatory and extends the experience.

These three empirically identified features of what makes gaming so potent, tell us what will matter in the metaverse, satisfying these needs with compelling applications.

Game theory

Self-determination theory explains why hundreds of millions play *Fortnite*, *Minecraft* or in Roblox. They allow you to express yourself, going on to create your own virtual environments and games, an even stronger expression of autonomy. Being a gamer is to be a learner, where you survive, gain or get to a destination through acquired skills. That sense of affirmation, not only in your own self but also in the eyes of others, makes these profoundly social environments, real proto-metaverses.

Rigby and Ryan went on to show, in *Glued to Games* (2011), that superficial stories or narratives are far less important than these deeper psychological needs and experiences. This lesson is often lost on learning games' designers. It is not the 'content' of games but the feelings and achievements through playing the game that matter. Novels, TV programmes and movies rely on the narrative or story but in games it is the experience of doing, the player interactions and gameplay, that matter. The authors dismiss the idea that games work because they are 'fun', as they observed and had players report that they involve intense experiences of focus, challenge, failure, effort and discomfort.

Ryan and Rigby give a solid explanation for the huge success of games, beyond mere entertainment, differentiating computer games from other media. This explanation also suggests why the metaverse will be a place where gaming learning experiences will lift learning games out of their rather simplistic and Pavlovian use in e-learning.

Games are therefore a form of confirmation that, if virtual experiences match up to the same self-determination drivers one finds in real life, they will be sought after. The metaverse will work if it satisfies these needs. Learning in the metaverse may well be far more gamified than in the real world, as the opportunities for 3D gaming and simulations are clear.

Coming back to learning, it is clear that autonomy or agency is important in learning, as is the acquisition of competences and their social reinforcement. Let us now see how self-determination theory can act as a bridge to learning in the metaverse.

Autonomy in learning

Metacognition may be a strong feature of learning in the metaverse. When you have an avatar, you find yourself thinking about your own identity and behaviour in different, quite reflective ways. You are almost planning your own behaviour, certainly self-monitoring more and far more aware of your own performance. In learning, one becomes more critically aware of oneself as a learner and how one is going about learning.

Some specific indicators of agency in learning are when learners identify their own learning needs and preferences, and are able to seek out appropriate learning opportunities and resources to meet these needs, set their own learning goals, and are able to monitor and evaluate their own progress towards these goals, choose their own learning strategies and tactics, and are able to adapt and adjust these strategies as needed to suit their individual learning needs. They may even self-assess their own learning, and are able to reflect on their own learning experiences in order to identify strengths, weaknesses and areas for improvement, even seek out and use feedback from others to support their own learning, and are able to use this feedback to adjust and improve their learning.

Competence in learning

What is fascinating in all of this is the bridge it forms between gaming and learning in terms of mastery or competences. 'Competences' is the currency of the learning world and self-determination theory gives us a way of seeing gamers gain and exercise abilities in a range of different contexts. Learning becomes fundamental in gaming, indeed games derive their power from learning experiences within games. So how do we help people learn how to do things? We place them in the context in which they will be autonomously motivated to learn and become more and more competent by overcoming difficulties, learning from failure.

Social in learning

These game spaces are also spaces for social interaction, connecting with peer groups within that multi-user world. In a world where real interaction is limited to just the people you know in your class at school or world and family, many find solace in meeting like-minded people in such virtual spaces. Games can be rich social experiences in themselves with slick communications within the game, playing in social context or in teams playing other teams. A rich ecosystem also exists outside games with game streamers and e-sports.

All of this sounds suspiciously like the metaverse. We can see all of this as an important frame for activity in the metaverse, a pull for meaningful activity in virtual worlds, satisfying deep and identified needs of autonomy, competence and relatedness.

Conclusion

The case for a rebalancing of learning has been made, along with several researched areas in the psychology of learning: metaphorical thinking, spatial thinking, ecological psychology, embodiment, along with episodic and semantic memory. On motivation we also identified intrinsic motivation as an important premise. These all relate back to a need for taking learning to the virtual or physical 3D world. Our evolutionary past seems to have given us a brain that works in 3D and expects 3D environments for many aspects of learning that are not semantic and not language-based.

To further unlock the role mixed reality and the metaverse will play in learning, we have seen how a general learning theory proved useful in explaining an already successful and compelling application, namely 3D computer games. We saw how its promise matches self-determination theory with its three canons:

1 autonomy

2 competence

3 social.

We will now explore how all three conditions are satisfied in the 3D world of the metaverse.

Bibliography

Barker, R G (1968) *Ecological Psychology: Concepts and methods for studying the environment of human behavior*, Stanford University Press, Stanford, CA

Caplan, B (2018) *The Case Against Education: Why the education system is a waste of time and money*, Princeton University Press, Princeton, NJ

Chang, H-J (2010) *23 Things They Don't Tell You About Capitalism*, Penguin, London

Chemero, A (2003) An outline of a theory of affordances, *Ecological Psychology*, 15 (2), 181–195

Deci, E L and Ryan, R M (1985) *Self-determination and Intrinsic Motivation in Human Behavior*, Plenum Press, New York

Geary, D C (2005) *The Origin of Mind: Evolution of brain, cognition, and general intelligence*, American Psychological Association, Washington, DC

Gibson, J J (1979) *The Ecological Approach to Visual Perception (17th pr)*, Psychology Press, New York

Goodhart, D (2017) *The Road to Somewhere: The populist revolt and the future of politics*, Oxford University Press, Oxford

Goodhart, D (2021) *Head, Hand, Heart: Why intelligence is over-rewarded, manual workers matter, and caregivers deserve more respect*, Simon and Schuster, New York

Krokos, E, Plaisant, C and Varshney, A (2018) February. Spatial mnemonics using virtual reality, in *Proceedings of the 2018 10th International Conference on Computer and Automation Engineering* (pp 27–30)

Lakoff, G and Johnson, M (2008) *Metaphors We Live By*, University of Chicago Press, Chicago

Lakoff, G and Turner, M (2009) *More than Cool Reason: A field guide to poetic metaphor*, University of Chicago Press, Chicago

Narula, H (2022) *Virtual Society: The metaverse and the new frontiers of human experience*, Random House, New York

Norman, D A (1988) *The Psychology of Everyday Things*, Basic Books, New York

Pinker, S (2003) *The Blank Slate: The modern denial of human nature*, Penguin, London

Pritchett L (2001) Where has all the education gone?, *The World Bank Economic Review*, 13 (3)

Rigby, S and Ryan, R M (2011) *Glued to Games: How video games draw us in and hold us spellbound*, Praeger, Santa Barbara

Ryan, R M, Rigby, C S and Przybylski, A (2006) The motivational pull of video games: A self-determination theory approach, *Motivation and emotion*, 30 (4), 344–360

Sandel, M J (1998) *Democracy's Discontent: America in search of a public philosophy*, Harvard University Press, Cambridge, MA

Sandel, M J (2020) *The Tyranny of Merit: What's become of the common good?*, Penguin, London

Sandel, M J and Anne, T (1998) *Liberalism and the Limits of Justice*, Cambridge University Press, Cambridge

Schank, R C (2015) *Teaching Minds: How cognitive science can save our schools*, Teachers College Press

Schank, R C (2016) *Education Outrage*, Constructing Modern Knowledge Press

Tulving, E (1972) Episodic and semantic memory, in E Tulving and W Donaldson (eds), *Organization of Memory*, Academic Press, New York, pp 381–402

10

Autonomous learning

Our starting point for learning must therefore be the mind, namely consciousness, that irreducible experience. It has developed over millions of years through natural selection to allow us to survive, be attentive and adapt to different environments. What our brains, sense, think and imagine allows us to extend our cognitive and physical reach into the world, even create new technologies and worlds. Whether it is an extension of what we think in words, what we physically build or create digitally, as a species we have, for at least 50,000 years since the cognitive revolution, been metaverse builders, creating spaces within our minds and externally, so that our minds can experience things differently. To understand the possibilities of the metaverse, we need to understand that we have a propensity towards them, and have been building them, from the very origin of our species.

Mind and metaverse

Consciousness

Consciousness is a sort of spotlight, constantly searching and settling on things of interest to us. We are constantly selecting and at the same time discarding information, so that what we deal with is an insignificant fraction of what hits us from our senses.

Even in the real world your brain is partly reconstructing reality in consciousness and what you see is always a reconstructed view of the world, and always a view of the past in being a few milliseconds after reality. Consciousness is already a metaverse of sorts.

What we see, sensory memory, is a fraction of the electromagnetic spectrum and what we see as colours are created qualities of the brain, not things that exist in the real world. What we hear is a limited set of frequencies. Even what we taste is a limited set of flavours within a vast field of possible tastes. What we experience is a tiny slice of possible subjective experiences.

Working memory is merely 20 seconds of scanned experience in which we can only hold three or four ideas or concepts at one time. We can manipulate no more than this. It is the small entrance hall that lies between what we experience in a small portion of real time and actual learning, which is persistence in long-term memory. Recalling things from long-term memory is to recall stored knowledge and experiences, semantic knowledge about the world and episodic memories of the world. What we remember is from all the time we have lived, but long-term memory fades with time and such memories are reconstructed and fallible when recalled. We truly are bounded in a nutshell of memories, despite seeing ourselves as kings of infinite space, and these different forms of memory hold our very limited, self-created conscious metaverse together.

Our omnipresent feelings are always there, that low-level feeling of being in the world with layer upon layer of attention, interest, seeking, avoidance and attraction that is being awake and attentive. The physical feeling of doing things while moving around is another layer of impressions, external and internal, along with reactions to the world we move through. This occasionally rises with feelings towards others, such as recognition, sympathy even empathy, into intense feelings of sadness or excitement. We may even be overwhelmed by feelings of love or anger. Our own metaverse is also a world of subjective feelings.

Emotional consciousness

In psychology, the neuroscientist Jaak Panksepp sees play as a fundamental part of our emotional lives. Play, as a form of social joy, is a fundamental, primary, innate part of our evolutionary, emotional legacy, along with seeking (expectancy), fear (anxiety), rage (anger), lust (sexual excitement), care (nurturance) and panic or grief (sadness).

We do not learn these emotions, and Panksepp thought they were the basis for different personality types, but we can learn to modulate them. Unlike other species, we are cognitive animals but we also have emotions commonly found in many mammalian species. In terms of learning, his work showed that although the use or alignment of instinctive emotions may enhance learning, they may also inhibit or hinder learning. Rage, fear and panic are not conducive to learning.

On the other hand, the emotion of 'seeking' benefits learning, that feeling of enthusiasm, purpose, anticipation and curiosity. The absence of this emotion signals a diminished disposition towards learning. Another powerful emotion in learning, for Panksepp, is 'play'. Instinctive in children, also found in the animal world, he separates physical, social, exploratory and object play. They are, for him, also learning experiences, essential for healthy, social and mental development as they create neural growth. In fact, he sees the lack of opportunities to play as causing increases in ADHD and other mental health issues.

We are seeking beings, in that we seek out challenges and find fulfilment in overcoming those obstacles. This is not just about learning, it is about mental health, a sense of purpose in life and finding meaning in life. These are the same virtues and psychological needs we experience in real life, in our jobs, hobbies, sports or intimate relationships.

Extending consciousness

When we stretch consciousness, it easily encompasses all sorts of things that are not actually the 'real' world, in recalling episodic memories from long-term memory, daydreaming, dreaming, reading, watching a movie or playing a game. None of these things involve engagement with the real world; rather, we naturally or willingly enter other worlds.

Consciousness itself is a world created by the brain in real time. It is your own metaverse, with perception your user interface, so you are under the illusion that it is real. We can switch immediately from one thing to another, which is why the switch in consciousness in VR works so quickly and so completely. We can swap it out in a second and believe that this newly presented world is now real. This is the essence of the metaverse as a medium. This idea of the metaverse is an extension of the mind; it takes consciousness beyond its normal bounds.

If we take as our starting point the definition of a metaverse as any extension of our minds, a place where we can take ourselves somewhere else to experience something different, then we can understand how the metaverse came to be, how it may evolve and how it can be used for learning.

Presence

Digital presence

Your digital presence has been growing in the virtual world and although you may not yet have an avatar, your image is in profiles, details of your life held and displayed online. We spend more and more time online and the technology is more and more a part of our selves. Our very identity is increasingly defined by who we are online. And that presence is about to become much more tangible, haptic and realistically unreal.

More and more of us are drifting towards looking at 3D worlds on TV, film and video, as well as hundreds of millions inside 3D games. We are gradually becoming metaverse beings, part of a digital, virtual, increasingly 3D world. What we have seen is a movement towards creating that world, user-driven content, from text, images and video in 2D social media, towards 3D games in younger audiences. Generative AI will accelerate this process. Yet it is people that matter. People give 3D worlds meaning, not the mechanics of just being in these worlds. And people need to be able to create and do things in these worlds. They are not there to be advertised to, like peripherals hanging off the network, they are living entities who want to take control of their lives and roles in those worlds.

VR has the unique ability to swap that reconstructed real world of consciousness for another and that involuntary, unconscious acceptance of you being in that new place is called 'presence'. 'Presence' is a word you hear often in VR but it is not a simple concept. It is as if, like a child, you are experiencing 'presence' again, learning to deal with the world, other people and objects all over again. It is the magic dust of VR and has huge implications for learning in the metaverse.

It varies from the visual feeling of just being in that world, through to fuller senses of presence, moving around and being with and interacting with other people and things in that world. It is this fundamental sense of self in VR, what it is just to be there, move slightly, look around, be aware of your own presence, that makes it so different. Also that sense of strangeness, awkwardness, even fear and angst, then curiosity about the possibilities. The fact that you are there, with all sorts of possibilities, starts to unfold and reveal itself. This feeling of presence depends on all sorts of factors: the field of view, fidelity of the images, smoothness of the experience.

Headsets shut out the external world. They have the advantage of greatly increasing your field of view and, being stereoscopic, present a powerful 3D

effect. While inside these worlds, the learner can move around and participate in the learning experience. This depends, first, on what is possible
within the limits of the technology in terms of physical movement, along
with other functionality, such as sensors and haptic devices and, second,
how much freedom one allows or designs into the learning experience. It is
far from being a wholly functional second world.

Presence as metamorphosis

Peter Rubin has written a journey, *Future Presence* (2020), involving
testimonies from people when inside virtual worlds. He is more interested in
what that does to us as humans, how it makes us feel and how we interact
with others. The subtitle is *How virtual reality is changing human connection, intimacy and the limits of ordinary life*. Of course, it will change
entertainment, work and learning but how does it change us? Are we already
seeing, in Japan and elsewhere, the replacement of real-world relationships
with online and virtual relationships, even virtual relationships with virtual
people? Rubin explores how the metaverse is likely to upend the world of
relationships, intimacy and sex.

His starting point is presence. At the very heart of virtual-world experiences is that sense of presence, of yourself, other objects, other people, even
of other AI-driven entities. Being in a virtual world is a form of being, similar to real life but also different.

What presence brings is a rather wonderful but dangerous present –
intimacy. Here we enter the world of closeness, trust, relationships and
titillation. This will be the first time in history we as a species actually
encounter *each other* in a virtual environment with real *presence*. We have a
lot to learn from these concrete experiences with this strange new medium
even from early experiments. As Rubin shows, this is quite an adventure, as
he delves into friendships, therapy, relationships, sex and marriage.

In truth, we metamorphose and exaggerate online. It is not that avatars
replace us in virtual worlds, it is that we can be transformed in VR. It is
often assumed that we remain as we are in the metaverse, but it is more
likely that we will metamorphose into something we are not. It is a point
made repeatedly by Jaron Lanier, the pioneer of VR – that we are changed
by it. He describes that astonishing moment that many of us have had when
we are suddenly transported to another place by VR, but he was even more
surprised by the fact that he could morph into a lobster with multiple
appendages.

Will this also upend relationships in learning? Does it fundamentally change the traditional role of a teacher, lecturer, tutor, coach or instructor when dealing with learners online? Virtual worlds are inhabited by our minds, not our bodies. It is vital that we understand what it is to be in such worlds in terms of presence and identity. This is fundamental to seeing whether or not it is a suitable environment. And in order to see the metaverse as a place to learn, we must see what cognitive affordances would possibly confirm that we can learn in such environments. This allows us to identify what type of learning is possible and most likely to be successful.

If the metaverse is to work, users cannot be mere visitors. We must have a fulfilling role to play in building, owning, working, playing, buying, being and learning in that world. It is not platforms or brands that will define the metaverse but people.

Good training mirrors real life and as the metaverse mirrors real life it can be a good place to learn. Yet the reality of learning this way, in real or imagined worlds, by donning a headset, has only been around relatively recently. One could assume that learning in other contexts is the same or similar to learning in immersive environments but there are other considerations with VR media, such as immersion, presence and what you experience visually, and agency.

Agency in the metaverse

We feel ourselves as agents with agency in virtual worlds. But what does this mean and how far can it go? Agency, the feeling of initiating action, is well researched when doing something in the real world (David et al, 2008). We associate our prediction in doing something with our perception of the action and then on execution we associate the action with the outcome. This works and encourages further action.

What is less researched is *social action*, which is no less common, another type of agency, where we have agency in interacting with others. Again we predict action, the difference is that we get feedback from others; eye contact, facial expressions, picking up social cues such as body language, actual language and behaviour.

There is also the attribution of mind and agency to others. This is not something we think about much, all of this we just assume, but it matters in virtual worlds. It may seem obvious but we are interacting with someone's avatar and must be aware that we may be interacting with a bot avatar, driven by AI.

Of course, there is more to this than meets the virtual eye, as the type of environment, the outcome and emotions also play a part in agency. An adrenaline-fuelled Battle Royale game environment, where the last person standing wins is very different from a yoga class in VRChat.

This is a neat schema for considering agency and action based on Wolpert (2003). It turns out that virtual reality, with its eye, face and hand tracking capabilities, allows us to see and feel 'presence' in terms of our basic sense of self as an agent with a body (avatar). This agency in virtual worlds can be broken down into the several components shown in Figure 10.1:

1 I can think about and predict the outcome. Note that this can be automatic and unconscious or more considered, conscious and planned.

2 I can get feedback and associate my action with the outcome, say touching, feeling, lifting and manipulating an object.

3 I can think about and predict the outcome in interaction with another person(s).

4 I can get feedback and associate my action with the outcome from another person(s), say eye contact, expressions, gestures, touching and so on.

5 Then there is the 'assumption' that this is a person with mind and agency of their own.

FIGURE 10.1 Agency and action

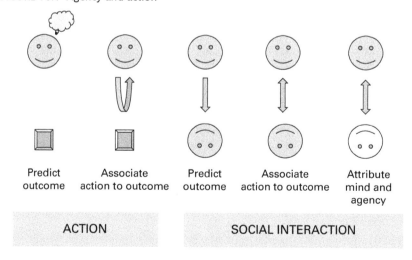

| Predict outcome | Associate action to outcome | Predict outcome | Associate action to outcome | Attribute mind and agency |

ACTION   SOCIAL INTERACTION

The 'minimal self' is a good start point for defining what it is to have a sense of self in the world as defined by point 1. In the rush towards social presence it is often forgotten that this personal agency and presence is also a powerful force in learning. The ability to know oneself, reflect and learn on one's own is still powerful. All learning need not be social. There is also that personal feeling of handling and manipulating objects, the presence of touch or haptic presence.

Haptic presence

An extension of presence in VR is your interaction with other objects in this new world. Places and objects will appear and, depending on the technology and design, you will be able to touch, feel, lift and manipulate these objects (point 2). For new users this often comes with a sense of wonder, even awe.

This is certainly an important component in learning by doing, in practical work, where tools and objects have to be handled, manipulated and applied. This form of presence offers the greatest technical challenges but will be vital if experiential learning is to be anything other than moving around, talking and being social.

Part of your personal presence may also be your feeling of status in owning virtual objects such as property and the sorts of things one would own in the real world, even objects natural to the virtual world but alien in the real world. Fashion and luxury brands may lead the way in avatar design and clothes. Status is status, whether in the real or virtual world. It is also likely that real clothes and other goods will appear in virtual worlds, where you can try them on virtually before you buy. This try-and-buy phenomenon may explode in virtual worlds. We will see the real and virtual blur, as clothes and shoes bought in the virtual world start to handle sizes, movement and touch. Buying online reduces transaction costs and the better the online shopping experience, the higher conversions to sales and fewer returns. Fashion shows are also appearing in virtual worlds and will only get better as the experience will be personal and immersive.

So let's now come to points 3, 4 and 5 which are also important as multiuser virtual worlds have lots to offer on social learning.

Social presence

You feel my presence as you read these words from the page or screen but it is a limited presence. If you heard me read them on a podcast you would get some other dimensions of me as a person: my sex (male), accent (Scottish), intonation (assertive) and personality (extrovert). You may even hazard a guess at my age. If you were to see me on video, age would be an easier guess and you would pick up on my body language, maybe the background I have chosen. In VR, you would see my avatar, hear me speak and see my head, eye movements and expressions. I may approach you and you will feel as though another person has approached you. So, in addition to your own presence, you feel the presence of me and others.

Immersive headsets which use eye, facial and hand tracking, so that your looks and facial expressions can be transferred to your avatar, increase the fidelity of social interaction. In the absence of these cues, you can feel as though others are slightly robotic in appearance and expression. As this technology improves it increases social presence between people in virtual worlds.

Then in multi-user worlds, there is the sense of seeing and interacting with different others, as either other avatars, software-generated avatars or people outside that world, for example an external tutor giving you voice instructions. Social behaviour and interaction in virtual worlds may not be quite the same as in the real world. This social dimension can, to some extent, be impoverished by the lack of social signals but also enriched and varied in ways not possible in the real world. The social side can also extend over time, as one sees in VRChat, where multiple encounters, even relationships, form over time. This is told well in the documentary *We Met in Virtual Reality* (2022), where real relationships form that then flourish back in the real world.

Embodied learning

All of these forms of presence add up to a form of embodied learning, the widening out from too tight a conception of learning as just pure solipsistic cognition. Embodied learning, sometimes called embodied cognition, includes a range of bodily movements, from gestures to the use of the body as a whole, the enactment of learning, as well as extension out into the use of physical and digital technology. Embodied learning looks for a causal relationship between the body and the learning task.

A good starting point is to see consciousness as a simulated construct of what we receive from our sensorimotor processes and situation in the physical world, an embodied simulation. This recognizes the role of sensorimotor data as an active, dynamic component in learning. There is the general physical context in which we learn that does have an effect on learning and recall, say learning inside a lab or aircraft, the places where the knowledge and skills will be applied. Multisensory approaches in general have proven to be useful (de Koning and Tabbers, 2011).

Embodied learning is the recognition that we are both body and mind. There is a tendency to think of learning wholly in terms of cognitive development but many of the skills we use in the real world require feeling our own embodiment, as well as recognizing the embodiment of others. Body language is an obvious example but so is eye contact and many dimensions of the language we use, not just content but tone, timing and intonation.

Moving on to something concrete, consider gestures. Showing animations of gestured hands has been shown to be superior to simple arrows in teaching (de Koning and Tabbers, 2013). The use of gestures seems to aid language learning (Iverson and Goldin-Meadow, 2005; Mavilidi et al, 2015). This has also been tested in mathematics (Cook and Goldin-Meadow, 2006). Gestures in general seem to be good for teachers and learners (de Nooijer et al, 2013; Stieff et al, 2016; Toumpaniari et al, 2015).

Enactment is a bolder technique, where learners act out the task. It can help with reading, for example, if the learners act out the story they are reading, as well as teachers drawing out what they teach (Fiorella and Mayer, 2016). We even have evidence that for some forms of learning, even things that are assumed to be wholly cognitive, like maths, and of course skills that require bodily movement, may find a receptive home in the metaverse. One need not have a fully fledged belief in embodied cognition or learning to see the worth of including physicality into the learning process.

Embodiment must naturally be seen as a feature of learning in immersive environments, virtual-reality applications and mixed-reality systems (Johnson-Glenberg et al, 2011; 2016; Lindgren et al, 2016). Even though in immersive learning there is the passive viewing of content on 2D screens, interactivity with physical movement through to tracked bodily movements, through to whole-body involvement, this is all embodied learning.

The metaverse may therefore provide an accessible, open and powerful environment for embodied learning to flourish. The move towards VR with more sensors, more tracking, less latency, wider field of view, frictionless hand and body interfaces and haptic sophistication, allows more embodiment into the learning process. We can see how this view of psychology reframes learning as something that takes place in a situated environment. If such situated environments can be re-created, then the metaverse becomes the environment for embodied learning. It is a place that can mirror contexts, allow for embodiment, even focus on what elements of these really matter for learning.

Embodiment can be easily measured through sensor data, such as head and eye tracking, hand and finger movements, body movements, all in reaction to targets within the virtual world. This allows detailed corrective feedback, real-time or delayed until the task is complete. If one has an ideal student model of perfect or expert behaviour, we can nudge learners towards that ideal. One can see how useful this can be in everything from sports to surgery.

Enactment in soft-skills training may also provide data on desirable manager behaviours in interviewing, meetings and coaching. Branching simulations could deliver behavioural change in a guided fashion that is quick and personalized, with time to competence dramatically reduced, rather than fixed-length courses with little formative action, feedback and assessment. This can be escalated into truly adaptive simulations that get learners over gaps in their knowledge and skills as they are performing. Rather like the satnav in your car, if you go off course, it recognizes this and gets you back on course.

This, of course, can be taken up to the next level with cohorts, groups and teams of differing sizes. The metaverse will allow multi-learner simulations, tracking complex interactions within complex practical or business simulations. We can train in a simulation of the real word, with real people, all in a virtual environment. Experts can be inside that virtual environment or sit outside and deliver feedback by voice. Software agents within the simulation may also act as guides or tutors.

Technology generally moves towards doing more with less and with digital technology different orders of magnitude around productivity are made possible, especially in learning, as it can be scaled. The metaverse offers lots of opportunities for increasing productivity in learning. It is particularly suited to situated learning, as learning is about intangible communication, cognitive change, knowledge, skills, memory and performance.

'We have Paleolithic emotions, medieval institutions and godlike technology', said EO Wilson. This is the problem we face with technology in general and will have to face in the metaverse. Oddly, it may be less of a problem than the current form of the internet. Our evolved brains deal well with 3D environments, as we have stereoscopic vision, stereoscopic sound and sophisticated embodiment and a sense of touch. These are not VAK learning styles – a common misconception and myth – they are common to all learners. We have evolved to exist, adapt and be within such environments.

The shift to AR and VR has brought us mixed reality, with AR, pass-through and fully immersive VR. These produce different levels and forms of presence around the self; what you see, touch and hear are different and depend on the nature of the technology and devices you use. It is time, therefore, to take a deeper dive into the three main senses that create presence:

- vision
- sound
- touch.

Vision

Stereo vision, our ability to see in stereo, just in terms of engineering and physics is a good solution to seeing in depth. We know that the brain is proactive in trying to predict the 3D environment, hence famous optical illusions, such as the Necker cube, where it guesses until it has enough confirmatory data to fix the most likely perspective. This is one of the many reasons VR works so readily. As we move through a given 3D environment, we construct a constrained virtual reality in our mind, a model of that world. Richard Dawkins goes one step further and claims that our brain functions, having adapted to a huge succession of 3D worlds, have survived to include these virtual worlds constructed by our ancestral brains.

Place two cameras a couple of inches apart to simulate our eyes and the two images can be viewed, when presented simultaneously, one to each eye, to re-create what our eyes actually see. This is what VR does with moving images. As all normally sighted people have the ability to see in three dimensions, exploiting something called 'parallax' (an apparent displacement of an object in relation to its background), we can estimate the distance that objects are away from us. Eye movement is also interpreted by the brain and turned into depth appreciation by the individual.

Evolution of stereoscopy

The ability to replicate this function with overlapping pictures has been appreciated since the earliest days of photography in the mid-1800s. Invented by Wheatstone in 1839, the Scottish physicist Brewster later developed an optical stereoscopic viewer in 1849, to allow the brain to re-create the illusion of three-dimensionality. They were hugely popular in the Victorian era for both education and entertainment. Brewster's device was originally used with drawings, as it came one year earlier than the invention of photography. The 3D stereoscope came before the 2D daguerreotype but was quickly eclipsed by 2D photography, film and TV.

Moving stereoscopic images could be viewed as early as 1855, when Claudette patented a viewer and many revolving stereoscopes in the late 19th century. Variations on these were also common in arcades well into the 20th century. They also had a brief revival in the View-Master, a successful toy patented in 1939.

But stereoscopic media was short-lived. It had a brief period of fame in the 1850s but disappeared under the onslaught of 2D photography, film and TV. Depth of field is real and interesting but clearly not a necessary condition for successful entertainment or education. It is not that depth of field was not valued, just that it was replaced by the moving image. Motion stereoscopes were limited to fairly simple scenes but film quickly used a variety of shooting and editing techniques to create the illusion of space and played with time through editing, to hold the spell of the viewer. Widening the field of view, to create the illusion of immersion in cinema, trumped depth of field, with its awkward binocular devices and limited field of view. Stereoscopy just couldn't compete.

Stereoscopes were also presented as fairground spectacles, not as long-form, serious forms of education and entertainment. They also had no significant effect on art that was still deeply rooted in 2D drawing and painting, then supplemented by photography that in turn influenced painting. 2D art remained the paradigm. We are, of course, excluding sculpture, which has been an art form, almost as long as we have been a species.

As stereoscopy declined in use as a form of entertainment, in education it continued to be used, with the invention in 1861 of a mass-produced, portable model, sold by companies such as Underwood & Underwood and Keystone. Geography was a popular subject and the devices were seen as stimulating scientific and cultural development, often supplemented by books and instructions on using them in teaching. They were still in use well into the 20th century in schools.

Stereoscopic TV was demonstrated by John Logie Baird in 1928 and the first 3D TV produced in 1935. Meanwhile 3D movies were released throughout the 1950s. Hitchcock's *Dial M for Murder* was released in 3D. Other revivals with movies such as *Jaws 3* were tried in the 1970s and 1980s. In 2009, the movie *Avatar* was released in yet another attempt to sell the 3D concept, but from 2013 sales of 3D TVs declined and were discontinued in 2016.

Stereoscopic images continued to be used for practical tasks, especially by the military. Aerial photography started in the First World War and continued throughout the Second World War. The RAF created the Photographic Intelligence Unit (PIU), and used planes, often high-speed Spitfires, to take images, and if something of real interest was spotted, missions to take 3D stereoscopic images were run. The images used the motion of the aircraft to take the separated images. One famous success for 3D images was the identification of the rocket launchers at Peenemünde for the V1 and V2 bombs. The use of stereoscopic imagery continued into the Cold War, with the addition of satellite imagery and now with drones.

For nearly two centuries, this stop-start process of innovation and commercialization has not yet resulted in 3D stereoscopic devices, and their dependent media had short-lived success. If the stereoscopic 3D world is so enticing, why has it failed so often? This suggests that a metaverse that relies solely on VR may be secondary to one which is viewed on 2D screens. Alternatively, the overwhelming, immersive nature of VR may sustain a metaverse that is truly 3D.

VR headsets

The virtual-reality headset is a stereoscopic device with sensors, such as accelerometers and gyroscopes that match the position of the head relative to the 3D world that is being viewed. Other devices, such as eye-tracking sensors and hand controllers, have been added. Early headsets began to appear in the 1990s, but it was a crowdfunding company, Oculus, who released development kits and eventually a consumer version in 2016. In the same year, Sony released the Playstation VR and HTC the Vive.

I had the first development kits DK1 and DK2, which were impressive in themselves. That is when I got the VR bug, as despite the weight, low resolution, latency and dizziness, the swap was total and convincing. With these early headsets, I saw wobblers, fallers, screamers and some frozen in silence when demonstrating those first headsets in 2013/14. A decade later, the weight, comfort, resolution, refresh rate and functionality have all improved and, importantly, the device is untethered. Head and eye tracking are built in and no doubt other sensors will come in for increased face tracking. Mixed-reality headsets allow you to be in a virtual world, while also seeing outside that world with pass-through. You can even see yourself within a virtual world.

Moving from head to hands and body, haptic devices are now common, smart gloves are available, even bodysuits for motion capture. Bodysuits have surprised a lot of people in virtual worlds, as one can make moves that are beyond the norm! Cameras can also be used to track movement and the possibility of a metaverse room for tracking and immersion is being offered, such as Google's Project Starline, where you see photorealistic, 3D people who you speak to through a glass screen. It is like being present in the same room as the person. Facebook's CTRL-labs uses a wristband to tap into electrical signals from the brain to your hands, so that you can spark off actions just by thinking. The advantages in a fully immersive, headset world are obvious. You can move around and take action in the metaverse just by thinking.

Eye tracking can be used for selecting items from menus, navigating around 3D environments, but in learning its most useful function is probably to help teachers and learners focus attention on the relevant items while learning; from learning to read to performing tasks such as maintenance to surgery. Even though the eye is better than the hand when pointing, the head is not a joystick, so using gaze as an interface device could have some uses, but this may not be its primary use. The problem is not the looking, it is the clicking or confirmation of an action.

As autonomous learners, it is clear that the technology gives us what we need to learn and perform.

Sound

As users moved from writing to typing to swiping to speaking, talking to your smartphone has become normalized, as has talking to Alexa or Siri in your home, or in your car. It frees one from the tyranny of touch. Technology can even distinguish between different voices in one home and respond differently.

Easy to overlook, 3D audio has been around in 3D games and VR for some time. Sound-delivery systems moved from mono to stereo, then to surround sound for cinema and TV, but all of this is essentially on one plane, surrounding you horizontally. 3D sound is different. The idea is simple: you can place sound 'virtually' anywhere around the listener in 3D space. Sound is intrinsically 3D as sound waves are not flat. The physics of sound is 3D – it can only be 3D.

Just as we have two eyes that give us stereoscopic vision, giving us depth of field, we also have two ears. The brain then does a lot of work in taking data from both sources; among other things, the difference in time in receiving the sounds in either ear to work out the direction from which the sound has come. This was mimicked by 3D headphones, largely used in gaming, as it is obviously useful in shoot-'em-up and similar genres of games, knowing where someone is shooting from.

Our eyes have a limited field of view, around 200 degrees, and it gets indistinct around the periphery. 3D audio really can fill out your virtual experience by placing sounds anywhere in 3D space. Its potential is huge.

So how does stereoscopic sound work?

Stereoscopic hearing, also known as binaural hearing, is our ability to locate the direction and distance of sounds in space. This ability is based on the difference in sound arrival 'time' and the 'intensity' between the left and right ears, which allows the brain to perceive the location, movement and spatial characteristics of sound sources.

Stereoscopic hearing is made possible by the unique anatomy of the human ear, our two ears separated by about 6.5 centimetres. The folds in the ear with their unique shape and position on the head allow us to perceive the location and movement of sounds in the environment. These folds are made of cartilage and covered with skin, and they are shaped in a way that helps to collect and direct sound waves towards the ear canal. They play a critical role in sound localization, which is the ability to determine the direction and distance of sounds in space.

The sound then passes through the ear canal and strikes the eardrum, and the vibration transmitted through the middle ear bones to the cochlea which generates an electrical signal that is sent to the brain through the auditory nerve. The brain then processes this signal, using information from both ears to determine the direction and distance of the sound source. The brain is able to interpret this pattern of sound and use it to determine the location and movement of the sound source. It uses this information to create a mental map of the sound environment, which allows us to locate and track sounds in space.

Stereoscopic hearing is a complex and highly developed ability, and it allows us to perceive the location and movement of sounds in the environment with great precision. This ability is important for a wide range of activities, including speech perception, music appreciation and spatial orientation. If we want authenticity and presence in the metaverse, stereoscopic sound really does matter.

We can expect much more sophistication in audio for music concerts in the metaverse, where that feeling of being at a live concert will be important, the sounds from not only the artists but also attendees. But it is also important in settings as simple as a meeting, where we intuitively know where someone is speaking from. The quality of audio has been shown by Reeves and Nass (1996) to be important for learning in video; more important than visual quality, as we have evolved to cope with variable light and conditions visually but expect, in conversation, high-fidelity audio. It would be a mistake to see the metaverse as a visual medium only, when audio needs to be one of its primary strengths, especially in learning.

The metaverse will be an audio-rich environment and will require as much care over audio as we now see in the 3D games world, where professional audio engineers and companies create sophisticated audio to match not only the visuals but the actions of the users.

Sound and learning

Of course, the real world is rarely completely silent and silent simulations can sound oddly dislocated and empty, as our ears are always on. In simulations, you can re-create the ambient sound of being inside an aircraft or on a busy street. This can add desirable fidelity and context. Then there are specific sounds that are desirable and designed into the learning, such as the specific sound of a problem in an engine or piece of equipment that is diagnostic of a particular problem. Specific sounds, relevant to the learning itself, can be delivered in their precise and correct location. Sounds are particularly important in maintenance and problem solving on mechanical systems. Hugely diagnostic in healthcare, as heartbeats, breaths from lungs, diagnostic wheezes and so on, sound is essential in general practice, the stethoscope being an essential piece of physician equipment.

Going up a level, the spoken word is obviously useful for instructions, guidance and exposition. Teachers have spoken and listened to learners for millennia, and so it will be in the metaverse.

In learning experiences, 3D-positioned sound can be used to guide and instruct learners. We will see simple lectures but that, one hopes, will be limited. Any form of dialogue can be delivered as well, especially from generative AI.

A teacher, tutor or instructor outside the virtual world can deliver voiced cues, guidance or direct instructions to learners, individually, in a group or subsets of the group. This has been used to good effect in health and safety training. Peer-to-peer dialogue is also possible, as is audio feedback. Teachers can also take part as avatars within the virtual training world, physically speaking, directing, showing learners what to do.

The spoken word is primary in language and critical to both teaching and learning. We sometimes teach through direct instruction but also questioning and feedback. We also have much to learn by speaking, responding and being more oral in our learning process.

Performance support

Learning in the workflow by getting quick definitions, job aids, answers to specific questions, is becoming normal. We often turn to Siri, Google Assistant or Alexa for an answer. Bob Mosher (with Conrad Gottfredson, 2012) has identified five moments of need, moments of truth, when we require such support:

1 learning something for the first time

2 learning more

3 applying and/or remembering

4 when something goes wrong

5 when things change.

These real needs drive learning, as they are delivered at the very moment you need them. This makes them more relevant and more likely to be remembered.

Audio can play a key role in this, not interfering with other activities as you work. It is hands free, allowing you to do what is instructed, does not need to be read and, just as we all do, when you ask for help from someone, they reply, you overcome your problem and move on. Audio-delivered performance support makes good sense.

Language learning

Learning a second language is hard and could be revolutionized by the metaverse – intense immersion with structured deliberate practice with avatars who speak to you using generative AI so that you become competent much faster. Duolingo already has this immersive feature, explaining what you got wrong as well as allowing immersive conversations with feedback. Immersion is often used in language learning to describe what is needed after the basics of vocabulary and grammar have been mastered. Immersive listening and speaking in context is then necessary, which is why so many people travel to a country where that language is spoken. The demand for language learning is increasing, yet supply is limited, expensive and impractical.

We can deliver that immersion through technology that floods the eyes and ears with immersive language-learning experiences. With 3D audio, we can simulate real contexts, such as railway stations and restaurants where the spoken word can be performed, along with listening comprehension. Software that understands what you have tried to say is now with us. Adaptive learning systems like Duolingo, when turned into virtual experiences, are inevitable, given the pedagogic advantages that immersion offers, especially around speech. It is not difficult to imagine this being a huge growth area within the metaverse.

Listening skills

Sounds can also provide useful content for learning if it involves listening skills. This is a staple in management training and if scenario driven, can both train and assess learners, personalizing the learning experience. Active listening involves paying real attention to what is said, confirming that you are paying attention, asking for clarification, paraphrasing, often giving judicious feedback and encouragement, asking questions, avoiding quick judgements then summarizing or responding appropriately. With practice you really can be more focused, even paying more attention to body language.

All of this can be delivered in virtual environments with data tracking progression in real time. In fact, a focused set of scenarios may be ideal, as your responses can be tracked and measured and provide the basis for improvement, either from a live tutor or automated and generated by text-to-speech software.

Translation

Generative AI now produces text and the spoken word to whatever age, gender or accent you want. Real-time translation is also possible, both of your speech and that of people speaking to you. This is useful in meetings but also in language learning and training in general, where instructors in one language can be effective to a range of different language speaking learners. Huge numbers of languages will be available from generative AI, both generated and quickly translated.

Touch

There is little doubt that various forms of learning could be delivered in the metaverse; some we know about, other exciting opportunities that we have yet to imagine will emerge. Much will depend on touch or haptic experiences.

In 3D worlds, the learner can manipulate objects. As this happens in real life – in factories, loading trucks, medical procedures, scientific labs, construction, maintenance and so on – there are no end of opportunities for training. More specific training in using hand-held tools and equipment will also be possible. This haptic effect can be felt through clever controller and glove technology, where you feel the object as it would feel in the real world. From a scalpel to hand-held objects through to the steering wheel of a huge vehicle, procedural training will be possible, safely and without risk.

Touch and learning

In Rec Rooms, a popular virtual world, you can not only create your own 3D objects using a brilliant simple tool, you can also manipulate these objects. This translates into the creation of 'circuits' in Rec Rooms, where you take components to program functionality. This feature alone shows how useful the metaverse could be, not only in programming and electronics but also in STEM subjects, in lab work, engineering, use of equipment and maintenance. There is a tremendous amount of practical, concrete education and training that could be executed, counterintuitively, in virtual worlds.

Soft skills will prove more difficult but learners can be given context and opportunities to learn and practise using touch. Virtual patients are already being used for the vast array of medical procedures that need to be performed on actual bodies when patients present: investigative, diagnostic and treatment. Avatar technology can provide an endless supply of virtual patients in medicine where all sorts of procedures could be possible.

Meaningful metaverse learning must allow learners to move in or through 3D spaces, manipulate 3D objects or use real 3D equipment in difficult, even dangerous places. It can replace learning that, in real-world set-ups, would be impractical or prohibitively expensive. Initial projects are likely, therefore, to be 'experiential' learning, of physical processes and procedures, self-awareness or team or group learning, where decision making can be safely simulated.

Physical and psychological issues may also be dealt with in this new environment. We have seen how VR has helped with physical disabilities such as paraplegia, stroke and amputations. It can also be used for psychological problems such as PTSD, phobias, depression (delivering therapy such as CBT), even dementia. Body swapping, where you become someone else through avatar swaps, can help teach about sexual harassment, racism and disabilities, also in soft-skills training.

The metaverse is unlikely to be used primarily for knowledge, text-based resources and 2D media. Neither is it enough to see the metaverse as a proxy for delivering 'fun' or 'novelty' in learning. There will, undoubtedly, be plenty of such projects in the opening phase, by those who think it is all about graphics or that media rich means mind rich or that learning is easy. We have to be careful with mistaking fidelity, novelty and excitement for learning. The allure of the new should not blind us to actual evaluation and research. Actual learning in 3D environments with 3D avatars and 3D objects will emerge as the most powerful learning experiences.

Autonomy and generative learning

Work by theorists like Merlin Wittrock has shown that generative learning is a powerful force in learning (Wittrock, 1974). An autonomous learner can fit new knowledge and skills into their existing schemas through generative experiences. An autonomous learner will not just learn but create their own meaning and reorganize their learning. Wittrock recommended that teachers create the content for this generative learning rather than impose set content.

Four major processes define his model:

1 Attention – directing generative processes on relevant incoming material and stored knowledge

2 Motivation – willingness to invest effort to make sense of material

3 Knowledge and preconceptions – prior knowledge, experiences and beliefs

4 Generation – sense making.

Learners effectively build their own models through generative activities. A classic example is imaginative note taking, especially in one's own words (Wittrock and Alesandrini, 1990) which one could do using audio in virtual worlds. But 3D worlds may offer much more in the way of generation. Fiorella and Mayer (2016) recommend generative strategies that involve creating connection maps, drawing, application, practice, explaining to others and enacting what you have learnt.

At the next level, problem solving can be taught using generative principles. Wittrock worked with Mayer on this in domain-specific problem solving, near transfer to a limited range of similar problems and the use of guided problem solving to acquire knowledge. Wittrock was particularly interested in training teachers using these methods.

The issue of cost is important here. The return on investment when using immersion can result in significant savings against alternatives that are more expensive, dangerous, even impossible in the real world. It is also clear that one must design learning experiences specifically for VR, with a focus on immersion and interaction. Too many projects assume that immersion will be enough, but these may simply encourage and exacerbate cognitive overload and distraction. Deliberate design with simplification to reduce cognitive overload, along with strong signalling, chunking and generative activities, make all the difference.

Implementation of autonomy

Vanity learning projects are common in very new and different types of technology, where many simply want to look innovative or seem contemporary. This results in lots of short-lived mosquito projects, which quickly die with no long-term impact or implementation, as opposed to turtle projects, which may be a lot duller, but where long-term impact is the goal.

It is important, when considering the implementation of learning in the metaverse, to make sure that these are 'learning' not just VR/multiverse projects. The way to ensure this is to do a serious task analysis before starting, in terms of actions and feedback. Real decisions have to be made with the right balance of user autonomy and structure.

There are two main forms of overreach with immersive learning. The first is overreach with the technology, promising things which the technology cannot yet deliver or delivers in such a crude way that it fails. The second is overreach with the goals, where immersion is not only unsuitable but can be destructive, where it hinders rather than helps learning. It is important to do the up-front analysis to prevent both types of overreach and failure.

Details can be found in *Learning Experience Design* (Clark, 2022), which first considers the *learning* namely the type of learning being delivered, then choosing the right type of *experience*, finally implementing the *design*.

For example, highly theoretical learning may be far less suitable than practical, vocational, learn-by-doing, experiential learning. On the other hand, theoretical learning may be enhanced through application, doing and enactment. There has to be a match between the technology, the use of that technology and learning outcomes. One must also be careful in assuming that more embodied learning is always better learning, as it can lead to increasing cognitive load (Post et al, 2013; Ruiter et al, 2015; Skulmowski et al, 2016). Simplified learning processes may, in some cases, actually be better.

The chosen experiences need to consider the degree of autonomy required, the role of the tutor (if any), others, process and meaningful, effortful learning, so that they are more than just passive exposure to 3D environments. Open, structured, highly structured or generative activities need to map onto the learning objectives. The degree of autonomy, from fully open and exploratory to semi-structured and highly formalized through a process or procedure must be carefully considered.

Finally, the design must focus relentlessly on the learning outcomes, not how the graphics look or frivolous activities. The medium is exciting enough without injecting much extra activity – less is often more.

An optimal approach is often a blend of immersive and other techniques, where other online and offline activities are carefully designed into an optimal blend to deliver your chosen outcomes. Blended learning, where you are in a 3D world but also interact in the real world, is almost always a reasonable approach for outcomes that have, eventually, to transfer to the real world.

Conclusion

The metaverse is a profoundly human idea and experience. It is about individuals interacting with imagined worlds, objects and other people. It is autonomous humans, with presence in mixed reality and the metaverse, who will learn. This is a new medium and we have to understand how we as individuals will operate within the medium. We must take advantage of the various dimensions of presence, both individual and social.

Stereoscopic vision is the essence of immersion. It provides the illusion, environments, objects, avatar presence and social presence of others in mixed reality and the metaverse. What we see, the others we see and the fact that we can see ourselves, lie at the very heart of immersive learning.

Sound and speech is a part of our everyday world; it is inevitable that it will be a natural dimension of our virtual worlds. It has crept into our lives and devices, in our homes, cars and smartphones. Sound assets can be triggered from code, as they often are in games, but also driven by logic systems to create reactive and adaptive sound. An underestimated aspect of virtual worlds, sound is what will make such worlds sing. Generative AI will also be driven by sound as input and output.

This is also true of touch, an affordance that comes into its own when doing things with objects in virtual worlds.

The affordances of stereoscopic vision, 3D sound and touch are important as they demarcate what can be learned and how. There are clearly limitations but also exciting affordances that offer more than other digital options.

Bibliography

Clark, D (2022) *Learning Experience Design: How to create effective learning that works*, Kogan Page, London

Cook, S W and Goldin-Meadow, S (2006) The role of gesture in learning: Do children use their hands to change their minds?, *Journal of Cognition and Development*, 7, 211–232

David, N, Newen, A and Vogeley, K (2008) The 'sense of agency' and its underlying cognitive and neural mechanisms, *Consciousness and cognition*, 17 (2), 523–534

de Koning, B B and Tabbers, H K (2011) Facilitating understanding of movements in dynamic visualizations: An embodied perspective, *Educational Psychology Review*, 23, 501–521

de Koning, B B and Tabbers, H K (2013) Gestures in instructional animations: A helping hand to understanding non-human movements?, *Applied Cognitive Psychology*, 27, 683–689

de Koning, B B and van der Schoot, M (2013) Becoming part of the story! Refueling the interest in visualization strategies for reading comprehension, *Educational Psychology Review*, 25 (2), 261–287

de Nooijer, J A, van Gog, T, Paas, F, and Zwaan, R A (2013) Effects of imitating gestures during encoding or during retrieval of novel verbs on children's test performance, *Acta Psychologica*, 144, 173–179

Fiorella, L and Mayer, R E (2016) Effects of observing the instructor draw diagrams on learning from multimedia messages, *Journal of Educational Psychology*, 108, 528–546

Gottfredson, C and Mosher, B (2012) Are you meeting all five moments of learning need?, *Learn Solutions*, 18

Hunting, J and HBO (2022) *We Met in Virtual Reality* [documentary]

Iverson, J M and Goldin-Meadow, S (2005) Gesture paves the way for language development, *Psychological Science*, 16, 367–371

Johnson-Glenberg, M C, Birchfield, D, Savvides, P and Megowan-Romanowicz, C (2011) Semi-virtual embodied learning: Real world STEM assessment serious educational game assessment, in L Annetta, and S C Bronack (eds) *Serious Educational Game Assessment: Practical methods and models for educational games, simulations and virtual worlds*, Sense: Rotterdam (pp 241–257)

Johnson-Glenberg, M C, Megowan-Romanowicz, C, Birchfield, D A and Savio-Ramos, C (2016) Effects of embodied learning and digital platform on the retention of physics content: Centripetal force, *Frontiers in Psychology*, 7, 1819

Lindgren, R, Tscholl, M, Wang, S and Johnson, E (2016) Enhancing learning and engagement through embodied interaction within a mixed reality simulation, *Computers & Education*, 95, 174–187

Mavilidi, M F, Okely, A D, Chandler, P, Cliff, D P and Paas, F (2015) Effects of integrated physical exercises and gestures on preschool children's foreign language vocabulary learning, *Educational Psychology Review*, 27, 413–426

Post, L S, van Gog, T, Paas, F and Zwaan, R A (2013) Effects of simultaneously observing and making gestures while studying grammar animations on cognitive load and learning, *Computers in Human Behavior*, 29, 1450–1455

Reeves, B and Nass, C (1996) *The Media Equation: How people treat computers, television, and new media like real people and places*, Cambridge University Press, Cambridge

Rubin, P, (2018) *Future Presence: How virtual reality is changing human connection, intimacy, and the limits of ordinary life*, HarperCollins, New York

Ruiter, M, Loyens, S and Paas, F (2015) Watch your step children! Learning two-digit numbers through mirror-based observation of self-initiated body movements, *Educational Psychology Review*, 27, 457–474

Skulmowski, A, Pradel, S, Kühnert, T, Brunnett, G, and Rey, G D (2016) Embodied learning using a tangible user interface: The effects of haptic perception and selective pointing on a spatial learning task, *Computers & Education*, 92–93, 64–75

Stieff, M, Lira, M E, and Scopelitis, S A (2016) Gesture supports spatial thinking in STEM, *Cognition and Instruction*, 34, 80–99

Toumpaniari, K, Loyens, S, Mavilidi, M F, and Paas, F (2015) Preschool children's foreign language vocabulary learning by embodying words through physical activity and gesturing, *Educational Psychology Review*, 27, 445–456

Wittrock, M C (1974) Learning as a generative process, *Educational Psychologist*, 11 (2), 87–95

Wittrock, M C and Alesandrini, K (1990) Generation of summaries and analogies and analytic and holistic abilities, *American Educational Research Journal*, 27 (3), 489–502

Wolpert, D M, Doya, K and Kawato, M (2003) A unifying computational framework for motor control and social interaction, *Philosophical Transactions of the Royal Society of London*, Series B: Biological Sciences, 358 (1431)

11

Competences

Autonomous learners need real autonomy in terms of where, when, how and what they learn but it is also a matter of being able to acquire *competence*. To acquire real knowledge and especially skills beyond just knowledge, the metaverse can free learners from the tyranny of the real, place, time, flat media and passivity. If there is one goal that mixed reality and the metaverse promise, it is the efficient acquisition of actual competences.

Tyranny of the real

Competences, as knowledge and skills, are things that live in the mind, are reinforced in the mind and applied by the mind. Yet learners are so often placed in classrooms and lecture rooms that have no relation to or connection with the tasks they are expected to do in the real world. It is rare for actual application, attitudes, skills, behaviours and performance to be learnt in situ, in context, practised and assessed. Most formal learning does not measure actual consequences of that learning or impact on the organization. It is assumed rather than evaluated.

One may think that most skills would be done best in the real world. Yet there are several arguments that show that this is a mistaken view. There are many reasons for taking learning into the virtual, not least that in the real world it can be:

1 Risky – physical risks to trainees and other people

2 Dangerous – injury or even death is possible

3 Harmful – psychologically harmful to the self or others

4 Time consuming – setting and resetting places and equipment

5   Costly – using expensive places and equipment

6   Resource heavy – human resources for physical places

7   Environmentally damaging – using physical resources and emissions

8   Physically limited – fixed places and objects

9   Non-manipulable – worlds cannot be changed quickly

10   Impossible – being molecular, in space, inside nuclear reactors and so on.

Think of each of these arguments in terms of flight simulators, where other methods would entail all of the above. Just as books and academic papers have been the virtual spaces for theoretical learning, so virtual places can be the virtual spaces for experiential learning or learning by doing.

EXAMPLE
Presentation training

Within VR, one can learn to present in different contexts: meetings, small-room presentations up through medium to large venues on stages. Position, body language, gestures and eye movements can all be tracked, as well as speech.

By virtue of being virtual, you have risk-free, inexpensive and manipulable worlds that are far more flexible than the real world. Scenarios and simulations can also be constructed way beyond what is possible with physical places and resources.

Tyranny of place

This is not to say that all learning by doing can be executed in the virtual, only that there is a tremendous opportunity to do things differently. As the technology improves, in terms of resolution, haptics and other sensors and data gathering, so do the opportunities for learning. If we look at what has been achieved, for example in Microsoft *Flight Simulator* or flight simulators in general (Clark, 2022), we can start to predict what is possible when the virtual consumer technology becomes cheap, multi-user and accessible.

We can dispense with those physical classrooms and lecture theatres, where ranks of young people sit, in sometimes windowless rooms at a prescribed time and place to listen to someone say and show things that are often not even recorded. It would never occur to a journalist or novelist not to publish their work, yet it is regarded as acceptable and normal in higher education to lecture without recording that lecture. Student attendance for lectures can be shockingly low and occupancy rates for educational buildings much lower than non-campus use, as they close for much of the year.

As 3D worlds are built, we will be able to be in any place, existing or imagined. Digital Twins will also exist for any place in the real world. This is not unimaginable as we are almost there with Google Maps. We will be able to put ourselves in any place and get the necessary information about that place, visit any famous gallery or museum, see the paintings and exhibits, and hear interpretations from experts, before we go there for real.

Visiting the past will also be possible in re-created historical worlds. Whether past or present, we can teleport to any place and time. From archaeological sites such as the painted Palaeolithic caves of Altamira to the interiors of ancient pyramids, we can enter, feel the presence of the place and learn whatever we need to learn. We can be inside the enormity of the Hagia Sophia in Istanbul, the wonders of the Sistine Chapel and all the cathedrals of Europe. There is no place, even those that are closed and inaccessible, where we cannot go to learn.

The authenticity of place and context will be provided by past worlds, also inhabited by avatars from the past. We may hear from real people, such as Lincoln at Gettysburg. People from the past, from Socrates to Wittgenstein, will speak to us of philosophy. Inventors from Archimedes to Tesla will show us their achievements. Darwin will show and explain the finches from the Galapagos Islands. Artists from the caves of Chauvet to Duchamp will explain their work. Having dialogue with all will be possible and in all cases will be aided by context.

In the workplace, training from onboarding to every species of management, compliance and competence training will be delivered *in 'virtual' situ*; not just places but manipulable objects and other people. Learning will free itself from the tyranny of place.

Competence needs context

A body of evidence has grown to show that we remember things better in context. The reason for this, according to Tulving (1974), is that we encode environmental elements, both physical elements of our surroundings (context) and elements of our own psychological mood or feelings (state), into our memories when we learn. So both content and state matter and when it comes to needing and remembering things; the closer we are to that original content and state the better, as these cues aid retrieval.

On physical context, a still-quoted study by Abernathy (1940) took separate groups of students taught by the same teacher. One group studied and sat an exam in the same room; the other group studied and sat the exam in separate rooms. The students who did both in the same room performed better. In a bolder experiment, Godden and Baddeley (1975) took 18 deep-sea divers and asked them to memorize 36 unrelated words. The first group were asked to learn these words on land, the second underwater. Half of each group were then asked to remember the words having moved underwater or onto land. The results showed that both learning and recalling in the groups had done both on land or in water, that is, in the same context, were better.

On psychological states, state-dependent memory also suggests that we remember better when the same or similar emotional or psychological cues are present. Goodwin et al (1969), in an experiment with no shortage of volunteers, took 48 students and asked them to remember words when they were sober, then drunk. They were asked 24 hours later, with some sober and others drunk again, to take four tests: an avoidance task, a verbal rote-learning task, a word-association test and a picture recognition task. Those who did both learning and tests while sober for both or drunk for both, performed better, supporting the idea that learning and performing in the same emotional state is beneficial.

Context and cues

Tulving focused more on the retrieval of specific 'cues' in memory (Tulving, and Thompson, 1973), recommending that such cues be designed into the learning experience by doing, along with retrieval and spaced practice. This has obvious applications in virtual training, where both factors can be aligned – the physical and psychological. It is important to focus not on general environments but specific cues, as these can be deliberately designed into virtual experiences.

The physical environment can have likely cues, such as general environmental factors: time of day, most-common place, objects most commonly found in that place, the tools used, types of people, their behaviours and so on. It can be a mistake to have too high-fidelity an environment or the unrealistically perfect and complete representation of a factory floor, hospital ward or oil rig. Simpler representations and less-cluttered environments are likely to work better. They are also more likely to result in less cognitive load, leading to better decision making and learning. It may seem counterintuitive but stripped down and stripped back environments may work better for learning. On design, a detailed critical-task analysis that identifies tasks and sequences can uncover these cues. They can then be used as a checklist for design and should prevent the overdesign of learning.

The psychological environment is more difficult to design and control, but again, settling the learner into the appropriate mood, not overstimulating for example, or creating the context of surprise, may help. Calm attention and avoiding negative emotions such as fear seems beneficial when learning.

Tyranny of time

We can also free ourselves from the timetabled period and one-hour lecture that only exists because the Sumerians had a base-60 number system. Adaptive, personalized learning fuelled by AI in virtual contexts, using physical, physiological and psychological data, will allow learners to vector though learning experiences at their own individual pace. They may take different routes and different times to get there, but failure because you failed to run fast will not be the main feature of learning. Competency should take as long as it takes.

Benjamin Bloom's research, in *Human Characteristics and School Learning* (1976), led him to conclude that learners could master knowledge and skills given enough time. Flexibility in time to competence, he thought, would free learning from the tyranny of time. Learners are rarely good or bad, they are fast and slow. Fixed periods of learning, timetables and fixed-end-point exams all act as constraints on learners and for many become an impossible hurdle. Learning is not a timed race but a process, one where learners need to progress at their own pace.

Bloom saw three ways of freeing learning from the constraints of time:

1 Entry diagnosis and adaption (50 per cent) – diagnose, predict and recommend at the start and throughout the learning process

2 Address maturation (25 per cent) – personalize and adapt to the learners' progress in real time

3 Instructional methods (25 per cent) – match to different types of learning experiences and be flexible on time.

Going one step further, he did a piece of research that remains fundamental in learning theory. In fact, Google's Peter Norvig claimed that it is the one paper, above all, that should be read by those interested in learning technology – 'The 2 Sigma Problem' (1984). Bloom takes three methods of delivery: lecture, lecture with formative feedback and one-to-one tuition. Using the lecture as his baseline, his results showed an 84 per cent increase in mastery above the mean for a formative feedback approach to teaching and an even more astonishing 98 per cent increase in mastery for one-to-one tuition. He concludes that one-to-one has the most on-task learning, so gets by far the best results. If technology can deliver something similar to one-to-one learning, it should achieve mastery. The trick is in not relying on another human being but the technology itself to deliver the feedback and intensity of this one-to-one tuition. If we can provide context in the metaverse, and measure the learners, alongside top-class delivery, this is possible.

EXAMPLE

Eye gaze

Gavin Buckingham at the University of Exeter is using multiple cameras and force transducers on objects varying in size, shape and material, along with hand tracking and eye tracking to improve surgical skills. The potential for personalizing learning experiences in VR with biofeedback is also interesting. Eye tracking and other sensors can provide feedback on the mental state of the learner. This feedback can be used to feed forward by adapting the presented material to learners as they proceed in the training. Researchers at the university have looked at two states: anxiety and flow. They have applied this technique to patients who need to go through scans, where tens of thousands of appointments per year are missed. Adaptive exposure through VR could help alleviate anxiety and claustrophobia. The strategic gaze or expert gaze control can also be used in this adaptive way with soldiers doing weapons training.

In schools, higher education and the workplace, whether in offline and/or online learning, time is something that can destroy the efficacy of learning. We would do well not to carry this obsession with time over into the metaverse. We should dispense with metrics such as the hour-long lecture in higher education and 'an hour of learning', commonly used in the commissioning and production of online learning.

In that respect it is rather disheartening to see lecture rooms being built by the dozen in digital twin metaversities. Easy to timetable, these are rooted in the physical world of buildings that need to be administered and time scheduled. In the virtual world there are no such constraints. The real world may need these constraints, opening hours, times of operation, but the virtual world does not. It is not time that matters but outcomes. On top of this, in the real world, dropout or non-attendance is common. It is not unknown for faculty to report zero attendance at lectures.

Universities are locked into old law-profession timetables, religious and agricultural timetables. If you want to start a degree course, you may have to wait for up to a year until the start date. Then there are the long, meandering three- and four-year degrees with months of holidays, periods of steep forgetting, baked into the model. Finally, the end point is often purely theoretical final exams, with resits after impractically long periods, sometimes up to a year later. There is no area of human endeavour so stuck in the tyranny of time than higher education.

Schools are similar. The 'period' is the school equivalent of the 'lecture'. The physicality of a school, with millions walking from one classroom to another down narrow corridors to an identical room, is the hallmark of school life. This staccato rhythm of the school day is a massive waste of time as students need to pack up, walk to the next place, then settle again. Schools also need to feed students into higher education, so have to be in sync with that timetable.

In the workplace, courses, many on compliance, are delivered as timetabled events, often a set number of hours, half- or multiple-day events. The content is often padded out to fit the allotted time. Learners have to travel to the location, sometimes from afar, wasting even more time and money, only to sit in a fairly anonymous room around tables with a flip chart and screen. Little attention is paid to context. Workplace courses may also be dislocated in time from the actual time of application in the workplace. It is obviously better to deliver learning as close to the point of need as possible. This has led to delivery at very specific moments of need, when one needs moments of truth, in context, in the flow of work.

The 'conspiracy of convenience' is the idea that learning and development can be seen like servers in a restaurant, simply taking orders from a fairly predictable menu of courses, taking months to make the food, then delivering that food long after the moment of need or hunger. There is a culture that expects this rhythm of course delivery – order, make, take, repeat.

Online learning is a little better, but again procurement is often by the 'hour of learning'. This has led to a commoditized approach where the same authoring languages produce similar types of content, often over-engineered, by the hour. There is a reluctance to move away from this model, of text and graphics and media assets strung together and thinly punctuated by multiple-choice questions. More recent generative AI has changed this forever. Mastery in education is so often assumed to be writing – there's the problem. If generative AI can do what you do, you shouldn't be doing what you do. In real life, few become 'writers', yet all are corralled into this funnel. We have abandoned practical and performative skills for text-obsessed institutions. Academics produce text for a living but they wrongly assume that this is the primary skill in real life – it is not.

So the tyranny of time comes in many forms: lecture, period, semester, term, course, module and degree. Rather than work from the real needs of learners, the variety of their locations, the different types of learning, flexibility in approach and delivery, we force things into the artificial constraints of time. With the metaverse we have the opportunity to rethink these models and free ourselves from this constraint. Blended learning can be extended as a concept to include learning inside virtual worlds with more flexibility on time. The new focus on value for learners, as opposed to value for institutions, would be refreshing.

One odd consequence of the tyranny of time is padding out learning experiences to fit allotted times; this leads to over-engineered content, often unfeasibly long slide decks or long online learning courses deliberately designed to a number of hours. Even in the use of media, research is now illuminating how video, for example, is used poorly in learning. The transience effect, among others, shows that six minutes may be indicative of the sort of maximum length we should inflict upon learners.

One often sees video, podcasts and other learning experiences produced, rather arbitrarily, to the half or full hour. It is rare to find a course that cannot be shortened and less is almost always more. This needs a relentless focus on what learners 'need' to know, not throwing everything at them in the hope that the essentials will stick. Task analysis, chunking and the general delivery of specific competences all help reduce time to competence.

This shift would ensure that learning experiences are not one-off events. Learning experiences need to be persistent, as we rarely learn from single exposure to any learning event. Learning requires repeated access, practice, reflection, note-taking generative activities, application, retrieval and prac-tice across time.

One feature of learning theory almost mandates this shift – forgetting. From Ebbinghaus (1885) onwards, we have known how acute forgetting can be. This requires open and accessible resources for effortful learning and deliberate practice. This problem is more complex than we imagine as, in institutions, we tend to physically batch learners into groups, by age, subject or course. In practice, this creates a distribution curve with varying numbers clustered in the middle but more worrying, long tails of slower and faster learners. This is why non-timetabled, personalized, adaptive delivery matters. One can cope with any differentiated group of learners, keeping all on course, to achieve less dropout and higher completion and attainment.

Time can be tragically tyrannical and when we free ourselves from such a tyranny, we feel liberated. Technology has liberated us from the fixity of watching movies at a fixed time in the cinema, even on television. Most consumed media is time-shifted, on demand. We are in control, which is how it should be. Just as in entertainment, time is truly tyrannical in learning. Time-shift is the answer. All of this leads to a single conclusion, that we should be digital by default, sensitive to asynchronous, on-demand, recorded, self-paced learning, especially if it is personalized by being adaptive, driven by AI. Above all it means making learning available 365 days a year, 24 hours a day in the metaverse.

Tyranny of 2D

Since the invention of writing over 5,000 years ago, it has gained momentum as a tool for learning (Clark, 2023). Mass schooling and literacy, which were often linked, saw text in most major religions as something to be studied, memorized and, above all, believed. Textbooks appeared and writing, in the form of a bewildering array of writing tools – cut reeds on clay tablets, brushes on papyrus, on wax, eventually ink on paper – became the primary tool in teaching and learning. The rise of the codex, printed book, blackboard, whiteboard and PowerPoint made display easier and writing ubiquitous. Computers and the internet gave us another renaissance in writing, with users becoming publishers of text, in email, messaging, texting, social media, blogs and other screen-based forms. We have an education system that is obsessed with text.

Yet text has always been problematic for teaching and learning. Listening and speaking, as Geary shows, are primary skills. Reading and writing are secondary skills, which take years to learn. In truth, few actually master good spelling, punctuation and writing. It is also a system that disadvantages those with serious literacy problems, such as dyslexia.

Note taking from lectures and the essay became the two teaching mainstays in universities. Although these institutions were always primarily research focused, again with vast amounts of text in papers, much of this is barely read with limited or no impact. The vast expansion of journals now creeps into the nooks and crannies of every conceivable subject and topic, with diminishing returns.

The workplace is just as text-ridden, with over-written emails, plans and reports that few regard as concise and actionable. Even in learning and development, courses that purport to teach behavioural and attitudinal topics such as leadership, management, soft skills, diversity, equality and inclusion, are often delivered via substantial amounts of text, often in text-heavy PowerPoint, the death of motivation and learning often being the outcome.

EXAMPLE
DEI attitudinal and behavioural training

'I did not find a single study that found that diversity training in fact leads to more diversity' said Harvard Professor of Public Policy Iris Bohnet.

Changing minds is hard, attitudes are deeply embedded, as are behaviours. Billions of dollars are spent annually on diversity, equity and inclusion (DEI) training; there is little evidence that it works, but indeed lots of evidence to show that it does not. Major studies from Dobbin and Kalev (2006; 2013; 2016) and Kochan et al (2003) show that diversity training neither solves the diversity problem nor increases productivity. An additional problem is the backlash effect. 'Research to date suggests that... training often generates a backlash' said Dobbins. Tracie Stewart, a Professor at Georgia University, identified this 'backlash' or 'victim blame', where the courses themselves induced resentment based on the way trainees had been made to feel.

One problem has been the use of 2D approaches, PowerPoint presentations, tests, flat online learning to solve real-world problems. A shift to 3D can help by situating the problem in the real, represented by the virtual, workplace. Bohnet's recommendation that we 'use data on what works to inform our decision' means making interventions that we measure. The data we can draw from actual actions and behaviour is so much better than simple paper tests.

In training, we can implement attitudinal and behavioural training where we really do take part in scenarios that challenge what we think and do. The active participation in 3D training allows us to face up to the problems, deal with them, even feel what it is like to be on the receiving end of racism, exclusion or sexual harassment. Such problems in the real world are also frequently reported in VR worlds. We can use this to our advantage. VR worlds tend to allow users to mute or keep others at a distance if they offend. This is perfect for online training. Things can be experienced, discussed and reflected upon in real situations and scenarios.

> Action matters more than words. Recruitment is an important point of action. If recruitment is done anonymously, even interviews can be done using avatars that are not related to race, sex, age, disability, social class or accent. A level playing field could be implemented in virtual worlds with virtual candidates. Operational tasks could also be implemented as part of the recruitment process in virtual worlds. This could be much fairer than traditional 2D paper CVs and a cursory, bias-ridden interview process.

It is not just the quantity of text that leads training astray, it is the obsession with individual words. The written word literally hijacks training when singular abstract words, such as leadership, along with the many adjectives lobbed on to the front of the term, begin to dominate training. Never have we had so much exaggerated rhetoric and books around leadership and so little of it. So carried away did training departments become that everyone became a leader, rendering the word completely meaningless.

Compliance training, deeply disliked by most employees, delivered from learning management systems, largely designed by HR to protect organizations from their own employees, now dominate what used to be a learning environment based on personal development. Lots of diversity, equality, inclusion and resilience courses were layered on top of this, making things even more abstract. In all of this, text lies at the heart of delivery, as if text could change attitudes, which it rarely does. It often deadens, rather than enlivens, these important subjects.

So wordy has organizational training become that organizations now define themselves by sets of abstract nouns, called values. Lists of words, sometimes starting with the same letter (as if the real world really were that alliterative) or forming a mnemonic, where the words are clearly chosen to fit that word, have become commonplace. Foisted upon people by over-eager, text-obsessed HR departments, they are, of course, rarely remembered.

One would imagine that computer-based training would have brought this to an end, but it largely compounded the error by producing over-composed courses with screens of text, accompanied by often merely illustrative graphics and stock photographs. Hours and hours of text-based e-learning hit the 2D screens, containing far too much content and text. So the march of text-based delivery has continued.

Badly written instruction manuals, largely unread, lie in drawers in our homes, as people actually learn to operate most things by trying things out or asking others. The same mistake made in training departments is made by product designers. Most humans would rather learn by doing than by reading text. AI tools that generate text may show us that all of this text content – endless essays, third-rate research papers, PowerPoint slides, screens of text and graphics – is largely a waste of time, as once commoditized it becomes less valuable.

Writing is a technology but other technologies came along and swung the pendulum away from text towards images, audio and video, not only in books but through broadcast then computer and internet-delivered media. Social media swung away from text towards images on Facebook, Twitter, then Instagram, now TikTok.

YouTube became a medium that challenged text formats, especially in delivering 'how to' learning. Video is now the medium of the age, with streaming services and delivery to smartphones. Along with photographs and other 3D diagrams, video does make a shift towards 3D, albeit the illusion of 3D. You are perceiving a 2D image but constructing a 3D event. Audio-based devices are also becoming more common in our homes, cars and on our smartphones. Audio's frictionless appeal now often replaces text interfaces.

The weakness of text for teaching has also become apparent through the appearance of AI. Students have access to generative AI tools for essays, written assessments and coursework; a tsunami of text that escapes plagiarism checkers. It can be written in different styles and, in many contexts, is astonishingly accurate, structured and literate. This undermines what was always a uniform and rather lazy form of assessment, where the same essay questions are asked year after year with often cursory feedback. It is not that this technology will destroy learning, only the learning game as currently practised. It heralds a new era of co-creation, a new 'pedAIgogy', which changes our relationship with knowledge and skills. This generative technology has a lot to offer in terms of dynamically helping students to learn, not only how to write, but also research, complete tasks, apply and transfer into the real world. Teaching, learning and assessment all have to adapt to this new world of abundant text, not by producing yet more text but by producing less but better text.

However, while generative AI text gets all the attention, it is not more text we need, but rather 2D and 3D images, objects and video. Here there has been huge progress. This shift from 2D to 3D may well be affected by generative AI as it matures. Progress is impressive as AI can already read and create 2D images. It has quickly moved on to create 3D objects and now 3D worlds from 2D images and avatars. Then there is its ability to determine avatar behaviour, recommend pathways, interpret behavioural data and so on. We see that generative AI itself has moved from flat text production to 2D screen delivery and then on to 3D production, as it is fundamentally a generative technology that can produce any form of asset in any medium.

Humans produce gargantuan amounts of dull, workaday text, most of it over-written. We are drowning in this sea of badly written text. Editing is rare, cutting text until it bleeds even rarer. We are far too text obsessed in education and training. The unfortunate consequence of this has been a corresponding obsession with abstract, theoretical learning, at the expense of practical and vocational learning. We need to learn for both life and a living. Many modern economies have diminished the work of the heart and hand, seeing only the head as the proper domain of learning. Universities have soaked up the budgets, while other forms of learning have atrophied. This has led to considerable skills shortages.

The solution is surely to recognize that technology is not just about teaching and learning theory but also application, skills and practice. We learn to both live and make a living. For too long learning has been the domain of the head, as theory can be learnt and managed in the mind and is easy to deliver in the classroom. We have progressively diminished and demolished practical and vocational learning. Skills in dealing with people, even dealing with oneself, also practical skills such as management, the professions and innumerable jobs and trades that keep the world turning must surely switch towards more performance-based solutions and, as we 'perform' in the real 3D world, that means simulating the real world to learn. These real-world skills need virtual spaces and time where they can be performed. Given that the real world is not always available, affordable and practical, imagined 3D spaces and places can be created to rebalance this lopsided state of affairs.

Only now do we see, on the horizon, technology that can solve this age-old problem: how to develop skills without wasting the time of the skillful. 3D worlds can teach, nurture and develop such skills. That technology includes VR and the metaverse.

Tyranny of passivity

With passive learning, the transience effect (Kalyuga, 2011) comes into play, where we read, listen and watch, but are lulled into thinking we are learning when we are not. It is easy to watch people speak or watch a video and assume that we are learning, but learners are often delusional about how they have actually learnt.

First and foremost, we can have a renewed interest in evidence-based, effortful learning. Rather than passively watching and listening to lectures or presentations or screenfuls of text and graphics in online learning, we can have real effort, agency and action by learners. What has been called learning by doing can be realized in ways not possible in the real world.

Learning science suggests that the metaverse will be a powerful place for learning, as it can deliver several strong conditions for good learning:

1 Attention – complete visual and total cognitive attention

2 Emotion – positive emotions to enhance learning

3 Action – learn by doing

4 Context – useful virtual environments

5 Collaboration – virtual multiplayer tasks

6 Transfer – transfer from learning to performance.

There is ample research and evidence for these principles in simulated environments, although the research has also uncovered some downsides. Media rich does not always mean mind rich.

What has emerged with VR, and points towards possibilities in the metaverse, is the possibility of using our natural affinity with 3D perception to put the metaverse to good use in learning. We know that virtual 3D worlds hold attention, indeed it is hard to escape being wholly attentive and this is a necessary condition for learning. It also provides emotional stimulus; this affective dimension in learning, identified as important by Anotonio Demasio, Imoldia Yand and Jaak Panksepp, is at its most powerful in these evocative worlds. As an experiential learning tool, one can also learn by doing, almost always a 3D activity, something that education and training struggles to deliver. Context is also provided, as the world in which you learn, the metaverse, is a designed context, whether place, things or other people.

There is therefore a strong argument for the metaverse being a place where there is a high probability for retention and transfer. Transfer to the real world is easier if you have learnt and practised in a similar, congruent virtual world. We know this with certainty from flight simulators. All pilots train extensively on simulators. Why? Well, the pilot goes down with the plane, but we also know it works. Learning in the Multiverse is likely to involve more 3D simulation learning and, in particular, training.

EXAMPLE
Onboarding

Joining an organization can be a nerve-racking experience. You know no one, don't know the lie of the land physically or psychologically, yet have to adapt and fit in as fast as possible. It is also erratic, as people do not generally join in batches, but as individuals. This makes running formal, batched training courses quite difficult.

The best time to welcome new people is before they join. So having a digital twin of your workplace is perfect as they can explore, know where they will be working, find the coffee area, toilets, and get generally familiar with the whole environment. Treasure hunts have been used to give a more structured approach. Health and safety can certainly be delivered in virtual worlds, including the whole process of what to do and where to go when the alarm goes off, position of first aid equipment, escape routes and so on.

There may be further introductions to the company's physical products, actual presentations in context, seeing them made in the factory, virtual visits to other nearby national or international sites. The entire geography of the organization can be revealed. The organizational structure can also be shown virtually, with individuals explaining their roles. You may even be introduced virtually, for the first time, to your colleagues and managers. The tools you will be expected to use can also be introduced. The place of work becomes the place you get to know work.

Learning transfer

Transfer is doing and practice. Virtual simulations have long provided powerful practice and transfer. Pilots really do learn how to take off, fly, land and cope with rare emergencies using simulators. So why are simulators not more commonly used in learning? Well, the pilot goes down with the plane. There is not much doubt when your imagination and the reality of your job takes you to 35,000 feet in 300 tonnes of metal and 600 passengers. It really does matter whether the learning delivered results in actual transfer and therefore performance in the workplace. But, transfer is often ignored in learning design as it is difficult to implement in most flat, 2D online contexts.

Learning design must have transfer in mind, leading towards agency, activity and action. It needs practice to turn the learning experience into performance, which in turn has real impact on the organization. In truth, this means learning by doing, with training pathways that allow you to take personal responsibility for such practice, as well as the organizational willingness to let you learn by doing, with a tolerance of failure. We know that knowledge can remain inert and fail to transfer (Renkl et al, 1996). What makes good transfer is congruence between what is learnt and the practice activities (Singley and Anderson, 1989).

Near and far transfer

'Near' and 'far' transfer are useful design concepts for learning in mixed reality or the metaverse. Near transfer involves simple, specific and routine tasks, such as learning how to apply a formula in a spreadsheet, where the contexts are similar. Far transfer involves more varied problem solving, where learnt knowledge and skills, such as fault finding or management competences, need to be applied, as the contexts in which such skills need to be applied are likely to be varied. Near transfer is easy to design for using methods such as varied worked examples, retrieval, deliberate, directed and spaced practice. Far transfer is tricky as the training needs to be as realistic as possible, not in terms of graphics but in terms of tasks and cues. Far transfer needs variation in worked examples, scenarios and applications to give the learner the flexibility to adapt what they learn to future problems. Flight simulators provide a good example of congruence between the training and environment. It is not that everything needs to be hyperreal, only that the tasks are trained well, with relevant cues.

One design feature that really matters is the degree of autonomy one gives the learner. Too much, especially for novices, will result in cognitive overload, even confusion. In general, the constraints can be loosened as new knowledge and skills fit into the learners' existing schema (Marshall, 1995) and competence builds.

Classrooms are generally a poor environment for transfer, whereas simulated or on-the-job training provides real cues and context. What is needed is something akin to the old apprenticeship model, now perhaps renamed as blended learning. A true blended-learning experience integrates theory and practice, providing a process for progress, from novice to expert, from virtual to real.

The process may be spread over weeks or months and not be restricted to a simple one- or two-day course or online learning experience. Learning needs transfer and transfer takes time. Specific features of an optimal blended-learning design may be experiences that allow you to apply what you learn in the metaverse, working through case studies, models of expert performance and changing scenarios to see how they affect the outcome, learning from mistakes. Learning experiences benefit from actual experiences, both virtual and real.

EXAMPLE
Surgical training

Surgery is far more than wielding a scalpel. It has become an area of rapid technological advances in devices and methods. Yet it is still a hands-on, performance-based profession – until, that is, precision robots do most of the work. Skills are still gained through practice and experience, but the field is likely to be transformed with virtual training.

VR operating tables are now here, allowing for a range of specific, surgical procedures, using a range of surgical tools. The advantages are obvious, as surgery is a high-stakes game, with lower risk to patients, less harm to patients by surgeons learning on the job and greater measurement of skills during the training with faster time to competence. With a good critical-task analysis, processes can be taught well, along with rare incidents and mishaps. Headsets can be lower than the cost of one night at a hotel for a workshop and the solution is scalable. You can do a procedure as many times as you wish, at very low cost.

A 2019 study conducted by UCLA's David Geffen School of Medicine found that in surgical performance using VR, the VR group significantly outperformed the traditionally trained group. They were, on average, 20% faster and completed 38% more steps completed correctly in the procedure checklist, with an overall improvement in the total score of 230%.

Further randomized blind studies using Osso (see Blumstein et al, 2020) have been impressive, showing increased procedural accuracy and completions, with a 300% increase in accuracy. It is clear that the procedural workflow and movements required to perform surgical procedures can be taught and assessed using VR.

This is also about accurate and objective assessment. With an ageing population, demand for surgery is soaring. If VR can deliver training to anyone with a headset, anywhere at anytime, we increase the throughput, as well as being able to measure performance more objectively.

Fidelity

Full fidelity is not always advisable, not just on the grounds of cost but on the distinction between 'physical' and 'psychological' fidelity. If attention is paid to psychological cues and decision making, the physical fidelity matters less (Cox et al, 1965). Complexity should be just enough to train and acquire competence and no more. Simple and mini-simulations are often effective. Having designed many scenario and branched training simulations, with regular choices and decision making, it is the careful selection of the scenarios that matters. What are the most common and critical scenarios in relation to the real world? To what problems, their frequency and criticality, is this a solution? Where customers, patients and potential employees are performing tasks, choosing the right and representative mix of people is also important.

Making transfer work

Weinbauer-Heidel's *What Makes Training Really Work* (2018) warns us against being too lazy on transfer. She recommends issuing *no* course certificates, unless transfer has been shown. For her, transfer needs to be leveraged at the personal, training and organizational levels:

1 Personal – you must want to push through to action and take calls to action into your actual work

2 Training – you need to be clear about what is expected in terms of application and doing and include this in the training

3 Organization – practice, with time available and support from line managers is important for real transfer.

When it comes to transfer, you must take the horse to water and then make it drink. Transfer needs to be designed into the process and not left to chance.

Assessing competence

In assessment, the move from writing to typing to talking is happening. If you are assessing skills that do not need writing, why complicate and reduce performance to writing, or worse, a series of multiple-choice questions.

With the rise of AI-generated text, allowing learners to produce credible text on demand, one solution is to rely more on practical and observational assessment. Subject to the tyranny of time and place, it has long been inefficient, with learners having to wait for up to a year for a resit, then travel to a specific site to sit a paper exam. This is why assessment has been moving online for many years – it frees assessment from the tyrannies of the real: place, time, 2D only and passivity.

Organizations realize that assessment needs to be free from traditional physical locations and held more frequently. This not only benefits learners but the organizations that need reliable and secure assessment. Sophisticated systems now include the creation and validation of tests, management, scheduling, authentification, invigilation, verification, as well as analytics. The pendulum swing towards online assessment is well underway.

One problem that continues to plague assessment is assessing competences and skills that lie beyond knowledge. Paper tests only go so far in testing knowledge and certain levels of understanding. They are limited, sometimes inadequate, even dangerous, in assessing competences that need to be proved in the real world, with real equipment and real people. Assessment, in this sense, holds education and learning back, as we tend to teach what we can assess. This results in over-theoretical, text-heavy teaching, learning and assessment.

Immersive assessment can push the boundaries and provide secure immersion, free from cheating, as well as virtual environments where one can test for far more than knowledge and understanding. We have, at last, a 3D medium where actual application and physical performance can be truly measured and assessed.

Total immersion gives you total control over what the learner sees, hears and does. It cuts out cheating, as it cuts out visual, oral and physical methods of cheating. One can present a test sure in the knowledge that others cannot see what is shown and heard. Secure testing is therefore assured. You can also track movements that suggest cheating; head movements can be tracked, even eye movements through eye tracking.

Assessment of knowledge and skills is still possible along with voice assessments. What is new is the ability to assess physical psychomotor skills. This can be pilot training, driving a vehicle, operating apparatus and machinery, so saving fuel, emissions, wear and tear, time and money on real but expensive equipment and vehicles. Detailed tracking through sensors give increasingly fine detail about performance, which can be tracked over time, in different situations.

Rather than the theory of health and safety, actual scenarios in simulated worlds can be presented and assessed. There are now full simulations for fires on oil rigs, where you really do have to find the evacuation point, with realistic fires and flames, right through to helicopter take off. Contextual training is important in these stressful, emergency situations.

We built just such a training and assessment system for gas installers in the USA. You entered a 3D home and as variables such as open windows were tracked, you could fail if you did not check, as the draft would blow away any gasses you were trying to detect. It is not just the task that one can assess but the task in different contexts. You are assessed on selecting the correct tools, spotting dangerous installations and situations, going through the correct checks and processes. Real-world scenarios can be designed that save huge amounts of time and money, as the tests can be taken online.

Soft skills, those to do with people interactions, can also be assessed in terms of being with others in multi-user virtual environments. Again, sensors can track useful indicators, such as body language or eye movements, to test behaviour in meetings, recruitment interviews, presentation skills, sales skills, customer-facing skills, patient-facing skills, team skills or general management situations.

The key word here is *performance*; whether in life, sport or work, virtual environments, as they track at more fine-grained levels of performance, provide ever deeper levels of assessment. Even fine-tuned motor skills, from sports to surgery, could eventually be assessed in this way. Being assessed in relevant environments and contexts is also important.

The fact that such assessments are easy to deliver means that one can practise the assessments, safely, risk free at very low costs. One can practise and self-assess towards a desired level of performance.

As assessment starts to cover physical, as well as psychological performance, we can expect areas to be better taught and assessed. Not waiting on expensive skilled assessors will save substantial amounts of time and money, also shortening time to assessed competence, getting people on the job quicker. Assessment will no longer be a bottleneck but flow naturally from the learning experience, a smooth transition from training to assessment to work. Lessening this time means less forgetting and more on-the-job application and reinforcement of what is learnt.

Assessments on large, even vast, scales could also take place in the metaverse, where large teams, groups, emergency services, venue staff, even armies, could be put into simulations that deliver and track assessed outcomes. Digital twin environments could obviously host such assessments, providing the place with multiple scenarios to deliver and track complex interactions across the whole airport, venue, hospital or battlefield. This could all be done safely with minimal environmental impact.

We could dramatically reduce the human, logistic and administrative costs associated with traditional exams. The metaverse reduces time to assess competences that rely on legacy processes and increases the flexibility of assessment delivery to an anywhere, anytime model. It also reduces the administrative burden and complexity of paper-based examinations, increasing assessment security and integrity, with higher levels of useful and relevant data to be used in assessment, as well as producing final assessment data through good reporting and analytical tools. Finally, we can reduce the environmental impact of traditional methods.

One can imagine a future where cheap assessment is available on almost any form of knowledge, understanding and skill in a virtual environment, a full range of assessment opportunities that takes you as far as being able to step into a job. Like the driving test, you learn, get tested and off you go to fine-tune your skills through real driving.

This extends into recruitment. Jobs are about doing things in the real world, yet recruitment is largely 2D with verbal interviews. Few actual capabilities or competencies are demonstrated across the entire process. People will be able to create their own performative acts, rather than just presenting a paper CV to show competence. Competences could actually be performed as part of the job application process. The metaverse will allow this to happen as we will look for jobs, offer jobs and look for evidence that demonstrates competence, all in 3D, in the metaverse.

Conclusion

It is clear that extended realities, whether wholly immersive, mixed or augmented, are already playing a role in learning in terms of the acquisition of real competence. The question is not whether they will be used, only the degree to which they will be used.

Bibliography

Abernathy, E M (1940) The effect of changed environmental conditions upon the results of college examinations, *Journal of Psychology*, 10 (2), 293–301

Bloom, B S (1976) *Human Characteristics and School Learning*, McGraw-Hill, New York

Bloom, B S (1984) The 2 sigma problem: The search for methods of group instruction as effective as one-to-one tutoring, *Educational researcher*, 13 (6), 4–16

Blumstein, G, Zukotynski, B, Cevallos, N, Ishmael, C, Zoller, S, Burke, Z, Clarkson, S, Park, H, Bernthal, N and SooHoo, N F (2020) Randomized trial of a virtual reality tool to teach surgical technique for tibial shaft fracture intramedullary nailing, *Journal of Surgical Education*, 77 (4), 969–977

Bohnet, I, (2017) Focusing on what works for workplace diversity, www.mckinsey.com/featured-insights/gender-equality/focusing-on-what-works-for-workplace-diversity (archived at https://perma.cc/V3VJ-LB73)

Clark, D, (2022) *Learning Experience Design: How to create effective learning that works*, Kogan Page, London

Clark, D, PedAIgogy [blog], Plan B, 2 March 2023, donaldclarkplanb.blogspot.com/2023/03/pedaigogy-new-era-of-knowledge-and.html (archived at https://perma.cc/4KHS-WYUG)

Cox, J A, Wood Jr, R O, Boren, L M and Thorne, H W (1965) Functional and appearance fidelity of training devices for fixed-procedures tasks (No. HUMRRO-TR-65-4), George Washington University Alexandria VA Human Resources Research Office

Dobbin, F and Kalev, A (2013) The origins and effects of corporate diversity programs, psycnet.apa.org (archived at https://perma.cc/SDF8-DSQE)

Dobbin, F and Kalev, A (2016) Diversity: Why diversity programs fail and what works better, *Harvard Business Review*, 94 (7–8), 52–60

Geary, D C (2005) The Origin of Mind: Evolution of brain, cognition, and general intelligence, American Psychological Association, Washington, DC

Godden, D R and Baddeley, A D (1975) Context-dependent memory in two natural environments: On land and underwater, *British Journal of Psychology*, 66 (3), 325–331

Goodwin, D W, Powell, B, Bremer, D, Hoine, H and Stern, J (1969) Alcohol and recall: State-dependent effects in Man, *Science*, 163 (3873): 1358–1360

Kalev A, Dobbin F and Kelly, E (2006) Best practices or best guesses? Assessing the efficacy of corporate affirmative action and diversity policies, *American Sociological Review*, 71 (4), 589–617

Kalyuga, S (2011) Effects of information transiency in multimedia learning, *Procedia-Social and Behavioral Sciences*, 30, 307–311

Kochan, T, Bezrukova, K, Ely, R, Jackson, S, Joshi, A, Jehn, K, Leonard, J, Levine, D and Thomas, D (2003) The effects of diversity on business performance: Report of the Diversity Research Network, *Human Resource Management*, 42 (1), 3–21 https://psycnet.apa.org/record/2003-99258-001 (archived at https://perma.cc/ZL47-NPYT)

Marshall, S P (1995) *Schemas in Problem Solving*, Cambridge University Press, Cambridge

Renkl, A, Mandl, H and Gruber, H (1996) Inert knowledge: Analyses and remedies, *Educational Psychologist*, 31 (2), 115–121

Singley, M K and Anderson, J R (1989) *The Transfer of Cognitive Skill*, Harvard University Press, Cambridge, MA

Siwicki, B, How virtual reality is turning surgical training upside-down, 9 September 2022, www.healthcareitnews.com/news/how-virtual-reality-turning-surgical-training-upside-down (archived at https://perma.cc/9EYU-AFK7)

Thomas, D (2003) The effects of diversity on business performance: Report of the diversity research network, *Human Resource Management*, 42 (1), 3–21

Tulving, E (1974) Cue-dependent forgetting, *American Scientist*, 62, 74–82

Tulving, E and Thompson, D (1973) Encoding specificity and retrieval process in episodic process, *Journal of Experimental Psychology*, 87, 353–373

Weinbauer-Heidel, I (2018) *What Makes Training Really Work*, Tredition, Hamburg

12

Social learning

In my childhood, I lived in a small town in Scotland with little or no contact with the outside world, other than a single penpal in the US. We corresponded once a month by letter. Our social reach was limited by who we knew locally, in school or at work. My social network now reaches around the world. I can speak face to face with anyone, anywhere around the globe for free; email and message anyone on social media for free; blog, post and publish for anyone to see on the web. In one lifetime I have gone from living physically in a world of hundreds to a virtual network of billions. You most likely heard about and bought this book in that virtual world. We are now connected in that world.

Indeed, we lived for most of our evolution among a relatively small number of people, with not much direct communication with others. Technology brought agriculture, settlement and transport to other places, then communications via letters, then telegraph and telephone expanded our social reach. Then we had the jump to screen communication via computers, tablets, smartphones, watches and home devices. We now speak to people at any distance, often for free. The next step is not just to communicate but to be communal and be with those people in the same virtual space. Online worlds in 3D will vastly expand our social connections.

Social metaverse

Social interaction exists for different reasons, at different levels, among different numbers of participants, with varying degrees of participation. It is not one thing. Julian Stodd is an expert on the social age and how social phenomena manifest themselves. That social power is now exercised largely through technology, as this has increased our networked reach, through social media and email, Zoom and formal communications.

Stodd's research has shown how the social now permeates everything, especially learning. Teachers and learners are no longer in a formal relationship but sit within a network of online options. Those options have grown, especially in the 21st century, to include wider and deeper sets of social tools on more and more devices. Starting with simple communications between computers, it has grown through the huge adoption of social media, messaging tools and video conferencing through Zoom, document sharing tools like Google Docs and on into audio through Discord. We have seen the social expand into using all media, not just text but images, video, AR and VR. Social has become a truly multimedia phenomenon.

Evidence for social activity in virtual worlds is also overwhelming. The three largest 3D creating games environments in the world, *Fortnite*, Roblox and *Minecraft* have social dimensions that are fundamental to their popularity. The computer games industry has seen the social dimension within games, and the social ecosystem that games exist within, grow enormously, not only from the early single-player games into multiplayer games, but also from the huge industries of social support, streaming and e-sports that now surround gaming.

In her common framework for collaboration in social games, Danielle D'Amour (2005) focused on collaboration and uncovered a complex set of social dimensions in playing computer games: sharing, membership, interdependency, power and process. *Sharing* includes shared responsibilities, decision making and values, also recognizing roles and responsibilities. *Membership* involves open communication, mutual trust and respect, that feeling of being part of a social group. *Interdependency* is mutual dependence, collaboration to complete tasks and achieve shared goals or to exchange social support, recognizing your role as part of a team. *Power* is in building relationships and interactions, with the recognition of the roles of leadership. Finally, the social *process* changes over time, with changing relationships between the social members.

Virtual environments such as VRChat are, in essence, social environments. The whole point of taking oneself into a 3D environment is usually to interact with others. From meetings to training, we are social beings and the metaverse is the one medium that by definition promises to bring us together as meaningful groups, with full presence, agency, communications and capability. We increasingly spend time in virtual worlds and we can expect this to continue into the metaverse, where the social opportunities become very tangible. Presence, avatar design and choices, audio, eye tracking, hand tracking, body tracking, the ability to move around and above all participate in social activities suggest that the metaverse will be an intrinsically social space.

It is not enough to simply appear as an avatar in the metaverse; one must also communicate with others. The metaverse will be an alternative social world. Some see it as similar to a massive social media platform where we hang out and meet others in the way we do in the real world, but with safeguards and affordances that make it a whole new world of possible social engagement.

Social learning in the metaverse

Social spaces change over time. The big shift has been our move from the physical to the virtual with a number of virtual spaces, tools and services. Learning has tracked this progress with a huge swing towards online learning, using many of the same tools as our everyday social interaction.

At one level this just happens. We use social tools for interaction and learning often just accompanies the communications. We learn a lot informally, incidentally, even accidentally. The tools available – search, knowledge bases, such as Wikipedia and Google Maps, and now powerful generative AI tools – all put learning at our fingertips. This simply happened, it was not designed to happen by learning professionals and institutions, yet we all have had to adapt and recognize their importance and validity.

Social learning in the metaverse increases opportunities for people to get together to plan things, show others how to perform a task, even formally train others. There are all sorts of possible virtual spaces to learn in, as any possible context could be designed, from a pure white world for planning and prototyping, through to more research and exchange of knowledge environments with available resources, through to small situated simulations, team training projects and large-scale sims. The social possibilities in the metaverse are limitless.

Social freedom

I met Andy Fidel in Berlin, when she was presenting her vision of the metaverse as a social space where one could be yourself, without judgement. As you can have any appearance you want as an avatar, you need not worry about your actual appearance or background. She argued that you discover people from the inside out, not the outside in. She is no introvert but makes a good case for introverts preferring smaller groups and one-to-one interaction, even preferring text or chat to speaking. There is also plenty of room for body language, gestures and eye movements to make communications more natural and authentic. Far from being a wild and dangerous place, the metaverse offers a safe space for interaction for people who may find it difficult to deal with real people in person in the real world.

Practising social skills in such spaces is also possible. You can find your place in the metaverse when it is difficult to find such places in your geographically limited real world. It frees you from the tyranny of place. With most media, you are on the outside looking in; with VR you are on the inside looking out. This sense of presence and agency is immensely powerful in learning. We talk a lot about empowerment in life, work and learning; this is a medium that does just that, as it puts you in charge.

Presence allows you not only to be yourself, but also anything else. Appearance, gender, race, socio-economic group, height, weight, age, accent and most other physical and psychological features can be changed, so that they do not interfere with social interaction and learning. You can be whatever you want to be. This is, indeed, what happens in open VR chat environments.

Collaboration

Social virtual worlds are spaces where groups of people can collaborate and work towards a common goal. So what type of collaborative activities for both work and play do people often conduct in social, immersive worlds? How do people go about collaborative activities in these social worlds? How do people perceive their role in collaboration in such worlds? These questions were asked in 'Working together apart through embodiment: Engaging in everyday collaborative activities in social virtual reality' (Freeman et al, 2022).

The authors explored what sort of things we actually do in social, collaborative virtual worlds and found a surprising range of collaborative activities for both work and play. A consistent theme was the need to build and customize places, which is not easy on your own, so collaboration made sense. Building places with other people, creating digital assets using third-party applications and then importing them into social VR are very popular forms of social collaboration. Playing simulated, physical social games like paintball or card games is another. More serious collaborations take place in meetings, conferences, workshops and studying with friends. All sorts of collaborative methods are used, including different modes of communication, from voice to full-body tracking; also the use of tools such as virtual maker pens, virtual brushes and virtual screens. Participants want engaging, fun, immersive activities that involve being and interacting with others in generative collaborative experiences.

Social learning

Social and collaborative effort can also be used to great effect in learning. You can be yourself, as role play is easy. You can be anyone and anything. Manager, nurse, physician, sales person, teacher, trainer – any professional role can be enacted. This includes the choosing of relevant workwear, important in construction and other dangerous and risky environments. You are then seen in whatever way you wish to be seen in social interactions.

You can also see yourself. This is important as seeing yourself in recordings of learning experiences may be where most of the learning takes place. Seeing yourself as a presenter, teacher, trainer, customer-facing person, is almost always a rich learning experience, as it provides direct feedback about your performance. It can lead to fast self-driven improvement, especially if you are open to advice from experts.

Beyond this you can do body-swaps. John Locke was one of the first to explore the power of the body-swap in *An Essay Concerning Human Understanding* (1690), where he made the point that although we do have a real body that is entirely personal, it is our minds that play the key role in personal identity, or sense of self. We have consciousness and feelings of our bodies, as an embodied self. More importantly, we have changing thoughts and beliefs. Locke and other philosophers, such as David Hume, have also stressed that our real identities have more to do with our minds, where identity is felt, defined and fluid.

Locke made the point that we often swap into the consciousness of another person. We do this when reading novels, watching movies and playing games. We can be so immersed in 3D worlds that this becomes the dominant mode. We can become saints and sinners, victims and heroes. This is how conflict and moral issues are dealt with in the world of fiction, by putting ourselves in the shoes of invented characters. Imagine now that you are not under the control of the narrative of the author, director or designer, but free to be that character, make choices, take action and do things. This is where real learning can take place, as you start to take things more seriously, even make mistakes. You also see how other people may like or dislike what you do in practice. For example, as a nurse, health professional or physician, you can become the patient. To see ourselves as others see us, we must be able to put ourselves in their shoes. VR literally allows you to put yourself in other minds.

An interesting feature of VR is the claim that one can also make partial body-swaps. Lanier found in the earliest of VR experiments, where a computer bug produced a lobster-like version of him, that he very quickly adapted to having extra limbs. This has been taken further with gender swaps, where a female and male can have the avatar of the other person, so that when you look down you see the other person's body and experience what they see, along with their movements and gestures. We can see how avatars and social presence open up all sorts of new possibilities and pedagogies for learning.

Group learning

It is relatively rare to need huge numbers of people in the same place in real life but especially in learning. Even group work in learning tends to be in small groups. But even in small groups, learning can be challenging. When poorly executed, it can result in lots of social loafing by those less motivated, lots of wasted 'not on task' time, dominance by extroverts and so on. Poorer students can often suffer from not being in the right 'peer' group, introverted, nervous students often being put at a particular disadvantage.

Virtual group work can solve some of these problems by dampening down these issues. You often find introverts, even those with autism, finding more freedom online, where there is a certain distance and they can have more control. The use of avatars is a clear example. In virtual worlds, we can find room to move around, breathe, express ourselves, be in control and be less open to embarrassment in learning. It takes off some of the pressure of real groups and embarrassing role plays.

There is also the advantage of relevant context. You also have the advantage of placing cohorts, groups and teams, in any number, into any chosen environment and context. Roles can be better shown and expressed when you are in a relevant context – the washer, sous chef, head chef, maître d', head server and servers are better trained in a restaurant setting than a lecture room. When roles are made clear, interactions between these roles can be learnt, along with critical problems that often occur in such settings.

A cohort, team or social group can also be brought together from lots of different places into one virtual environment to have learning experiences in one common virtual place. This saves a lot of time and money in travelling to specific busy locations just to have a team learning experience. One can also have the teacher, tutor, instructor or trainer being anywhere, guiding from inside that virtual environment.

One concrete example of the shift from 2D to 3D in training are escape rooms, which are now available as group training exercises. The aim is to provide a motivating 3D environment to develop the skills one needs to work in groups and problem-solve. Rather than largely 2D online learning with text, graphics and video, intense multiplayer challenges force teams to work together to discuss, reflect, make decisions and perform. This learning experience is then carried over into the workplace to effect transfer. We can expect lots of small simulations that teach and test specific skills, rather than PowerPoint slides that have little effect on attitudes and behaviour. In these online 3D escape room exercises, we have a glimpse of how such experiences can be structured.

COHORTS

Often in formal learning, cohorts of learners have to be taught and learn together. Assignments or discussion groups may have to be held, and virtual worlds can help. The text-only discussions forums and discussions often peter out through lack of sustained interest. The flat world of Zoom can also feel psychologically flat.

Being in a full 3D world, which is how we normally socialize, may induce the correct context and atmosphere for optimal cohort interaction and discussion. As a teacher or trainer you can be part of that group, or sit outside it, giving students more freedom to discuss as a peer group. More complex peer-group activity, such as pairing up, pioneered by Eric Mazur, Professor of Physics at Harvard, can provide a mix of direct instruction and peer learning, as explained in his book *Peer Instruction* (1997). He stops his direct instruction to deliver what Dylan Wiliam calls 'hinge' questions, diagnostic questions that tease out whether learners have understood a concept, principle or process. Mazur then groups learners in peer instruction groups and waits until all have understood and moves on. This approach led to significant improvements in attainment.

Mazur's work on redistributing learners within a physical space is also fascinating. He found correlations between sitting in a lecture hall and attainment – the further back you sat, the lower the attainment. His solution was to mix it up, so that different abilities were closer to each other, making peer learning more effective. This peer planning can be executed so much easier in a virtual space, where learners can be placed in an optimal pattern.

When Harvard moved all classes online, Mazur (2021) went all in: 'I have never been able to offer a course of the quality that I'm offering now. I am convinced that there is no way I could do anything close to what I'm doing in person. Online teaching is better than in person.' Seeing that most learning could be done by minimizing the synchronous components, he came to the realization that it is 'almost unethical' to return to classroom teaching.

In a radical move, Mazur realized that students needed to be free from the tyranny of the clock, so he set small assignments, in a structured sequence, with students posing questions and answers for each other. This provided lots of space for failure and multiple attempts. As he says, 'When you teach online, every single student is sitting in the front row.'

These are the approaches that will be made easier in the metaverse, where time and real places are less relevant. You can do things in your own time in constructed spaces, where learners are situated in the right context, with the right people in the right place at the right time for optimal learning.

TEAMS

Teams really matter in organizations, and in the military, aviation and healthcare they can be critical. Team learning is quite different from social learning, in that specific, critical team structures and tasks are the focus. Yet much teamwork is sub-optimal, as it does not come naturally to people. You need to be taught as a team, in a team, in team-oriented environments. This is an area ripe for training in VR and the metaverse.

Eduardo Salas has researched what makes a good team and how to develop teams and train for teamwork. He is a world expert on teams, even used for astronaut training for Mars! His analysis of what makes optimal teamwork feeds into his views on the training of teams, with its emphasis on doing team-based work or simulations.

He reminds us that what is also needed is a clear view of what teams are and how they should be supported and trained; how real collaboration takes place in teams that have a common purpose and that research can inform what makes a good team and how we can train teams. The research shows that better team processes, along with better training, increases performance, saves money and saves lives.

Mazur's research involves studying real teams in action to uncover the behaviours and decision making process. It does not matter whether a team is fixed, temporary, in the same place or virtual; teamwork and collaboration is on the rise and becoming more complex. Salas identifies seven drivers for teamwork that could drive training in the metaverse:

1 Capability – right people with right mix of knowledge and skills
2 Cooperation – right attitudes and willingness to be in the team
3 Coordination – demonstrate teamwork behaviours
4 Communication – communicate with each other and outside
5 Cognition – possess a shared understanding of priorities, roles, vision
6 Coaching – leaders and team members must show leadership behaviours
7 Conditions – favourable conditions such as resources and culture.

The competence of individuals within a team really does matter, as do beliefs around collective responsibility and success. Team members need to be sure that they can speak up and will not be embarrassed in front of the rest of the team. But how do you train this? From PowerPoint? Not likely.

This is best done with teams working together in safe environments, possibly in VR or the metaverse, so that they understand fully the importance of good teams with the following characteristics:

1 Have clear roles and responsibilities
2 Driven by compelling purpose – goal, vision, objective
3 Guided by team coach (leader) – promotes, develops, reinforces
4 Have psychological safety – mutual trust
5 Develop team norms, performance conditions – clear, known and appropriate
6 Hold shared understanding of task, mission and goals – hold shared mental models
7 Able to self-correct – huddles, debriefs
8 Set expectations – clear, understood
9 Share unique information – efficient information protocols
10 Surrounded by optimal organizational conditions – policies, procedures, signals.

All team members need to be trained on team-based knowledge, skills and abilities. You also need to teach how to debrief and huddle, then ask: What worked? What can be improved? What needs to be done differently?

Think about all of this. The optimal solution is surely to use virtual worlds to make and learn from your mistakes. Simulation techniques, such as games and role plays with embedded instructional features, are all possible in virtual worlds and, importantly, competences can be measured. Everything about team training screams for the need to work within the team environment with other people to solve problems, not in a general way, but in domain-specific environments.

Large groups

Some training tasks involve very large groups. One could quite see how a CEO presentation to all employees could be held in these virtual worlds but also entire groups within organizations, say departments, a community of practice, the entire sales team; sharing 3D objects such as products on a product launch, introducing a new company and your plans after an acquisition. All can be done in virtual worlds.

Within a defined environment, such as large buildings, hotels, malls, public transport systems or airports, training for all can be delivered and integrated so that optimal outcomes are realized. The digital twin of that environment brings a unified approach to problem solving and training.

Large-scale incidents and emergencies can also be simulated, from natural disasters, such as volcanic explosions, earthquakes and floods, to human-created events such as mass shootings, hijacks and terrorist attacks. In all of these there are multiple possible scenarios, with multiple agencies that need to work in a coordinated fashion.

The military operates at the international, national, corps, division, brigade, battalion, company, platoon and squad level. Training must be applied at all of these levels. On top of this there are separate services – army, navy and airforce – along with international training across many national forces. One can see why virtual worlds are critical here. Simulations can be held for multiple scenarios, on a large scale, with large numbers of participants and equipment. Most of the time, military personnel are not at war, but must prepare and keep skilled for that eventuality. Conflicts have also got more complex with insurgency, improvisation, social media, cyberwars and politics. Multi-actor, complex scenarios can be run to prepare for what is to come. People do not get injured or die in these large-scale simulations and the simulations can be reset and rerun as many times as needed to reach competence.

Conferences

Conferences are essentially group learning experiences. There is, of course, the joy of travelling somewhere and being with real people. But in these days of climate change, that is looking increasingly difficult to justify. The sheer time, cost and environmental impact of the conference world now looks somewhat out of date. One can also question whether they really are as effective in learning or networking as so often claimed. Virtual conferences partly negate the need to spend huge sums of money and lots of time on travel and accommodation, as well as reducing environmental impact.

Large group events, with a variety of social and learning opportunities can be held in virtual worlds, from the big keynote speeches, to small, intimate breakout groups. Virtual conferences can be held on virtual campuses, in digital twin venues or in specially designed conference or event spaces. Your avatar can move around, speak to others, join and leave groups without the physical embarrassment of rising and leaving the room.

New formats could emerge, where you can dip in and out of the conference, get AI recommendations on what may interest you and what to see and do next. Additional resources may appear within events, such as links to books, papers or articles that are mentioned. The group participation could be far superior to the rather stilted Q&As we suffer with roaming microphones. Real experiences can be created where one is learning within another place or world, rather than sitting in rows in a large hotel conference room.

Social events

It is often difficult to get an organization, department or group to feel bonded. Yet social events popped up online during Covid, many of which continued long after that dark shadow passed through the world. Quizzes, get-togethers, Friday socials, book clubs, film clubs, all sorts of social events carried on as they clearly provide a useful function, a sense of community or relatedness. From 'getting to know each other' events to 'quiz' and 'board game' events, keeping people interested and interacting with each other can be a useful goal in itself. You can welcome new people into organizations and groups, as well as reinforce team spirit. Virtual worlds offer even richer communal experiences, with actual avatars and tasks in all sorts of virtual environments and virtual kick-offs for projects, company anniversaries and Christmas parties for remote teams. This is not just about virtual meetings but also to enthuse teams, even the entire organization.

Informal social groups

Informally, groups of practice and learners emerge socially, especially on social media but also in virtual worlds, like VRChat, RecRoom, AltspaceVR, High Fidelity and others. Users demand and build social interaction on the back of other things, such as games or learning. Virtual worlds allow learners to find and socialize with like-minded people and other learners. This is clearly demonstrated on social media, where you as an individual associate with huge numbers of people but then have varying strengths of ties, finding reliable sources, even getting to know strangers really well online. Twitter, for example, has become a valuable source of continuous professional development for many teachers, lecturers and trainers.

How do young people first engage with social VR and what attracts them to such worlds? Maloney et al (2021), in 'Stay connected in an immersive world: Why teenagers engage in social virtual reality', found that a common entry point was YouTube, seeing influencers try VRChat or through friends. The apps were often free or easily found on VR app stores. Games and play are big draws but so were just hanging out and talking to people. Building and creating things were also popular, either their own rooms or games, even just making new friends. Young people certainly connect, socialize and interact in social VR worlds. One should add that there was also some harassment and unpleasantness, as there is in real life.

Social skills

Special educational needs pose particular problems around distraction, social fears and fear of failure. One of my most vivid memories in VR was in Kampala, Uganda, when some school children crowded around to try the headset. At one point, they brought their friend in a wheelchair, who did a virtual bungee jump. His friends knew how this must have felt, how liberating it was for their friend who couldn't walk. VR allows learners to overcome physical problems they have in performing tasks. One can have any body shape one wants in any context, move with ease around virtual environments. Eye tracking now helps with navigation and menu choices.

Being inside a virtual world also gives those with social fears the freedom to do what they may not be capable of doing in the classroom. Social inter-action in a controlled environment, with avatars rather than real people can be ideal for those who are not confident in social settings. This is also true of any cognitive issues learners may have. A virtual world is a safe space to learn, free from peer judgement and potential embarrassment. The opportu-nities for repeated failure mean there is less social pressure on time to competence.

Those with physical, cognitive or social impairments may well benefit from being able to do in mixed or virtual reality what one finds difficult to do in the real world. The metaverse may well be a safe haven for those who find certain real-world contexts taxing, even impossible. It may even provide a safe place to prepare and train oneself to cope with these contexts.

Public speaking

Many are terrified at the very prospect of public speaking. It is a problematic area in terms of personality types and neurodiversity. There has been a flurry of research on the back of technology products that claim to help with public speaking, a social need in some organizational contexts. A meta-analysis of 92 papers on using VR to help reduce anxiety and fears in public speaking confirmed a statistically significant effect on reducing anxiety. They even identified an optimal number and duration of VR training episodes, at around six sessions lasting about 37 minutes. This VR approach proved as statisti-cally effective as other approaches such as CBT (Lim et al, 2022). Reflection and self-evaluation using an avatar of themselves speaking has also proved useful, especially for those who lack confidence (Zhou et al, 2021). The advantages of immersion and training in virtual worlds include being able to practise without fear of embarrassment in front of real audiences and observ-ers. Direct feedback also proved beneficial (Palmas et al, 2021).

Introverts

We should also remember that not everyone has high-level social skills. Most of us have felt socially awkward at some time. Could the metaverse provide a better space for play, activity and work for introverts? Will intro-verts thrive in VR and the metaverse in a way they often do not in real education and workplace environments? Over 20 years of research have shown that introverts often feel more comfortable in online environments than in real-life spaces. They identify their authentic selves on the internet, whereas extroverts tend to see their real selves exhibited in real-world environments (Amichai-Hamburger et al, 2002). As VR environments emerged, similar research replicated this effect in specific ways in virtual worlds. Introverts thrive online when they are encouraged to participate and share their often deep reflections (Callahan, 2021).

Another interesting question is how visually realistic the virtual environments have to be to treat social phobias in VR. When people are presented with three types of avatar, with different levels of human likeness – low, medium and high – anxiety was lowest for the highly realistic avatars. This gives us a guide to the necessity of realism for this particular type of training (Stefanova et al, 2021).

Autism

3D virtual worlds, where one can be someone else but also be yourself, have proven to be a boon for those who may have serious difficulties with social communication in the physical world. Many find opportunities to communicate and even make friends in virtual worlds that they would never have found in the physical world. The use of VR has also been used to study and attempt to support those who need help with speech therapy, social encounters and communication, especially in children with autism spectrum disorder (ASD), ADHD, anxiety and other neurodiverse conditions.

Some people are nervous about being overbearing with 'training' people with autism to be more 'normal' when simple acceptance may be better. Others value help on speech and social interaction. Parents and schools, however, seem to have welcomed VR technology from Floreo when it has well-designed and structured lessons about the real world. Practising crossing a road in VR is safer than doing it in real life. One does not want to practise crossing the road using discovery learning.

These systems have been used by parents, teachers and therapists, with an adult interacting with the young learner from outside the immersive environment with an iPad. They see what the child sees and coach them forward, as well as playing some of the characters. The idea is to capture a lot of everyday experiences in short lessons, and transfer the acquired skills over into the real world.

A study by McCleery et al (2020) looked specifically at the staying power of students in VR, to see if anxiety and sensory overload might limit the use of VR during such lessons, and showed that immersive VR was 'both safe and feasible', with 98 per cent of participants completing, across three 45-minute lessons. Lessons include taking a bus, going to a shop, dealing with other people in a team, going through airport security and simple social interactions in school.

On very specific real-world tasks, like job interviews, virtual reality has been used by adults with ASD to train for job interviews (Smith et al, 2014). Learners instructed using a virtual character in VR reported that they felt it increased their confidence and prepared them for real job interviews.

There are now research protocols (Lee et al, 2022) in place for research into studying metaverse social skills improvement. Real-time biometric data will be gathered to monitor the results. It is difficult to imagine a metaverse in which this avenue is not explored and implemented. There is even emerging evidence that eye tracking in VR can be used to diagnose autism, with a reported success rate of 86 per cent, although this is by no means a settled matter (Alcañiz et al, 2022).

Conclusion

People tend to play, work and live in groups and teams. There are intrinsic skills in dealing with this, often called soft skills, and harder skills around actual teamwork. Intrinsic, social expectations and behaviours are part of our cognitive make-up. The world is social, we are social beings, so learning is almost always social to some degree. It is not that the metaverse could host social learning; it will be a social learning environment where the social will manifest itself in many ways.

Bibliography

Alcañiz, M, Chicchi-Giglioli, I A, Carrasco-Ribelles, L A, Marín-Morales, J, Minissi, M E, Teruel-García, G, Sirera, M and Abad, L (2022) Eye gaze as a biomarker in the recognition of autism spectrum disorder using virtual reality and machine learning: A proof of concept for diagnosis, *Autism Research*, 15 (1), 131–145

Amichai-Hamburger, Y, Wainapel, G and Fox, S (2002) 'On the Internet no one knows I'm an introvert': Extroversion, neuroticism, and Internet interaction, *Cyberpsychology & Behavior*, 5 (2), 125–128

Callahan, K (2021) Valuing and supporting introverted students in the virtual design classroom, *International Journal of Art & Design Education*, 40 (4), 714–722

D'Amour, D, Ferrada-Videla, M, San Martin Rodriguez, L and Beaulieu, M-D (2005) The conceptual basis for interprofessional collaboration: Core concepts and theoretical frameworks, *Journal of Interprofessional Care* 19 (1), 116–131

Fidel, A (2022) Debate at OEB Conference, Berlin

Freeman, G, Acena, D, McNeese, N J and Schulenberg, K (2022) Working together apart through embodiment: Engaging in everyday collaborative activities in social Virtual Reality, *Proceedings of the ACM on Human-Computer Interaction*, 6, 1–25

Lee, J, Lee, T S, Lee, S, Jang, J, Yoo, S, Choi, Y and Park, Y R (2022) Development and application of a metaverse-based social skills training program for children with autism spectrum disorder to improve social interaction: Protocol for a randomized controlled trial, *JMIR research protocols*, 11 (6), 35960

Lim, M H, Aryadoust, V and Esposito, G (2022) A meta-analysis of the effect of virtual reality on reducing public speaking anxiety, *Current Psychology*, 1–17

Locke, J (1690) *An Essay Concerning Humane Understanding*, London, Thomas Basset

Maloney, D, Freeman, G and Robb, A (2021) Stay connected in an immersive world: Why teenagers engage in social virtual reality, *Interaction Design and Children*, 21, 69–79

Mazur, E (1997) *Peer Instruction: A user's manual*, Prentice Hall, Upper Saddle River, NJ

Mazur, E, Teaching: Why an active-learning evangelist is sold on online teaching, Chronicle, 27 May 2021, www.chronicle.com/newsletter/teaching/2021-05-27 (archived at https://perma.cc/HMU3-YM32)

McCleery, J P, Zitter, A, Solórzano, R, Turnacioglu, S, Miller, J S, Ravindran, V and Parish-Morris, J (2020) Safety and feasibility of an immersive virtual reality intervention program for teaching police interaction skills to adolescents and adults with autism, *Autism Research*, 13 (8), 1418–1424

The New York Times, Can virtual reality help autistic children navigate the real world?, 14 June 2022, www.nytimes.com/2022/06/14/business/virtual-reality-autism-children-telehealth-floreo.html (archived at https://perma.cc/T9QV-BLS5)

Palmas, F, Reinelt, R, Cichor, J E, Plecher, D A and Klinker, G (2021) Virtual reality public speaking training: Experimental evaluation of direct feedback technology acceptance, in *2021 IEEE Virtual Reality and 3D User Interfaces (VR)* (pp 463–472), IEEE

Salas, E and Fiore, S M (2004) *Team Cognition: Understanding the factors that drive process and performance*, American Psychological Association

Smith, M J, Ginger, E J, Wright, K, Wright, M A, Taylor, J L, Humm, L B, Olsen, D E, Bell, M D and Fleming, M F (2014) Virtual reality job interview training in adults with autism spectrum disorder, *Journal of Autism and Developmental Disorders*, 44, 2450–2463

Stefanova, M, Pillan, M and Gallace, A (2021) Influence of realistic virtual environments and humanlike avatars on patients with social phobia, in *ASME International Design Engineering Technical Conferences and Computers and Information in Engineering Conference*, Volume 2

Stodd, J (2012) *Exploring the World of Social Learning*, Google Books

Zhou, H, Fujimoto, Y, Kanbara, M and Kato, H (2021) Virtual reality as a reflection technique for public speaking training, *Applied Sciences*, 11 (9), 3988

13

Learning analytics

AR, VR and the multi-user world of the metaverse are computer-generated worlds, so can produce huge amounts of rich data. Within the bounds of privacy, such data can be used to help people learn more efficiently. It is data that can be made available to the learner to help with autonomy, self-awareness and reflection. It can also be made available to teachers and trainers who are helping you learn. More importantly, it can be used to automate the process by which technology can help you learn. It can be used to identify where you are having problems and get you back on track through adaptive and personalized learning. AI data can also start to identify your 'intents' so that when you need to find a solution to the problem you are dealing with, it will hit the target and provide a solution.

The metaverse is not evolving as a technology on its own, it is evolving alongside and with AI technology that demands a data-driven approach to learning. We are no longer in a world where learning analytics are simple course-completion stats around how long it took you to complete a course and your scores. We have moved well beyond simple histograms and pie charts on dashboards. This is a world where data drives action. It is used not only to train the tools we use in AI, but also to guide learners on personalized and adaptive learning journeys, provide detailed feedback to encourage forward momentum, deliver what is needed at the moment it is needed, create content, curate content and assess. This is not surveillance, it is data as the servant of progress in learning.

What the metaverse offers is descriptive data on everything we do in learning, as virtual worlds allow us to 'do' things. It can also analyse that data in real time to accelerate our learning and performance. Beyond this it can be used to predict what we should be learning next, guiding us on our learning journeys. Above all it can, behind the scenes, automate the support we need to learn effectively and optimally.

Although we have five senses, most of what we sense comes from the big three: vision, hearing and touch. Immersion allows detailed data to be gathered about you as a learner, in context; not only what you say and hear but importantly, what you do. We are finally looking at a holistic learning environment that can select a rounded set of data to help you learn.

Healthcare data in virtual worlds

Virtual worlds are data-rich worlds. Your body is a mass of data points. Like a second, virtual self, this biometric data has fuelled a digital health revolution for both consumers and professionals. Healthcare is an ideal area to explore in data and learning analytics, as it is already a data-driven field.

A range of popular consumer devices now monitor our mobility metrics, step length, walking asymmetry, fall detection, access to medical records and sleep routines, routinely designed into digital devices and watches. This feedback loop is a feed-forward learning experience. You adjust your personal behaviour in response to the data. High or low heart rates may also signal underlying problems, irregular rhythm notifications, ECG data, blood oxygen, along with general activity data, to give deeper and deeper insights for you as a user and your physician.

In virtual worlds this extends into whole-body data, where biometric data such as face recognition, head movements, eye movements, hand and arm gestures, body movements and movements through 3D worlds are all possible. This extends the breadth and depth of biometric healthcare data. As we shall see, it is also useful data in experiential learning.

Virtual patients

Virtual patients, represented by software-created avatars or real patients can present to physicians and other health professionals, making the scenarios realistic, allowing for more transfer to actual practice. Patients can present symptoms through voice and gesture.

The software creation of avatar patients can be complex and calibrated from simple to complex sets of medical problems. They can even be selected to represent the specific range of patients one is likely to be working with in your country, local area, hospital or practice. Different age expectancy, frequency of chronic illnesses, even likely genetic profiles can be built into the models. This can make training more targeted, and telescope training down in time, increasing the relevance and time to competence in the training.

Multi-user

Socially, in virtual worlds, learners share spaces with others and communicate, no matter where they are on the planet. While AR and VR allow enhanced learning, metaverse spaces allow multiple learners to communicate, interact with each other, access shared learning content and participate in learning activities. We can see, hear, move and feel ourselves move through environments as well as touch and manipulate objects.

In healthcare, many multi-user learning studies have taken place around that most 3D of entities, the human body. Its structural components, skeletal, as well as internal organs, show symptoms, move, get diseased and age. Patients also present, describe pain with gestures; investigations are often physical with stethoscopes and other techniques, as is training on techniques such as IV therapy or using equipment such as 3D scanners. It is a team environment with lots of interaction with 3D patients' bodies and equipment.

In social care, I was involved in a 3D project that trained care workers how to communicate and interact with senior residents in care homes. Dealing with dementia, being clear with communications, as well as many other patient interactions, were taught within a 3D environment with 3D avatar residents. Dealing with healthcare in actual emergencies, in patients' homes, at road accidents, on the mountain, in emergencies, are all possible with this technology.

Data in learning

A simple way to look at data in virtual worlds is to consider its use in learning. The danger is in assuming that descriptive data is all that is necessary. One can get stuck with an array of static dashboards with doughnuts, pie charts and histograms, say 'job done' and stop there. Dashboards, especially those that present too much descriptive data, can have a stultifying effect. If all you are doing is collecting descriptive data, you are collecting statements of the obvious and it is unlikely to give you many deep insights, other than completion and simple scores. *Descriptive* data is merely the start of the process.

The data schema in Table 13.1 forms a data maturity model that can measure how far an environment has come in using data to drive learning.

What really matters is the *analysis* and use of that data to move learning forward, analysis that provides insights. Insights often come as much from what people do wrong or not at all. The data gathered in the search box will

TABLE 13.1 Data maturity model

Type	Use	Virtual worlds
Descriptive	'What' is happening?	Data from sensors describing body, head, face and eye movements
Analytic	'Why' is it happening?	Insights from behavioural and other data sources
Predictive	What 'should' happen?	Recommended learning pathways
Prescriptive	What 'will' happen?	Automated adaptive and personalized learning experiences

show you more about what people need than menu clicks. Analysis of behavioural data in 3D worlds can tell you a lot about actual performance. All of this requires more and different forms of data. What tends to be gathered in learning is recall of simple knowledge; even then most of that is likely to be quickly forgotten. The really useful data about actual performance remains unharvested.

Beyond analysing data, one must look towards using that analysis to *predict* learning pathways, remedial pathways and resequencing of learning to help the learner overcome difficulties to acquire knowledge and skills.

Beyond prediction is *prescription,* where one automates the sequencing or spaced practice to improve the learning process. Learning is a process not an event and that process can, to a degree, be automated.

The first step is to gather more useful *descriptive* data: informal and formal, offline and online, knowledge and skills. Secondly, *analyse* that data to release useful insights. Thirdly, use that data to look forward and *predict* to sustain and accelerate progress. Lastly, use that data to *prescribe* or automate as much as possible, so that learning can be more accessible, faster, cheaper and better.

Metaverse and xAPI

SCORM has been the *de facto* standard in online learning for over 20 years. You can play SCORM packaged content on almost any learning management system. It is a rather limited standard in learning with its narrow focus on starting, completion, tracking time to completion and a single score. Frustration led to lots of hacks to increase its functionality but, as learning was increasingly seen as a process, not an event, it became a data bottleneck. It was like measuring your health by simply taking your pulse.

Experience API (xAPI), its replacement data standard, takes much more into account. Learning happens constantly, both formally and informally, offline and online, knowing and doing, and if you want to track, quantify and share what people have done and achieved, you need to look at their learning in a much wider perspective. xAPI looks at learning holistically over the long term, both offline and online. Multiple test results and scores, games, simulations; adaptive, informal learning, blended learning and real-world performance are all possible. You can also track individuals, teams or groups. This makes it particularly suited to performance and the ability to track this in performance environments, with experiential learning in real, mixed and virtual environments.

xAPI is conceptually simple and can be described as a piece of data that says 'I did this', a subject, verb and object. This format can be used to record almost any learning activity. So it can capture everything from 'Peter watched a video on generative AI' to 'Peter used generative AI tool x', right through to 'Peter successfully used generative AI tool x to do y.'

It frees data from the constraints of the LMS world and is device independent. Data can be harvested from mobile apps, websites, micro-learning, courses, as well as virtual and actual on-the-job performance data from the metaverse or business systems.

This *descriptive* data can be very fine grained down to learner data on tabs chosen, clicks, hovers, duration on a slide, question or course. On formative or summative assessment, you get not just the final score but also items chosen, distractors chosen, whether the user jumped out to find the answer to a question. Media types are also tracked, such as video, audio, images, text, self-paced online learning. With video, for example, was it muted, paused, rewound, played at x1.5 or x2 speed? You can also track data with negative outcomes, such as, did learners just click through the course without time for reading and understanding or do the wrong thing in the 3D simulation? At what point did people skip out of the video, podcast or simulation? Where did they go in the 3D environment, who did they interact with, what did they actually do?

The data then needs to be sent to a learning record store (LRS). This allows you to *analyse* your xAPI data. For example, consistently wrong answers or actions can be identified and diagnosed as either poor questions, points that need more explanation, or poorly defined actions. One can remove obstacles where people get confused or stuck and get rid of superfluous content. If the data shows that people are not spending enough time on a page or doing an action, then edit it down or redefine the tasks. Taking this a step further, A/B or split testing can also take advantage of xAPI to compare different learning interventions against actual performance in a virtual-world simulation or on the real job. The whole design of a course or learning experience can therefore be optimized for completion and competence.

You can measure not only how people did on their learning experiences but also on the job. How many took the short course? Did the people who watched the videos or took the branched simulation do better on the job than those who did not? This allows you to analyse by correlating between completed learning and actual performance data, say sales training correlated to actual sales.

On another level, xAPI data can also be used to *predict* what should happen next. What content in the learning experience should come next to personalize and optimize that experience for that particular learner? Everyone can then be educated uniquely towards competence, as the learning is tailored to the needs of every individual, with no one getting stuck or unable to close that necessary gap in learning that competence requires.

Events can also be *prescribed* or automated, so that your different learning pathways can be optimized as you move through your learning experience. This is increasingly using AI techniques, trained on data but also using new data to optimize such pathways. It can take you on a learning journey where the invisible hand of AI determines your learning path.

Importantly for mixed reality and the metaverse, you no longer need a learning management system. You can collect xAPI data from anything: a virtual environment, real environment, even real entities such as a machine or vehicle. You can collect data from lots of different learning or business platforms. All activity by a person or group of learners can then be brought together.

Smartphone sensors, such as compasses, gyroscopes and geolocation, provided a lot more data about user behaviour but little was used in learning analytics. With immersive learning, sensors are there to measure biometrics from head, heart and hands. It is a rich data environment where eye tracking, gesture tracking, movement through 3D spaces and interactions can be captured using xAPI as 'people thinking, feeling and doing' things. Spatial data can be descriptive about what happened in what context, analysis can determine why it happened and what we can learn from this. From eye tracking and user behaviour, analysis can reveal insights. Precise recording of steps and actions taken can be used to interpret intentions and behaviours.

This is real people doing real things in virtual environments, giving us real insights into intention and behaviour within precise contexts. Spatial data fuels learning analytics as it is rooted in behaviours and performance.

Also, if the goal of learning is to improve performance, *transfer* must take place. The need for transfer has been studied for a century and the criteria for success identified. Behavioural data within 3D worlds can measure actual performance, from fine-tuned motor skills in surgery to sports performance. Any skills that manifest themselves in physical movement can be measured. Beyond this, behaviour in soft-skills and management training, where eye movement and contact and body language are relevant, can be measured in precise detail. Then add the spoken word and language learning comes into play. Performance can not only be learnt but consistently assessed in defined contexts.

Eye tracking

One set of incredibly useful biometric data comes from your eyes. Eye tracking has been used in product development and marketing for some time. Large data sets allow heat maps and look-throughs to be created that show where attention is focused. These same tools can be used in training, where eye-tracking data can identify critical decision making, skills and situational awareness in critical jobs.

The traditional method in training is to do a critical-task analysis by interviewing subject-matter experts and practitioners, then collating that evidence to produce a critical set of steps. You then rank the steps in degrees of criticality, to put more focus on those where a training intervention or performance support will have the most impact. The problem with this is that it is long-winded and experts, even practitioners, often forget what they do as the process has become tacit or automatic for them.

Eye-tracked data objectifies judgement, as it avoids fallible verbal recall by instructors or learners from memory. It records, in detail, actual behaviour, whether in real life or in virtual simulations or worlds. Such data can capture expert behaviour then allow you to put yourself in the head and eyes of the expert. Eye data can also be used in conjunction with hand-movement data, in surgery or other hand-controlled systems. It can then be used to train and assess novices.

Identifying optimal assembly procedures through a critical-task analysis can have a huge impact on productivity. There can be wide variance in employee productivity, and standardized optimal processes and procedures can be identified, taught and assessed using eye-tracking data. Maintenance of equipment is literally about keeping an eye on things, and good training can keep equipment running to minimize downtime and extend the lifetime of expensive equipment. Safety is another topic, whether it is spotting safety hazards, formal safety inspections or solving problems when they happen. Eye tracking can prevent accidents, even save lives. Lowering defect rates in products from the factory floor is also big business and inspection skills can be taught to speed up time to competence on accuracy, consistency and better rates of fault detection.

Experts develop skills over time that they perform automatically. Novices can acquire these skills faster if they know precisely what experts do, can see things through their eyes or get corrective feedback to shift them towards expert performance. Eye tracking with instruction from experts is a powerful tool in the acquisition of these situational skills. The military often do after-action reviews (AARs) and recording sessions for review can be a useful training tool for pilots in cockpits, teachers in classrooms, presenters at conferences, surgeons when operating, maintenance engineers, all to improve performance.

With behavioural data, you can standardize a wide variety of operational procedures and processes. You can then both measure and assess performance to identify cognitive overload, unpack critical decision making and above all accelerate training and assessment. This is not to say that quantified behavioural data is the only data you need. There is almost always a need for other qualitative data from learners and experts.

Data, in general, unlocks the power of learning experiences for learners and those who deliver learning experiences. Having an agreed data format, xAPI, allows learning data to be used to improve, confirm and prove impact. It puts everyone on the same page as it allows data to be gathered from many different sources, on many different activities, in a rich, relevant and useable format. Mixed reality and the metaverse will provide far more data that is far more meaningful, giving far more insights, working faster towards improved performance.

Eye tracking has the potential to take VR to another level in terms of teaching and learning. It uses small, high-quality cameras in immersive devices such as glasses, AR and VR headsets. As it is now available in consumer devices, it can be used in learning.

There are some technical improvements that eye tracking makes possible, such as reducing the processing power needed as one can focus higher levels of fidelity on areas you are looking at, aligning lenses to the distance between your eyes for comfort and less eye-strain. Iris scanning could increase security, allowing one headset to have many users. The ability to interact, read faces and emotions, it is all in the eyes.

Interface design

Interface design usability commonly uses eye tracking, an early example being Nielsen (2006) on search and browsing, where the identification of scanning by the eyes formed distinct triangular and F-shaped patterns. This is, of course, very useful in the design of virtual learning experiences, where one wants to make interfaces as frictionless as possible to reduce cognitive load.

You can track exactly what the teacher or learner is looking at in real time within the 3D virtual environment. The two important types of eye movement are *fixations* (pausing still on something) and *saccades* (movements between fixations). Frequency of fixations, distances and the speed of saccades can all be measured. This is becoming a very exact, quantifiable science. Eye gesturing can therefore also be used for natural navigation and menu selection.

Teaching

Take one skill: teaching. Non-verbal communication, such as eye contact and communication, is a powerful tool. Yet eye contact is not always fully understood, practised, learnt or assessed in teaching. To look is one thing; to give a look is quite another. There is a big difference between a commanding look that demands immediate compliance from a learner, and glances around the room requesting attention.

Being in the class before learners arrive, looking at each in turn, making them feel welcome is good practice. Teaching itself requires rapport and looking at learners to hold their attention, not looking at the book, laptop, board or floor. The eyes are a part of instruction and can be used to ask, affirm, approve or disapprove. Watching student behaviour to see if they are on task, confused, lost, bored or distracted is also useful. It is enough to say that there are many ways in which eye contact can be used with a group, even an individual learner.

VR can be used to test teacher skills (Seidel et al, 2021), improve those skills, as well as to assess student(s)-teacher engagement (Haataja et al,

2021; Goldberg et al, 2021). Eye tracking can, to a degree, track all of this, providing data to a teacher or teacher trainer while being trained. This is invaluable feedback that can give teachers useful practice before entering the real or virtual classroom with real learners.

Learning

Learning itself can be tracked: time on/off task, focus, time note taking, tiredness and, in particular, the identification of cognitive load expressed by eye movement. With reading, eye tracking can track the way text is being read, and precise places in the text where the reader is having difficulties.

Within a learning experience, eye tracking can also be used as a data source for adaptive, personalized learning, to help re-sequence content, provide remedial help or decide on learning pathways. Tracking a student's eyes could be used to keep them on track or on course, by increasing levels of guidance within an adaptive learning environment. Piotrowski and Nowosielski (2020) have looked at this very idea based on diagnosing students' skills levels through the trajectory of gaze in an immersive environment. The use of visual, aural or haptic signalling can all be tested by analysing the eye tracking data. A/B testing and design improvements are then possible.

Eye tracking has also been used with medical students to improve their diagnostic skills (Litchfield et al, 2010). It has long been used to accelerate medical students' skills from novice to expert, especially when they are made aware of the data. Scanning trajectories can also identify situational awareness of an environment.

There is also the identification of negative behavioural traits such as peer pressure, forms of distraction, anxiety, potential problems, even dyslexia. Cheating in exams is another area of application, especially in virtual proctoring. Pupil diameter has also been suggested as diagnostic data, as it can be diagnostic of emotion (Zheng et al, 2020).

It is not that eye contact and eye tracking are isolated skills. They are intimately tied up with other presentation, management and teaching methods, such as head pose, gestures and body movements (Ballenghein et al, 2020). Tracking fingers in surgery or medical examinations is one example but any task that requires fine-tuned hand movements can benefit from a more holistic look at the learning experience and data collection.

Overall, we can see that educational research on the use of eye tracking is maturing (see Rappa et al, 2022; Gorbunovs, 2021) and a consideration of engagement and student-teacher interaction in Kaakinen, 2021.

Hearing

After sight, and therefore the importance of eye tracking, we also have hearing, what is said in virtual worlds. This has come of age on the internet with video, podcasts and audio-driven personal assistants. The metaverse will undoubtedly be a place where audio is normal. We will speak to each other in all sorts of contexts.

Speech-to-text now allows us to use what is said in a learning context to drive further learning. We can record what was said descriptively, analyse semantically what was said to see whether the learner's answers are correct, in terms of content and sentiment (through sentiment analysis) and use audio as a trigger for learning events.

Presentation skills can be taught as what is said can be tracked as well as how it is said, speed of delivery, intonation and so on. AI can then be used to suggest improvements on presentation performance.

Your abilities as an interviewer or interviewee in job interviews or appraisals can be measured, as can dealing with patients and customers, anything that involves human interaction.

All sorts of verbal behaviours can then be tracked and used in learning. This also opens up the possibility of using speech-prompted generative AI chatbots to help you get through learning experiences.

Haptics

Another source of data in VR and the metaverse centres on our sense of touch – haptic data. You will receive data that makes it seem as though you feel objects – their shape, forces, vibrations, movements – or others touching you.

Technology has already delivered some of this through the haptic design of objects such as computer keyboards, finely tuned to allow you to feel a key press, or touchscreens on computers and smartphones that give you fingertip control of the devices. Your smartphone can vibrate but it is the subtle vibrations and haptic engineering on keyboards and trackpads that don't move but feel as if they do, that have made haptics a feature of a lot of consumer technology. Feedback has also been built into devices such as joysticks, seats and suits for game players. Your watch may even vibrate when you receive calls.

In virtual environments, this is an area of intense development with several types of feedback technology driven by the games industry and, in part, by the need to enable those with physical disabilities.

The commonest type of haptic feedback is vibrotactile, which stimulates the receptors we have on our skin, which are especially concentrated in certain areas, such as our fingertips. A vibrostimulatir literally presses down on these receptors to create a sense of touch.

There are also mechanical-force feedback techniques that use the mechanical nature of movement to mimic or stimulate what our hands and arms do. The dynamics of resistive and active forces make you feel things. Mechanical resistance puts the brakes on your movement to make you feel force, whereas active devices restrict movement using motors. It can all seem a little clumsy.

A fascinating, and at first surprising, form of feedback is electrotactile, as it requires the application of electrical signals for its effect. Yet our nervous system is largely this, a body-wide system that transmits electrical signals to and from the brain and it dispenses with the need for crude mechanical devices. It is here that the long-term integration of the real body into virtual environments may bear most fruit.

Ultrasonic feedback uses high-frequency sound to create the illusion of touch, where several emitters are used. Together they create invisible, tangible interfaces in the air. Ultrasound waves from arrays of emitters generate turbulence, which humans can feel through the skin. You don't have to wear anything but the effects can be sub-optimal.

There is also the thermoelectric effect that uses electrically generated heat but this is imprecise and energy hungry.

All sorts of devices from the simple fingertip devices to full body suits have been and continue to be developed with huge numbers of patents being lodged. We have the controllers that come with VR headsets but there are all sorts of wonderful devices out there, such as gloves, vests and suits. There are even mouth haptics, which stimulate your lips, teeth, tongue or jaw!

Haptics in learning

Haptic feedback for a learner has to be appropriate for the learning experiences and outcomes. In the case of flight or vehicle simulators this has to be multifaceted and complex. For some simple tasks it may require a very specific feeling of resistance or application, when, for example, using a tool.

For many other learning tasks, it may not be necessary at all, such as soft skills. It is haptic horses for courses.

In terms of learning effectiveness, haptics are important as they enhance the immersive experience. If you really are learning by doing, then doing is likely to require not just sight and sound but also touch. It can contribute significantly to the transfer of a skill, say speed or lower error rates.

Haptic feedback is useful, for example, when physicians use touch to feel for abnormalities beneath the skin or do a physical examination of an avatar patient. But haptics come into their own in surgery, for feeling resistance and in laparoscopic surgery where you have to rely on sight to perform procedures. With haptic effects, you can feel the grab, the nature of the tissues (Tholey et al, 2005). Dental-implant training has also benefited from feeling the bone resistance when placing the implants (Wang et al, 2022).

On a physical task, like loading parcels optimally onto a truck or spray-painting a vehicle, you will want the user to feel the parcels and the recoil of the spray gun. In the manipulation of objects, such as maintenance and repair, feeling the resistance of tools and parts is essential. Training is also expensive; using haptic gloves for this type of training is therefore useful, as electrical and computer equipment is expensive to install and maintain.

The data from haptic devices again adds to the rich data sets that can be used to monitor, help and assess learning, especially in learning by doing. This matters as performance has in the past been poorly measured, assessed and evaluated. We rarely do much more in online learning than shoot out a few multiple-choice questions. We have the opportunity to allow learners to show that they can do things, rather than just recite the theory behind doing those things.

Conclusion

Learning analytics can be free from their usual constraints when we move from the classroom to virtual worlds. Things such as what the learner is looking at, what they are saying and what they are doing suddenly become measurable. Eye tracking, along with other data, is now a part of the learning technology toolkit, used to help design interfaces and improve the efficacy of teaching, learning and assessment. It is also likely to unlock all sorts of uses and applications in learning, some still unimagined. Hearing will also be relevant in any training task that requires the spoken word.

Haptics are now starting to provide detailed learning data that allows us to measure actual transfer. When you are asked to go through a learning experience where you have to perform the actual tasks, assessment may even be seen as a by-product of completion. VR and the metaverse may open up data and learning analytics to truly measure learning.

Bibliography

Ballenghein, U, Kaakinen, J K, Tissier, G and Baccino, T (2020) Cognitive engagement during reading on digital tablet: Evidence from concurrent recordings of postural and eye movements, *Quarterly Journal of Experimental Psychology*, 73, 1820–1829

Goldberg, P, Sümer, Ö, Stürmer, K, Wagner, W, Göllner, R, Gerjets, P et al (2021) Attentive or not? Toward a machine learning approach to assessing students' visible engagement in classroom instruction, *Educational Psychology Review*, 33, 27–49

Gorbunovs, A (2021) The review on eye-tracking technology application in digital learning environments, *Baltic Journal of Modern Computing*, 9, 1–24, doi: 10.22364/bjmc.2021.9.1.01 (archived at https://perma.cc/V94P-S7HH)

Haataja, E, Salonen, V, Laine, A, Toivanen, M and Hannula, M S (2021) The relation between teacher-student eye contact and teachers' interpersonal behavior during group work: A multiple-person gaze-tracking case study in secondary mathematics education, *Educational Psychology Review*, 33, 51–67

Kaakinen, J K (2021) What can eye movements tell us about visual perception processes in classroom contexts? Commentary on a special issue, *Educational Psychology Review*, 33, 169–179

Litchfield, D, Ball, L J, Donovan, T, Manning, D J and Crawford, T (2010) Viewing another person's eye movements improves identification of pulmonary nodules in chest x-ray inspection, *Journal of Experimental Psychology: Applied*, 16, 251–262

Nielsen, J (2006) F-shaped pattern for reading web content (original study), www.nngroup.com/articles/f-shaped-patternreading-web-content-discovered/ (archived at https://perma.cc/R5GU-2SUR)

Piotrowski, P and Nowosielski, A (2020) Gaze-based interaction for VR environments, in M Choraś and R Choraś (eds) *Image Processing and Communications, Advances in Intelligent Systems and Computing*, Springer, Cham

Rappa, N A, Ledger, S, Teo, T, Wai Wong, K, Power, B, and Hilliard, B (2022) The use of eye-tracking technology to explore learning and performance within virtual reality and mixed reality settings: A scoping review, *Interactive Learning Environments*, 30 (7), 1338–1350.

Seidel, T, Schnitzler, K, Kosel, C, Stürmer, K and Holzberger, D (2021) Student characteristics in the eyes of teachers: Differences between novice and expert teachers in judgment accuracy, observed behavioral cues, and gaze, *Educational Psychology Review*, 33, 69–89

Tholey, G, Desai, J P and Castellanos, AE (2005) Force feedback plays a significant role in minimally invasive surgery: Results and analysis, *Annals of Surgery*, 241 (1), 102

Wang, X, Shujaat, S, Shaheen, E and Jacobs, R (2022) Quality and haptic feedback of three-dimensionally printed models for simulating dental implant surgery, *Journal of Prosthetic Dentistry*

Zheng, L J, Mountstephens, J and Teo, J (2020) Comparing eye-tracking versus EEG features for four-class emotion classification in VR predictive analytics, *International Journal of Advanced Science and Technology*, 29, 1492–1497

PART FOUR

Metafutures

14

Artificial intelligence

Artificial intelligence is a much more profound shift in our relationship with all media but also with knowledge and learning.

For most of our history as a species, knowledge and learning were oral stories, cave paintings and simple 3D artifacts. Then, around 5,000 years ago, the big bang of writing generated an explosion of knowledge production. Even then our relationship to that knowledge was slight, as it remained in the hands of those who ruled, while the vast majority remained illiterate. For thousands of years, papyrus, paper and vellum remained expensive; reproduction a laborious task, executed by skilled scribes. It was printing that amplified text and took knowledge and learning to the masses in their vernacular languages through that most portable of media, books.

Another shift that brought our relationship with knowledge and skills closer was the second big bang that was the internet, where digital knowledge and learning became multimodal through multimedia. Text was available through Wikipedia, newspapers, articles and books online; audio through podcasts and music; video through YouTube; and 3D worlds through Google Earth and Maps.

The real pedagogic difference, however, was 'search' – not content, but easy access to content. Google, Google Scholar and other different forms of search for videos on YouTube, a different form of search, was the real pedagogic means to the end. 'Hyperlinks' also allowed us to leap across and drill down into knowledge. Search continues to be developed through semantic search, which promises to be more pedagogically precise.

This closer relationship with knowledge and learning was also amplified through our online relationships. We suddenly had ties to more than just our close friends, relations and work colleagues. We could communicate and share knowledge with anyone online, almost anywhere at any time through posts, re-posts, comments and messages and see knowledge and learning as accessible from others. This extended the breadth and depth of our knowledge and learning. The full story of this technological development is told in *Learning Technology* (Clark, 2023).

pedAIgogy

An entirely different form of dialogue surprised consumers in November 2022, with ChatGPT famously beating all records for adoption. A fiendishly simple interface, a bit like 'search', it draws on something approaching the sum of human stored knowledge. It is also a bit like 'social dialogue' as it has been trained by data that came from us. Its output is a social construction.

It is also multimedia, as, in addition to text, these large language models generate images, voice, music and video. It also helps create 3D objects, avatars and worlds. Multimodal generative AI reads, comments and generates content from and to all media types. Our relationship with knowledge and learning has suddenly changed. That change is profound.

No longer in a world with just teachers and learners, we are now in a world of human teachers and human learners but also technology that teaches and technology that learns. We can now use AI to learn and learn from it. We can also use it to teach by using it and it can also teach us.

This is a big bang with a difference as it is the dynamic creation of knowledge, in real time, in created and co-created dialogue. We are no longer using technology to simply find knowledge and learn. We have gone through a sudden shift to find, create, change, organize, synthesize, even evaluate knowledge and learning with technology. This is a new form of pedagogy, let us call it 'pedAIgogy'. We are co-creators, not just of text but in all media; multimedia creators.

We have only just begun to realize that we no longer keep knowledge and learning at a distance but engage with it by embracing dialogue. Socrates and Plato were rightly suspicious of writing and in *Phaedrus*, Plato cautions us about being too dependent on a technology as simple as writing. Rather than being an effective form of knowledge and medium for learning, it may have the opposite educational effect from that intended, as it creates a sense that something is learnt but actually results in forgetfulness. He warns us that writing may be the enemy of memory, as one is not generating from one's own mind and using real critical thinking but being reliant on the already-written text.

If we return to a core Socratic relationship with knowledge, new forms of co-created literature, images, audio, video and 3D entities will emerge; new knowledge, new research, new art, new worlds, new forms of teaching, new forms of learning. We have crossed a generative Rubicon and there is no going back. Neither should we want to, as this technology captures all of our thoughts. It is us. It reflects the many not the few, the hive mind, the supermind.

There are dangers, but scarcity in knowledge or learning was never a virtue. In many ways it is not a little knowledge that is a dangerous thing but too much of one thing. Perhaps we have been drowning in a sea of text in education, learning, research and work for too long.

Have we been under the yoke of text-heavy institutions for too long, with scarce, expensive courses, plunging many into debt, in some cases for a lifetime? We have extended periods of learning so far that our current model is 20 solid years of reading and writing text. Yet those most in need of education still seem furthest from it and despite serious practical skills shortages, vocational learning has been demoted and in some places, decimated.

Most people want a 'working knowledge' of things they want to do, not over-engineered, PowerPoint-led, abstract courses. This new era of 'pedAIgogy' may herald a more dynamic way of formal teaching and learning.

It may also swing us quickly toward performance support in the work-place, where the technology responds to needs; more focus on dynamic, personalized and contextualized learning: a demand-driven, not supply-driven model.

There is a sense in which all content has been 2D: as text and mathematics as symbolic information on the flat page, photography, painting, television and cinema on flat screens. Suddenly AI was creating these different media and we were no longer centre-stage, not that we had been since Copernicus and Darwin. Many, however, still thought we were at the centre of the universe, deluded for millennia in our own imagined religious and little, fictional metaverses, as consciousnesses invented stories about other worlds, without any evidence that they actually existed.

It turned out that these heavens could be generated on earth and that what we had could create our own augmentations to consciousness, using AI and 3D worlds. This shift has been well documented by Mike Pell in *The Age of Smart Information: How artificial intelligence and spatial computing will transform the way we communicate forever* (2019). For Pell, the world is being altered by two forces; one invisible, the other visible: AI and 3D virtual worlds. These are two different dimensions; one the world of mathematics, the other of the metaverse. Yet they are related. It is no accident that they have arisen in parallel. The same advances in technology, driven by consumer demand, such as chipsets and advances in software, are pushing us ever nearer to the metaverse.

In this new 'pedAIgogy', technology is our partner, with whom we engage in dialogue, not as a tool or instrument but to co-teach, co-learn and co-create.

AI and 3D

AI and the metaverse

Alan Turing developed a chess-playing algorithm before there was even a computer to run it on. AI has since become a common tool, used in many areas of human endeavour – interfaces, assistive software, search, filtering harmful content, catching spam, security and now learning.

The first AI success in 3D worlds, common in gaming, was to move software avatars from one place to another or change non-player avatar behaviours. Another was to get software to build worlds that generate themselves or build on command. We have seen generative AI create text, as well as fantastic graphics from simple prompts. It seems perfectly feasible to have text-prompted builders, even users, do the same within the metaverse. GANs (generative adversarial networks) have been successful in creating deepfakes but they can also be used to generate avatars. AI will eventually generate worlds, avatars and objects from text prompts, from both professional designers and users. Open worlds could then become much larger, designed by AI then auto-generated by AI.

AI will therefore make virtual worlds, design software avatars within those worlds, decide on the behaviour of these avatars and provide generative scale. This will carry through to learning, where engagement, support, content creation, feedback, learning pathways and assessment will all be driven, in part, by AI. AI will be one of the chief architects of the metaverse.

Generative AI and the metaverse

It used to be the case that learning content was always a trade-off between cost, quality and speed. Generative AI has blown this model apart with ultra-fast speed along with ultra-low costs and the quality is rising fast. Text and images that took hours, days and weeks in the past, can now be done in seconds. This displacement of expertise by technology is moving tremendously fast and surprising even those who work in AI.

Generative AI hit the world with text generation from GPT, then ChatGPT and image generation from DALL-E. Suddenly, credible text and images could be generated from text prompts. ChatGPT then became global, at a million users in five days, 100 million users in two months and now hundreds of millions of users. It was not just the speed and quality that impressed but the flexibility of generative AI. When used dynamically, it can create new stuff, quickly, even on the fly. Beyond speed, it can also create any number of prompted or triggered styles and variations, such as speak to me in the style of a famous person or for an eight-year-old. For 2D media such as text and images, you can also ask (prompt) the system to write text or create an image in a specific 'style'. It spawned a massive amount of imaginative, innovative and creative uses after launch.

What got less attention, but were just as important, were a whole range of generative tools where we also had the creation of 3D objects and worlds. The 3D world generated by AI can be as flexible as you want, certainly as flexible as the real world, even more flexible, as it is a created environment. This is a massively disruptive technology in the field of content creation, especially in learning.

Generative AI, in many forms, first generated text, images, audio and 3D content but it still had the problem of common sense, context, efficiency, updatability, accuracy and provenance. These are not easy problems to solve. Things that seem hard are often easy in AI and the easy problems hard. Common sense and context are hard problems and will take a considerable amount of time, even alternative approaches to AI, to solve. Efficiency is a compute problem, as the tech needs eye-watering amounts of energy. Interestingly, only five days after the launch of ChatGPT on 30 November 2022, we lit the fuse on fusion, with a breakthrough that makes the commercial application of fusion to the energy problem much more certain. Updatability can be solved by faster releases through faster training of the models by both data and humans. Accuracy and provenance will come with larger numbers of parameters and the use of ensembles of AI tools that work in tandem and can communicate with each other. Breakthroughs may even come from areas other than large language models, such as pure, symbolic AI. It is clear that progress on a number of fronts is certain.

In learning, AI can give answers, define structure, write text, write in any style, add links to other content, create 2D and 3D graphics, define and deliver spaced practice patterns, personalize, notify and create formative and summative assessments, as well as generate support, content and assessments (Clark, 2020). This will radically reduce the cost of learning content design, in some tasks to almost zero. One problem is that generative AI confuses educators, who see it as equivalent to search or Wikipedia. It is a radically different 'generative' technology. That is why it is so potent: it does what we do, only much, much quicker. Like us, it is fallible, which is why the idea that humans are always needed in the loop is not quite certain; that is one fallible system checking another. We more likely need other forms of AI to check content, so that accuracy and provenance are improved. In fact, generative text systems, such as ChatGPT, are already speaking to other systems that provide different functions, such as mathematical solutions, context and accuracy. They will improve with more efficiency, updatability and provenance.

Generating the metaverse

For VR and the metaverse, generative AI has hit almost every media type, from avatars and their voices and behaviours, to full 3D objects and worlds.

Generative AI also drives chatbot technology through language models. Replica and Anima are already in the business of creating friends. This has developed into character creation, where avatars with defined purposes, such as friends and various forms of assistants, are available. This will also move quickly onto tutors, teachers, trainers, instructors, experts, mentors, coaches, who will provide help on any imaginable subject. The pedAIgogic features of these avatar chatbots will include their specific educational purposes, such as subject expertise, age appropriateness, cultural sensitivity, and will be endlessly helpful and patient, available in hundreds of languages, 24 hours a day. They will also be personalized.

These teaching avatars will produce real speech as dialogue, in many languages, on the fly, avoiding the trap of fixed and expensive pre-recorded audio. Role-playing with specific characters then becomes possible, as, in addition to teachers, trainers, experts, mentors and coaches, they will speak as real employees, customers or patients do in the real world, for training. Adaptive music and sound effects will also be possible, created in real time to match the purpose and mood of a situation.

Generative AI in 3D worlds has largely been the domain of computer games with their huge budgets, built over several years with hundreds of characters in vast 3D environments, and there are hundreds of such games. AI is now fundamental to the creation of 3D worlds and components within that world. But this is exactly the technology that will be used to build the metaverse.

And in learning, those who harness abundance and use it wisely will become the scarce resource. *Learning Experience Design* (Clark, 2022) explains how learning designers need to reskill to cope with emerging technology. Rather than producing learning 'events', they have to see learning as a process; even their design of content will be dominated by tools that create media for them. They will have to become familiar with the new technologies of AI, mixed reality and the metaverse. The new pedAIgogy will require knowledge not only of how these technologies work, along with the new design opportunities they provide, but how to design to their strengths and weaknesses, and manage expectations.

This progress in AI is unlikely to abate. It is moving so fast it is difficult to keep up with the releases, not just the number of published academic papers, which is growing exponentially, but the release of functional product. The research and development spend is enormous as AI is producing tangible results with real impact. That impact is saving huge amounts of time and money. The generation of text, images, media, objects, places and intelligence is now orders of magnitude quicker and cheaper. Being able to generate high-quality assets quickly and cheaply allows the designer to explore more sophisticated solutions with more focus on learning as a process, and to explore more sophisticated solutions.

AI will cover the whole gamut of tasks for creating the metaverse: coding, the generation of 3D assets, textures, animation, speech, sound effects and recommendation-led experiences. In learning, learning experiences can be created within the easy-to-produce context of your own shop, hospital, building or workplace. Digital Twins will be quick to produce, allowing everything from onboarding to management skills to be delivered in a replica of your organization, not generic context. Ultimately, the metaverse will be possible because 3D worlds generated at scale will be possible as generative AI techniques will do much of the heavy lifting.

Generative AI, software that generates, creates and co-creates content, like the games industry, may turn out to be many times larger than current streaming or Hollywood. Film and TV production has already been boosted by CGI and advanced animation. Generative AI is a far wider and more productive technology that promises to be much more disruptive. Every aspect of media production will be affected: plots, scripting, storyboarding, direction, avatar actors, props, music and sets. It may allow creativity to break free of the larger institutions, as the creation of art or learning experiences will not be hidebound by skills, tools and cost.

With the metaverse, we will see something quite different, a social shift, where we as a species will reshape, augment and transcend what it is to be conscious and have minds. We will transcend our evolutionary past. We will become 'meta' in several senses.

This will also be true of learning experiences, where new, unimagined forms of accelerated learning will be built. New types of entertainment and learning experiences will emerge as innovators thrive on the new opportunities offered by AI and pedAIgogy.

Artificial intelligence

AI will drive the metaverse. Generative AI already creates meaningful media and has moved into the creation of 3D moving images such as video, as well as 3D entities and worlds. AI is also jumping forward in several areas that promise to accelerate learning in the metaverse. This is an irreversible trend.

AI interfaces

First, AI has also transformed interfaces. It has for many years delivered voice from text, as well as voice to text, enabling voice to be used with personal assistants, in the home, car or on smartphones. This is also useful in virtual worlds where voice is the easiest and most natural way to communicate with others. The metaverse may be a return to a more natural form of communication through voice and dialogue. In learning, this can be from real teachers, tutors or trainers on one side, or learners and peer learners on the other. This is the method of communication that has been used for millennia in teaching. The rise of voice, in podcasts and services such as Discord, also suggests that it will be the medium of choice within VR and the metaverse, as avatars will speak to each other.

The point, as Donald Norman, the design and interface guru, points out, is to make the 'technology' as invisible as possible. This is especially true in learning where the mechanics of the process of learning can waste cognitive effort, or worse, cause cognitive overload; time and effort that would be better spent attending to the process of learning. The addition of eye and face tracking also makes interfaces more invisible, as do sensors that track hand and other body movements.

Interfaces can also be personalized by AI adaptive learning techniques and recommendation engines (Clark, 2020). Adaptive learning ecosystems will emerge, driven by AI, to automatically construct dynamic learning pathways, monitored and visualized in real time across the learning space, the hidden hand behind the learning journeys taken by different learners, depending on their performance.

When either invasive or non-invasive brain-computer interfaces are fully developed, and all involve the decoding and interpretation of signals using AI, navigation and actions within the metaverse will also be made easier and more natural. It will, in a sense, replicate what we do in real life when we move around in the real 3D world, anticipate and decide where we want to go, being truly seamless.

AI places

AI will also help create virtual places from text descriptions, both creatively in look and feel but also digitally in form and physics. This is exactly how Google is transforming Google Maps with billions of images, used as data, to produce seamless worlds through which we can move. The generation of new worlds takes skill and time using expensive tools. But 3D worlds have long been created on the fly in game worlds. Increasingly, these tools are using AI to automate tasks such as lighting, sound levels and physics, so AI is already a designer of 3D spaces, places and worlds.

For learning, you will be able to build digital twins of any existing educational environment, such as a school, university, laboratory or training centre. Cultural places such as museums, art galleries and new forms of interactive learning environments will also be created using AI.

Real-world training environments will also be possible – hospitals, airports, factories and so on – to re-create environments that best match the learning to increase retention and transfer. It is important that these are relatively quick and cheap to build, and that means automating the process.

One of the surprising successes in AI has been its ability to generate content from text. Type in a description of what you want and it creates the text, image or video you have asked for. This has huge implications for learning, both positive and negative. These transformers were then adapted to create images, the most famous being DALL-E (OpenAI), also Stable Diffusion (Stability.ai) and Midjourney. Deep learning proved to be highly productive on the classification and creation of 2D images.

The search for similar success with 3D, constructing a 3D object or scene from 2D images, taken from multiple angles, came with a breakthrough using neural radiance fields (NeRFs). NeRFs and other AI techniques are already revolutionizing the generation of media. They learn to create 3D representations from 2D images, so that 3D scenes can be rendered from previously unseen angles, for example, 3D objects, a 360-degree camera tour around an object or a walk through the interior of a restaurant or art gallery.

Improvements using this technique reduce AI training times from data, as well as reducing the number of images needed to construct the 3D model. This line of research and enquiry has already seen remarkable results and points the way towards AI being able to automatically reproduce the real world as a 3D world quickly and at low cost. It is now possible to see that the creation of avatars, digital twins and virtual worlds will be easy, fast and cheap, opening up the possibility that user-generated 3D worlds are within our reach.

AI objects

AI will also help, augment and create the virtual objects that populate virtual worlds. This can already be done from text prompts but there will be tools that allow one to amend, personalize and fit objects into created worlds. Tools, like Rec Room's pen that creates objects on demand, will become intelligent co-creators and producers of objects.

For learning, all the technology one would wish to have in the real world will be available in the virtual world, such as search, transcription, translation along with the use of objects such as learning aids: coloured blocks for basic maths, globes, maps, brushes, design tools and calculators. More importantly, objects used for training, such as laboratory equipment, medical equipment, tools, construction equipment, factory equipment, robots, vehicles, aircraft, guns, sensors and maintenance equipment can all be used in a safe environment before use in the real world.

AI people

Avatars will also be AI created: personalized, designed avatars with skins or clothes but also autonomous avatars with human-like behaviours. This has long been true in games worlds. We will see a vast, automated army of helpers, guides, personal shoppers, priests and experts populate virtual worlds. These will be off-the-shelf but also personalized.

For learning, AI-created people will use voice and learning content, generated by AI, to teach and coach learners along their learning journey. Teachers, instructors, tutors, coaches and counsellors will be available to help you learn. They will embody the best of pedagogy in both teaching and learning to optimize your learning journeys. You will be able to speak to historical figures and they will reply, as the AI model will be trained using a corpus of their own works and literature about their works.

Whisper AI (OpenAI) provides AI-generated audio from text, and tools like this will most certainly be used to provide speech from sources such as AI created and behaviourally determined by AI.

It is not that the metaverse will mirror the real world, more that it will augment, enhance and improve on the real world. AI promises to accelerate the process as AI allows virtual worlds to be bent to our will, to be something new and better. It is gradually taking over some of the roles that a teacher performs, especially basic support tasks and assessment. This process is certain to continue.

AI content

AI has already been producing self-paced, asynchronous learning experiences with automatically created learning and assessment. This has included effortful, interactive learning that is created faster and therefore cheaper than traditional 'authored' content. This is invariably created in tandem with human designers but generative AI tools have allowed much more to be generated by the tools themselves.

Learning content in virtual worlds will be everything from exposition through to scenarios and full simulations. There are already AI tools and services that allow one to create 2D learning experiences; this will lead to AI tools that create optimal 3D scenarios and simulations.

Assessment will also be made through question generation and automated assessment of performance tasks. The tracking of body and eye movements and tasks in time will allow forms of assessment that promise to be done quickly and cheaply and be better validated than human observation.

AI pathways

AI is a process of optimal automation. It will solve several anticipated problems in the metaverse, not only in the creation and build of virtual worlds but also the objects and autonomous agents within those worlds. AI also promises not just to automate the design, development and delivery of learning, it promises to improve and optimize the learning process or learning journeys undertaken by the student.

AI can be used as a guiding hand, in tandem with the learner, in some form of dialogue or exchange, to get learners 'back on course'. It can do what your satnav or GPS does when you need to be pointed in the right direction to your destination, find yourself stuck, take a wrong turn or simply get confused. Adaptive learning, in its many forms, either as pretesting, or dynamically (see Clark, 2020), does precisely this.

Moments of need are psychological states one finds oneself in when working or learning. Learning, whether formal or informal, in education or work is a personal journey for every learner and is becoming increasingly personalized. You may not know where to start and need a sense of direction, a first road to follow; need a simple clarification – a simple decision, this way or that; find yourself lost and confused, even overwhelmed and need more focus; want to know about something in more detail; get stuck and need to get over that hurdle to move on; apply your skills and knowledge; practise your skills and knowledge; assess your skills and knowledge. You may even find that something has changed; company regulations, standards or procedures – the road has been rebuilt but you did not know of the change. The complexities of learning can be increasingly handled by adaptive, personalized, AI-driven software that keeps you on course and gets you back on course when necessary. This is important pedagogically but even more important in a 3D world where learning by doing will need to be learnt and assessed.

AI analytics

All of this operates on the assumption that data about the process is gathered and used to propel the learner forward. Personalization depends on data, not only to identify the needs of the learner but also to train the AI models.

This process of AI support can benefit from both personal and aggregated data to improve learning, in real time, as you progress on your learning journey. By seeing learning as a process, aided by AI, learning solutions can be data-led, feeding personalized learning experiences and progress along the whole learning journey from initial engagement through learning, support, feedback, application, practice, transfer and assessment.

In learning, AI will be able to determine optimal routes through learning experiences. Metanode, for example, has already used evolutionary algorithms to determine learning pathways. Other adaptive systems have used other predictive techniques. You can now see a single, dynamic relationship between learner agency, content and actions emerge on smart platforms that use pedaAIgogies, which in turn use data-led approaches to learning process and pathways.

AI hardware

Many generations of graphics chips, which offload tasks such as rendering and simulation, have been developed in response to the need for 3D environments in gaming, taking processing to edge servers and devices at the edge of the network, reducing the need for data transfer and so reducing latency and increasing performance. They also allow more sophisticated AR and VR experiences, suggesting their common use in supporting a more seamless metaverse.

This is why Nvidia is regarded as a significant player in the metaverse. Its graphics processing units (GPUs) are mainstream products with their real-time ray tracing and AI rendering for realistic virtual worlds. Its Omniverse platform is a 3D internet platform for creating and operating metaverse applications. It uses Pixar's Universal Scene Description (USD), an open framework for file formats, also open-source 3D scene description used to create 3D content. Nvidia will play a significant role in the metaverse story, not only in hardware but in visioning, standards and software.

We also have AI chips from a number of manufacturers and large tech companies, embedded in consumer computers, laptops and smartphones that allow local processing. These will also bring real-time graphics and AI into AR, VR and haptic devices, into headsets and other mixed-reality devices, especially wearables such as glasses.

Learning

My hope is that we will be able to learn in such places. Of all the things we can hope for, that education becomes bountiful and free is surely one. Those most in need of education are often not catered for within the current system, as the cost and problems with access mean entire parts of that system, especially higher education, are still built on scarcity. If it can be free or so cheap that anyone can receive it at any level, we will have achieved something most find unimaginable, the creation of a tremendous social good.

Many of the problems we face as a species are to do with physical resources, whether physical infrastructure or enough warm bodies to deliver services, even teaching. Imagine if we lessened the need for scaling education through warm bodies and managed to educate and train people for all of those roles where and when they are needed. The system will be able to react quickly to demand, as demand itself would be predicted through AI. As technology eliminates one role, existing roles not replaceable by technology, and new roles, will become more valuable and training available.

This is not just a matter of digital twins in learning; mimicry is easy. The point is not to mirror the world but to re-create the world or create new worlds. One would hope that learning in these new worlds would not just be about the existing world but unleash the creativity for people to create their own worlds. We have a generation who have grown up in *Fortnite*, Roblox and *Minecraft* creating their own worlds. Are we going to impose digital educational twins, like 3D classrooms and lecture theatres upon that generation? Are we going to make them conform to the narrow strictures and limitations of the real world?

Technologies start by mimicry; they parrot the real world, repeating the same old mistakes. They then mature, playing to their own affordances and strengths. Why repeat the architecture of the real world, which is subject to the forces and constraints of gravity and physics, when you have the freedom to break free of those constraints? We have seen how we can break free from the tyranny of place and time; we can also break free of the tyranny of old pedagogies.

Before dismissing the metaverse, think of the time you have spent inside 3D worlds, physical and psychological, worlds spun from our imaginations, with or without technology: to have entered a building so stupendously beautiful that all thought of the outside world disappeared; to have been so engrossed in a book that you emerge changed and surprised that mere words could so envelop the mind; to have watched a movie and come back out into the dark night seeing the real world in a different light; to have lost yourself on the web researching something of deep interest, losing all track of time; to have poured over Google Maps exploring a place you plan to visit. Then there are games, for many rich experiences so beyond the real that they seem real. Finally, virtual reality, to literally have the world swapped out for another. The metaverse is the continuation of this process of the imagination. We have always created new worlds, we always will. The point is to use them for the benefit of all. Learning, above all, will benefit all of those who have the imagination to see that it is about changing minds. You change minds by taking them somewhere else. That somewhere could be the metaverse.

Overestimated in the short term, underestimated long term, AI is making progress much faster than expected and is likely to hugely influence and shape the metaverse. For example, in learning, once you have a workable teaching assistant even in just one domain, that takes the knowledge and practices of a good teaching assistant in that domain and that can be replicated as many times as you wish. This would be a massive breakthrough that can be implemented in the metaverse across the whole of education, a sort of singularity point.

Conclusion

Barely a day passes without some astonishing service appearing, driven by AI. At first beating what we thought were unbeatable players of unbeatable games – chess, *Go* and poker have all fallen. Then beating us at our own game, science, with Alphafold. Now it produces its own text images, audio, faces and 3D entities, beating us in that last bastion of human exceptionalism, creativity. AI at first played, then predicted and is now productive. Truly creative production is still to come but that is not far off as it is difficult now to claim that AI-created text, music, images, even moving images have no merit, aesthetic beauty or worth. That is because we now find it difficult to distinguish between the AI- and human-created content.

We have always decried the introduction of technology into the creative process, thinking we were unique as creators. Yet if there is social acceptance of these new creations, as content, even art, we may have to think again and go further than Darwin ever did and accept that biological evolution in itself may be overtaken by the cultural revolution that gave us writing, mathematics, media types, the internet and AI. Our evolved brains seem to have created algorithmic processes that can create things on their own.

We are on the cusp, not of rocketing ourselves to second worlds on huge cylinders of explosive fuel to other planets but of creating second worlds here on earth. They will exist as invisible bits but be as visible as the real world. Why try to live on another unliveable planet when we can enhance our lives here and, with the aid of technology, create everything we need and want here on earth? Rather than escape from this world at great cost, and even then only a few of us, we must surely first try to save what we have. We may move to these barely inhabitable, rocky planets with their interminable, monochrome landscapes and impossible-to-breathe atmospheres but that solves nothing. We would be, in a sense, accepting that our fate is simply to trash one place and move on to another.

What is likely to aid in our search for ourselves and our futures is the new pedAIgogy, where we co-teach, co-learn and co-create a future which improves our lives here on earth.

It is far more likely that we will find other nearer virtual worlds, which we can co-create ourselves, to solve the crisis in meaning; worlds where we can do things differently, as yet unimagined worlds where we can solve problems. We may at last find each other in these worlds. We may find new things to explore – ideas rather than just places.

Bibliography

Clark, D (2020) *Artificial Intelligence for Learning: How to use AI to support employee development*, Kogan Page, London

Clark, D (2022) *Learning Experience Design: How to create effective learning that works*, Kogan Page, London

Clark, D (2023) *Learning Technology: A Complete Guide for Learning Professionals*, Kogan Page, London

Hackforth, R (ed) (1972) *Plato: Phaedrus*, Cambridge University Press, Cambridge

Pell, M (2019) *The Age of Smart Information: How artificial intelligence and spatial computing will transform the way we communicate forever*, Futuristic Design, New York

INDEX

Note: Page numbers in *italics* refer to tables or figures